WAR, EXILE AND THE MUSIC OF AFGHANISTAN

Dedicated to the memory of John Anthony Randoll Blacking, social anthropologist and ethnomusicologist extraordinaire, who encouraged and guided me from the start.

War, Exile and the Music of Afghanistan

The Ethnographer's Tale

JOHN BAILY

Goldsmiths, University of London, UK

Routledge
Taylor & Francis Group

LONDON AND NEW YORK

First published 2015 by Ashgate Publishing

Published 2016 by Routledge
2 Park Square, Milton Park, Abingdon, Oxon OX14 4RN
711 Third Avenue, New York, NY 10017, USA

Routledge is an imprint of the Taylor & Francis Group, an informa business

British Library Cataloguing in Publication Data
A catalogue record for this book is available from the British Library

The Library of Congress has cataloged the printed edition as follows:
Baily, John, 1943–
  War, exile and the music of Afghanistan : the ethnographer's tale / by John Baily.
    pages cm. – (SOAS musicology series)
  Includes bibliographical references and index.
  ISBN 978-1-4724-1582-0 (hardcover : alk. paper) 1. Music—Political aspects—Afghanistan. I. Title.
  ML3917.A34B35 2015
  780.9581–dc23

                                                                2015000814

ISBN: 9781472415820 (hbk)

Contents

List of Figures

John Baily claims copyright of all photographs and illustrations unless otherwise indicated.

Films on the Accompanying DVD

The four films on the DVD that accompanies this book can be obtained individually in DVD format from The Royal Anthropological Institute, 50 Fitzroy Street, London W1T 5BT, UK. The RAI Film Officer can be contacted at: film@therai.org.uk. Copyright of the films is owned by John Baily, with the exception of *Amir*, where copyright is owned by the Royal Anthropological Institute. I am very grateful to the RAI for permission to include *Amir* in conjunction with the hard- and paperback versions of this book. Any unauthorized copying, hiring, public performance, radio or TV broadcast, streaming and online publication of *Amir* is prohibited. Applications for an educational licence or public performance use should be referred to the RAI Film Officer.

The sequence of scenes in each film is listed below, but these are not digitally accessible chapters. Where particular scenes are referred to in the text they are identified in terms of minutes and seconds from the start of each film.

Amir: An Afghan refugee musician's life in Peshawar, Pakistan (Baily 1985a). Directed by John Baily. Camera Wayne Derrick. Beaconsfield, UK: National Film and Television School. Shot in 1985, released in 1986.
1. Introduction to Amir
2. Amir at home
3. The musicians' workplace
4. The wedding party
5. Ezat Jan's visit
6. At the shrine of Rahman Baba
7. *Ramadân* (*Ramazân*) in Swat
8. Amir plays the *rubâb*

Across the Border: Afghan musicians exiled in Peshawar (Baily 2007c) Directed by John Baily. London, Goldsmiths. Shot in 2000, released in 2008.
1. John Baily introduces Ustad Asif
2. The road to Peshawar
3. Amir Jan plays *rubâb*
4. Hayatabad Friday market
5. Khalil House
6. Homayun Sakhi plays *rubâb*
7. Mohammad Sadiq sings *ghazal*
8. Masjedi plays *dohol*
9. Ghulam Hussain plays *rubâb*

10. Wedding preparations
11. Daoud Hanif's modern band at a Hazara wedding
12. Ustad Asif's relatives
13. Ahmad Shah plays *tabla* for Ustad Asif
14. Essa Qaderi's workshop
15. The Sufi *khânaqâh*
16. The introductory *naghma* played by Hussein Jan
17. Alem-e Shauqi sings *ghazal*
18. Amir Jan sings *ghazal* accompanied by Ahmad Shah

Tablas and Drum Machines: Afghan Music in California (Baily 2005). Directed by John Baily. London, Goldsmiths. Shot in 2000, released in 2005.
1. Introducing Fremont
2. A trip to San Francisco
3. Ustad Asif arrives from London
4. Qader Eshpari's music store
5. An Engagement Party
6. Tabla classes
7. An Afghan Market
8. New Year Celebration 21 March
9. Zaki's Party

A Kabul Music Diary (Baily 2003). Directed by John Baily. London, Goldsmiths. Shot in 2002, released in 2003.
1. Introducing Kabul
2. The Kucheh Kharabat (Musicians' Quarter)
3. Ghulam Hussain plays *Râg Bhupali*
4. Music shops and music offices
5. Radio Afghanistan
6. Gol Alam plays *Râg Megh*
7. The children of Khorasan House
8. Kabul University's Department of Music
9. At the Ministry of Information and Culture
10. A concert at Kabul University

Acknowledgements

In authors' lists of people to be acknowledged, spouses usually come at the end, thanked for their forbearance in having put up with domestic disruption and long absences while the author was incarcerated in the ivory tower of an academic institution, or office in the garden shed. My wife Veronica Doubleday was with me from the start of my research on the music of Afghanistan, not just giving support, but very much involved in the work with her own study of women's music making, so that in due course we covered 'both sides of the curtain' in the largely separate social worlds of male and female music makers. It was music that brought us together in the first place, and it is music that has bound us together through the years, particularly as a duo performing the *mahali* (local) music of Herat. Moreover, she read through the penultimate draft of this monograph with her keen editorial eye. For all this, and much more, I owe her a huge debt of gratitude.

My thanks to all the Afghans who have helped me, especially my 10 *hamkârân*: Amir Jan Herati, Nashenas, Sattar Khan, Rahim Khushnawaz, Madadi, Homayun Sakhi, Ustad Asif Mahmoud, Ghulam Hussain, Haroon Yousofi and Zahir Yusuf.

I thank my music teachers: Krishna Govinda and Narendra Bataju from Nepal, who first showed me the practicalities of Indian classical music; Ustad Mohammad Omar, who started me off on the *rubâb*; Gada Mohammad and Mohammad Karim Herawi, my guides in learning the Herati *dutâr*; Amir Jan Khushnawaz and his son Rahim, my *rubâb* teachers in Herat. I acknowledge those other *rubâb* players from whose recordings I learned so much: Ghulam Jailani, Ghulam Mohammad Atay and Essa Qassemi. I thank that family of *tabla* players exiled in London with whom I have played so often: Ustad Asif Mahmoud, his son Yusuf Mahmoud, and Asif's younger brother Ustad Arif Mahmoud.

Many non-musician Heratis helped me greatly: Ghani Niksear, in the Herat office of the Ministry of Information and Culture; Safar Sarmed, my research assistant in 1974 and Abdul Wahed Saljuqi, who assisted my research in 1977.

I thank Bruce Wannell, Matthaios Tsahourides, Jolyon Leslie, Shirazuddin Sidiqi, Kate Clark, William Reeve, Patricia Omidian, Abdul Aziz Yaqubi, Tareq Mehdavi, Nasruddin Saljuqi, Hooman Asadi and Mohammadreza Darvishi, who all helped me in many ways. Thanks to Afghan scholars Nabi Misdaq and Sayed Qassem Reshtia, whose work has guided me in matters of Afghan history. I offer special thanks to Ahmad Sarmast for his friendship and deep knowledge of the music of his native Afghanistan. I have referred frequently to his historical work in Chapter 1 and he takes a final bow in Chapter 7.

I offer thanks to the funding bodies that have supported my research: the Social Science Research Council, the Leverhulme Trust, the British Academy, the Committee for Central and Inner Asia, the Arts and Humanities Research Council, and the Aga Khan Trust for Culture. Goldsmiths, University of London, has been my academic home since 1990 and has always supported, and encouraged my work on Afghan music culture, and in 2002 allowed me to establish the Afghanistan Music Unit, which basically gave me regular time off to continue the good work. I thank Nigel Fuller of the former Media Services Centre at Goldsmiths for all the help he gave with digital video editing. And I thank Ken Gregory, Ben Pimlott, Geoff Crossick and Pat Loughrey, four successive Wardens of Goldsmiths, who all had a keen interest in the Afghanistan music project.

From 2009 to 2011 I held a Leverhulme Emeritus Fellowship, which enabled me to work through all my data since 1985, and to conduct research on Afghan music in Australia. The promised output was this monograph. The Leverhulme Fellowship allowed me to employ as a part-time research assistant Yama Yari, a young Herati graduate in engineering and expert in the matter of Persian poetry. We passed many agreeable hours together listening to recordings of song and conversation from my fieldwork, and I owe him a huge debt of gratitude.

I also thank those with whom I worked in the world of anthropological film: Colin Young, former director of the National Film and Television School (NFTS), Herb DiGioia, my documentary tutor at the film school, Wayne Derrick, who worked with me as cameraman in Peshawar in 1985, Susi Arnott, who did the sub-titling of three of the four films on the DVD, and Paul Henley, my fellow anthropological film trainee at the NFTS.

I also acknowledge the help and friendship of several western scholars who have assisted my work on the music of Afghanistan. Lorraine Sakata and Mark Slobin are two American pioneers of ethnomusicological research in Afghanistan. I followed in their footsteps; they were always generous in sharing their knowledge with me and encouraging my own efforts. Jean During, Lloyd Miller and Jan van Belle helped a lot in their separate ways.

And my thanks to the editorial and production teams at Ashgate who made publication of this book possible, especially Laura Macy, Heidi Bishop, Emma Gallon and Barbara Pretty.

Some Notes on Terminology
and Transliteration

The Term Afghan

There is a terminological confusion here that continues to have resonance even today, for the term *Afghan* has an ambiguous semantic field. At one level *Afghan* (properly pronounced *Aughân*) is synonymous with Pashtun, the dominant ethnic group of the area, a largely tribal society, speakers of the (Indo-European) Pashto language, as distinct from the other ethnic groups inhabiting the territory, with their own languages (Dari, Hazaregi, Uzbeki, and so on). At another level, *Afghan* refers to any citizen of Afghanistan, irrespective of language and ethnicity. In this monograph I have adopted the term Afghan to refer to citizens of Afghanistan, irrespective of language or purported ethnicity.

The Persian language spoken in Afghanistan is properly called Dari. I have never studied literary Persian and my knowledge of vernacular Dari has been largely learned through talking with often uneducated Heratis. Speaking the common tongue gave an immediate rapport with the people of Herat. Regrettably, I know little of Pashto. Most of my research has been conducted in Dari, sometimes in English when working with Afghans who have acquired a good command of the language.

Transliteration

In this work I have adopted a simple system of transliteration. The italicization of Dari words is maintained throughout the text rather than just the first occurrence of the word. I have chosen to italicize *tabla* and *sitâr*; it looks odd in a list of instruments to see these ones without italics. Likewise, I render the Indian harmonium used in Afghanistan as '*armonia*. The word *mujahedin* is usually spelled *mujahideen* in books written about Afghanistan, and I follow this usage. I refer to the celebrated *mujahideen* commander as Ahmad Shah Massoud, rather than Ahmad Shah Masud. There are also some inconsistencies in transliteration of Dari terms from my earlier publications, which reflected Herati dialect. For example, *naghmeh* (instrumental composition) is rendered here as *naghma*. The only diacritical mark I use is â, the long a, sometimes rendered by other authors as aa. Finally, there are variations in the way different individuals write their names with Roman letters. So we have Nasruddin Saljuqi, but Nesruddin Sarshar.

Introduction

The subject of this monograph is the fluctuating state of Afghanistan's music culture from the 1970s to 2014, when the country was about to be left to stand on its own two feet after 13 years of occupation by western military forces. In the seemingly endless conflict that has devastated Afghanistan for the last 35 years, one might ask, 'What's so important about music when there are so many other pressing concerns to be addressed?' In answer, I reply that music does matter, for, as John Blacking put it, 'music is essential for the very survival of man's humanity' (Blacking 1973: 54). Afghans have a strong sense of humanity (*ensâniat*) expressed in their famous hospitality, their generosity, their concern for the comfort and welfare of others, and their expressions of warm and positive feelings reinforced by spiritual certainties. The survival of that sense of humanity has been challenged by the catalogue of cruelties and atrocities visited by Afghans upon each other during the years of internecine conflict. Music and the musicians who create and perform it have been, and continue to be, a counteractive force for good, and must be nurtured and supported. As Jean-Pierre Guinhut, former French Ambassador to Kabul wrote, 'In a country as devastated as Afghanistan, music is a gift in a dull and desperate struggle for survival ... The death of musicians from war should be commemorated in history as one of the worst crimes against humanity' (Guinhut 2005).

The present work is a personalized account of most of my encounters with Afghan music and musicians over a period of 40 years. I may call myself an ethnographer, but this is not a standard ethnography; it is an ethnographer's tale in which the author is closely bound up in the narrative. It examines how music making and music makers have been affected by the tumultuous and tragic events that have occurred since the communist *coup d'état* of 1978. This is not a musico-political history, though it does largely follow the chronology of political events, sometimes interrupted by flashbacks and prolepses. Chapter 1 looks at music before the war, the patronage of the Amirs of Kabul, the advent of radio broadcasting, and introduces the ethnographer and his fieldwork in Herat in the 1970s. Chapter 2 considers how the life of music was affected by the communist takeover, the Soviet invasion, and the origins of the *mujahideen* and their *jihâd*, with a visit to Peshawar in 1985 to make a film about Afghan musicians in exile. Chapter 3 describes three visits to work with Afghans in Islamabad, Peshawar and Herat during the time when the *mujahideen* were in power, under Presidents Mujadidi and then Rabbani. Chapter 4 outlines the rise of the Taliban and recounts visits to Peshawar, Mashhad and Fremont during the period of Taliban rule. Chapter 5 chronicles several visits to Kabul in the post-Taliban era, the recovery of music culture and the origins of the Aga Khan Music School. Chapter 6 narrates further work on music in the Afghan diaspora – in London, Melbourne and Sydney – and traces the global circulation of Afghan sonic art. Chapter 7 suggests some conclusions about music and politics, the role of music in the construction of an Afghan national identity and ends on an optimistic note with a visit to the Afghanistan National Institute of Music in 2011. Altogether this is a complex story that weaves together several strands: the political backdrop, the field trips, filmmaking as musical ethnography, and learning to perform as research in ethnomusicology.

The Political Backdrop

So much has been written in the last three decades about this inexorable conflict in Afghanistan and it is certainly not my intention to follow in the authorial footsteps of others. The 'political events' sections at the start of Chapters 2–5 are intended to enable the reader unfamiliar with the details of recent Afghan history to contextualize the ever-changing circumstances of musical life in Afghanistan and its diaspora in political terms, in the belief that music is often, perhaps always, a sensitive indicator of wider socio-cultural processes. And, of course, music is not simply reflective and indicative but can be proactive, supporting and even instigating political action. One might cite music used as state propaganda in the communist period and the Taliban use of *tarânas* (chants) as a form of religious propaganda. These sections proved the most difficult to write. The political narrative is so complicated, particularly with endless changes in alliances between different factions. It has been difficult to forge a new account that is both succinct and expresses (implicitly) my own understanding of what happened. Furthermore, since I am completely reliant on secondary sources, the political sections have a very different style to the voice of the ethnographer.

The 10 Field Trips

After setting the scene in the 1970s, my narrative proper begins in 1985, when I made my first journey to visit Afghans in exile, in Peshawar, Pakistan, in order to make an anthropological film about refugee musicians. Over subsequent years I worked with Afghan musicians in many places. I have condensed my engagement with them to 10 encounters, some in Afghanistan itself, the majority in the diaspora. Some of the visits were 'official', in the sense of receiving external funding from a research council or equivalent organisation, involving the submission of a well-crafted proposal in which the objectives, research methods and outputs were specified and justified. Others were shorter 'private' visits to find out what was going on at a particular time and place. These periods of fieldwork yielded a large body of data, collected in the form of audio and video recordings, and field notes. The recordings were often of musical performances, sometimes in their usual social contexts, sometimes staged for my benefit to record. Others were of interviews, conversations and music lessons. As for field notes, from the start of my work in 1973 I had been exhorted by my mentor John Blacking to keep regular and extensive field notes and to categorize my research materials such as audiotapes in a systematic manner.

Each of the 10 fieldwork expeditions recounted here brings into focus a key individual, encapsulated in 10 portraits or vignettes. Together, these protagonists, all male – I never had much opportunity to work with women musicians – constitute a kind of 'panel of experts'. It is hard to find the right word for them. Informant? Musician friend? Musician colleague? Research colleague? Research assistant? None of these feels quite right. So I opt for the Dari word *hamkâr*, meaning 'colleague' or 'co-worker'. The plural form is *hamkârân*, which sounds euphonious. My *hamkârân* are not treated in a systematic manner, for I know a lot more about some of them than I do about others. Each *hamkâr* profile tells a different kind of story and reveals a contrasting aspect of what it is to be a musician in Afghan society. Some of these individuals appear several times in my narrative, and in the process we get some sense of their migratory movements as exiles through diasporic space. For each fieldwork visit I have selected a song text that is relevant to the period under review. In four instances the song in question can be found on the DVD that comes with this book. Of the 10 songs, four are of a Sufi character, derived from classical poetry, two are patriotic songs about Afghanistan, three are about war and exile, and one is a modern wedding song. In addition, several other song texts are included.

Filmmaking as Musical Ethnography

From the outset filmmaking was an important part of my work with Afghans in exile: the objective of the first fieldtrip (1985) was to shoot a film. I was at the time a Leverhulme Film Training Fellow at the National Film and Television School, where I was encouraged to work in the documentary style known as observational cinema. This kind of filmmaking is regarded by its practitioners as a way of 'performing ethnography'. The outcome of the field trip was *Amir: An Afghan refugee musician's life in Peshawar, Pakistan*, shot with professional 16 mm camera and sound recording equipment. From this experience I later realized the possibilities of the video camera as a *research tool*. As video technology improved I graduated from Hi8, to Super-VHS and finally miniDV. It was not until 2002 that I started editing my research footage, when Goldsmiths set up a number of digital video editing suites. In this context I developed the idea of the 'fieldwork movie', embodying some of the principles of observational cinema, but breaking some of its rules, too. These films were not made for commercial purposes and were not constrained by popular styles of television documentary, with fast cutting and extensive voice-over commentary. There are four films on the DVD that goes with this book *Amir: An Afghan refugee musician's life in Peshawar, Pakistan* (1985), *Across the Border: Afghan musicians exiled in Peshawar* (2000), *Tablas and Drum Machines: Afghan Music in California* (2000) and *A Kabul Music Diary* (2002).[1]

Taken together, the films document some of the research described in the text. It is anticipated that the films will be viewed at home, in the office or in the library, probably on a computer. The loss of visual quality due to extreme compression means they are not suitable for projection in the classroom or auditorium. DVD copies of the original films are available from the Royal Anthropological Institute in London. The four films here should be regarded as a supplement to the printed text; a separate book would be required to do them justice. In my narrative there are frequent references to particular scenes in the films, and sometimes I quote from filmed conversations and song texts.[2]

Learning to Perform as Research

From the time when I first started reading about ethnomusicology, Mantle Hood's programme at UCLA, with its emphasis on the performance of a variety of musics from different parts of the world, was an inspiration. The idea of learning to perform on Afghan lutes as part of my research was alluring, but not mentioned in the grant proposals I put forward at the time for fear that hard-nosed funding bodies such as the Social Science Research Council would consider this too frivolous to count as serious research. What a long way we have come since then! In due course performing Afghan music on Afghan instruments became a very important part of my engagement with Afghan culture. As a guitarist with a strong interest in 'oriental music' it did not take long to master the basics of the *dutâr* and the *rubâb* (both plucked lutes) and by the end of my two years' fieldwork in the 1970s I had achieved a satisfactory level of competence on both instruments. By the time I had the opportunity to re-engage with Afghan musicians in 1985, my ability and knowledge of old instrumental compositions for the *rubâb* was a great asset and allowed for real musical communication. Playing their music gave me wonderful access to the world of musicians, not only because they might approve of how and what I played, but they appreciated my enthusiasm for and love of their music.

My field trips were not motivated by a need for further training, or *tâlim* as Afghan musicians would call it, though there were certainly gaps in my practical knowledge that required filling. But I was always on the lookout for ways to improve my performance, to learn new techniques, expand my repertoire and

---

[1]   These are the dates when the films were shot but not necessarily when they were edited, see 'List of Films'.

[2]   The four films occupy four separate tracks on the DVD. Reference timings are given from the start of each film, in minutes, indicated by the symbol ', and seconds by the symbol ".

arrive at fresh insights. The Afghans categorized me as a *shauqi*, an amateur enthusiast with a passion for music, and that gave me a recognized place in the social organization of musicians. Increasingly, playing Afghan music became part of my life and part of my self-identity.

Chapter 1
Before the Communist Coup of 1978

Afghanistan in British Popular Imagination

> I always say no one goes to Afghanistan once … once you go, you always go back. (Lyse Doucet, personal communication, 3 February 2009)[1]

Afghanistan has occupied a place in the popular imagination of the people of Britain for the last 200 years. The story has been told many times, yet it is necessary to say something about the history of the relationship for readers who may be unfamiliar with British colonial history. Afghanistan was closely linked with British economic and political domination of the Indian Subcontinent and with maintaining that jewel in the imperial crown; it was the land-route through which those who might wish to rob the British of their prize possession would come.

The remote land-locked country we know today as Afghanistan came into existence as a political entity in 1747. Celebrated as the 'Crossroads of Asia', the region had enormous strategic and economic importance, with trade routes from east to west along the many-stranded Silk Road, and north to south, connecting Central Asia with India. In addition, it was an important cultural crossroads, where different ethnic groups, often with individual languages, met and intermingled. The region was not called Afghanistan – the 'Land of the Afghans' – in 1747: much of the terrain was known as Khorasan (or Khurasan), once a great centre of urban civilization, scholarship and Sufism (Figure 1.1). In the eighteenth century the term Afghanistan, as used by European geographers, referred to a small area of the Pashtun homeland, as maps of the period indicate.[2] Naming the whole area Afghanistan did not come into general practice until the nineteenth century, and was probably a British invention.

Long before 1747 there had been significant populations of Pashtuns (Afghans) inhabiting parts of northern India. The British labelled them as Pathans, a name that has stuck persistently in the English language. *Pathan* is derived from *Pakhtanah*, the plural of *Pakhtun*, which is the same word as *Pashtun* in the dialect of the

---

[1]   Lyse Doucet, the BBC's Chief International Correspondent, is probably the best-informed and most well-connected journalist who has covered Afghanistan over a period of many years.

[2]   According to Thakston (2002: 481, footnote 6), Emperor Babur's 'Afghanistan' referred to the regions of Bangash, Bannu and Dasht, an area southeast of Kabul down to the Indus.

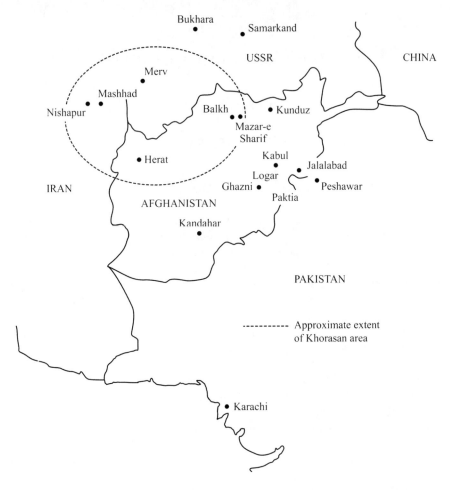

Figure 1.1   Map of Afghanistan, showing the extent of historic Khorasan

language known as *Pakhto* (Allen 2000: xii).[3] Pashtuns populated principalities we hear little of today, notably around the city of Rampur, in Rohilkand, which is today part of Uttar Pradesh. The Pashtuns of this area, also known as Rohillas, were professional warriors, mercenaries for the Moghul emperors and heavily involved in the lucrative trade bringing horses from Central Asia to India (Gommans 1995). The cavalry horse was an important military asset, and the importation of horses from the north was part of the arms trade of the time. The north–south transit routes passing through what was to become Afghanistan were of crucial importance, and were controlled by Pashtuns. Pashtuns were also an important element of the

---

[3]   That is, *Pashtun* is equivalent to *Pakhtun* and *Pashto* is equivalent to *Pakhto*. Here I use *Pashtun* and *Pashto* as being the more common words used in Afghanistan.

Iranian military forces and formed part of the army led by the Iranian ruler Nadir Shah that sacked Delhi in 1739. After the assassination of Nadir Shah in 1747 his Pashtun mercenaries defected to Kandahar, their ancestral homeland, where the young tribal chieftain Ahmad Shah from the Durrani tribe was elected paramount chief by a tribal gathering. He is revered as the founding father of Afghanistan, known respectfully as Ahmad Shah Baba. Capturing a caravan on its way to Iran that was filled with treasure plundered from the Punjab, Peshawar and Kabul, allowed Ahmad Shah to buy the support of other Pashtun khans, and he embarked on a period of rapid conquest in northern India. By 1762 the newly created 'Afghan empire' was at its peak, extending from the Caspian Sea to Delhi, and from the borders of Tibet to the Indian Ocean. It endured for little more than 50 years; the Afghans lost most of the Punjab in 1801, Kashmir in 1819, and Peshawar in 1832, all to the Sikh ruler Ranjit Singh.

In the sixteenth and seventeenth centuries the British in India, in the form of the East India Company, had little interest in what was going on in Khorasan. Their presence at the time was limited to a few East India Company coastal trading entrepôts in Surat, Bombay, Madras and Calcutta. The last of these became the main British settlement, and from Bengal British power slowly expanded westwards and northwards. By the late eighteenth century the British started to become concerned about the possible expansion of the Russian Empire across Central Asia (Hopkirk 2006: 22), foreseeing an eventual attempt to wrest control of India. In view of this threat the East India Company sent Mountstuart Elphinstone on a fact-finding mission to the 'Kingdom of Caboul', then ruled by Shah Shuja, a grandson of Ahmad Shah Durrani. At that time the rulers of Kabul still had an extensive territory that included much of northern Punjab, and their winter capital was Peshawar. Elphinstone arrived there on 25 February 1809 and remained for several months, collecting data of every kind. He never visited Kabul itself. Those were troubled times and Shah Shuja was deposed later that year by Dost Mohammad.

The results of Elphinestone's research were published in 1815 as *An Account of the Kingdom of Caubul and its Dependencies in Persia, Tartary, and India* (Janata 1969). It became the standard reference book for the British about Afghanistan for decades, and is still regarded as an important anthropological source. It includes some information about music and dance of the period (Elphinstone 1815: 236–7, 279; Baily 1988a: 17). Elphinstone summed up the character of the Afghans as follows: 'their vices are revenge, envy, avarice, rapacity, and obstinacy; on the other hand, they are fond of liberty, faithful to their friends, kind to their dependants, hospitable, brave, hardy, frugal, laborious, and prudent; and they are less disposed than the nations in their neighbourhood to falsehood, intrigue, and deceit' (1815: 253). Thus began the strange idealization of the Pashtuns in British popular imagination, which was prominent in the first half of the twentieth century; they were an enemy worthy of respect.

Elphinstone was followed by a long succession of adventurers travelling in Afghanistan, some of them intrepid young officers from the East India Company's

Bengal Army, conducting unofficial reconnaissance, often disguised as natives. Many of these visitors published books about their experiences, for example: Sir Alexander Burnes's *Travels into Bokhara* (1834), and his *Cabool. Being a Personal Narrative of a Journey to, and residence in, that City in the Years 1836, 7 and 8* (1842); Arthur Conolly's *Journey to the North of India, Overland From England, Through Russia, Persia, and Affghaunistaun* (1834); Charles Masson's *Narrative of Various Journeys in Balochistan, Afghanistan and the Panjab, including a Residence in those Countries* (1842).[4] There was clearly a ready market for travellers' tales of this kind amongst certain sections of the British public.

The perceived Russian threat to Afghanistan increased markedly in the middle of the nineteenth century. Their seemingly inexorable advance across the vast territory of Central Asia caused consternation in Britain and Afghanistan became a British pre-occupation. In 1839 the British restored Shah Shuja to the Kabul throne, supported by a British army of occupation. The British suffered an historic defeat in 1842, only to return as an 'Army of Retribution', razing towns and cities, culminating in the complete destruction of the Grand Bazaar of Kabul. After the debacle of the Anglo-Afghan War of 1839–42 many more travellers' memoirs were published, along with detailed examination of the conduct of the war itself (notably Kaye 1851, 1874).[5] The flow of new publications fed a lively political debate about British policy with regard to Afghanistan as the Russians successively conquered the cities of Tashkent (1865) and Samarkand (1868), and the three khanates of Bokhara (1868), Khiva (1873) and Kokand (1875). On one hand there were the advocates of the 'forward policy', which amounted to taking control of Afghan foreign affairs, and its converse, 'masterly inactivity', leaving the Afghans to get on with their own affairs in their own way. Afghanistan was the focus for many fierce parliamentary debates between the parties of Disraeli (Conservative) and Gladstone (Liberal), the former advocating the forward policy, the latter, masterly inactivity. Russian overtures to the Afghan ruler Amir Sher Ali Khan led to the Second Anglo-Afghan War (1878–79), which, like the previous conflict, resulted in a severe defeat of the British Army, this time at Maiwand. The British returned, won the decisive battle of Charasiab, near Kabul, followed by widespread destruction, executions and withdrawal. The strategy, which came to be known as 'butcher and bolt' (Stewart 2011: 111), allowed the British to claim victory in both these Anglo-Afghan wars. A positive outcome of the 1879–80 conflict, from the British point of view at least, was the coming to power of Amir Abdur Rahman, their former enemy, returned after a long exile in Tashkent.

Abdur Rahman's accession to the throne in 1881 led, unexpectedly, to an easing of tension between Afghanistan and British India, for now an agreement was reached by which the British took control of Afghanistan's foreign affairs, so

---

[4] Hopkirk (2006: 525–40) provides the essential bibliographic guide to this kind of literature.

[5] The most recent contribution to this body of popular historical literature in Dalrymple (2013).

effectively blocking Russian contacts with the Afghan government. The Durand Line of 1893 settled for the time being the contentious issue of the border between British India and Afghanistan, though it left a legacy of armed conflict that is a major political problem even today. In the First World War, Amir Habibullah resisted strong pressures to join the German–Turkish axis. His successor, Amir Amanullah, apparently in a move intended to appease his Pashtun tribal subjects, launched incursions across the frontier. In response, the British declared war. The Third Anglo-Afghan War was a relatively brief conflict of a few weeks only and is memorable for the British arial bombing attacks on Jalalabad and Kabul, not the first but an early example of the use of this new weapon. The Treaty of Rawalpindi of 1919 resolved the conflict and gave Amanullah the prize of Afghanistan's full independence.[6]

Until the partition of India in 1947 the British remained preoccupied with controlling the Pashtun tribes in North-West Frontier Province (renamed Khyber Pakhtunkhwa in 2010) and the Tribal Areas that were adjacent to the border with Afghanistan. This was the time when the romance of 'The Frontier' really flourished. A measure of the seriousness of the situation from a military point of view is the fact that in the 1930s there were up to 50,000 British and Indian Army troops on the frontier (Swinson 1967: 311). Blood feuds between Pashtun tribesmen were a serious problem, 'accounting for three hundred murders a year in Peshawar district alone … [as was] raiding for cattle, women and guns' (Allen 1976: 198). The British responded to these incursions from the hills with, 'a punitive foray, a light bombing raid after advance warning or, as a last resort, a military column involving several brigades' (ibid., p. 199). The fighting took place in very difficult mountain territory, where the Pashtuns had all the advantages of familiarity with the territory and support from local inhabitants.

Paradoxically, this was the time when British admiration for the Pashtuns reached its zenith; they respected their adversaries as warriors, tacticians and expert marksmen. Many were the publications that described the military actions undertaken by the British. The television film *KHYBER* (1979), directed by André Singer, contains some quotable statements by three of the most eminent British officers who served on the Frontier in this period about their dealings with 'the Pathan' (that is, Pashtuns).

I must say I have the greatest respect for them as fighters, particularly the Masuds, who I think were on a par with the Germans and the Japs as perhaps the toughest people I've ever had to fight against. (Sir John Smythe, VC)

Our dealings with the Pathan was a gentleman's game, you know, no matter how poor a Pathan was, he may meet the King of England or the Viceroy of India,

[6]   Stewart (2011: Chapter 8) has a lot of detailed information about the Third Anglo-Afghan War.

but he'll look him straight in the eye and shake hands with him as if to say that, 'I'm as good a man as you are'. (Colonel Buster Goodwin)

The Pathans were not treated as enemies really, rather as naughty children who misbehaved from time to time. They were all under the Indian Government, they were all in Indian territory, they weren't invading India, they had their own British Political Officers looking after them, but now and again they played up, being Pathans, and if they played up and made a nuisance of themselves by attacking each other, or by looting villages in Indian territory, they had to be punished. It's quite different to an ordinary war. You had to organise your columns and go and punish these people or show them where they got off, in their own country. One looked on it as rather a summer vacation really, and the other side looked at it the same way. Mind you, they were not the sort of people into whose hands you wanted to let your men fall, because they wouldn't last very long. (Field Marshall Sir Claude Auchinleck)

After independence and the partition of India and Pakistan 'The Frontier' became someone else's problem: with the liberation of India from colonial rule in 1947, Britain too was liberated from its colonial responsibilities of maintaining law and order there, at least until 2001.

Enter the Ethnographer

So much for history. What did I actually know about Afghanistan before I went there for the first time? Where and what was Afghanistan in *my* upbringing, in *my* education, in *my* imagination? Given the importance of Afghanistan to British interests throughout the nineteenth century the answer is, surprisingly, that young people of my generation knew very little about this part of the world and its place in our colonial history. I knew something of the 'Great Game' played between the expanding British and Russian empires, a term originally coined by Lieutenant Arthur Conolly of the 6th Bengal Native Light Cavalry, one of the earliest players of the game (Hopkirk 2006: 123) and the term was immortalized by Kipling in *Kim*, a book I never read as a boy, though my father did take me to see the film, starring Errol Flynn as the Afghan horse dealer and spy Mahbub Ali, probably in 1951, the year of its release. *The Great Game* is the title of Hopkirk's invaluable book on nineteenth-century history, and also features in the title of Ahmad Rashid's *Taliban. Islam, Oil and the New Great Game in Central Asia* (2000). When the communists staged their coup in 1978 the *International Herald Tribune* declared: 'The great game is over and the Russians have won it' (cited in Halliday 1978: 4). My father was a one-time devotee of the American magazine *Popular Mechanics* and I recently discovered an article entitled 'Around the WORLD on a MOTORCYCLE'. Intrepid motorcyclist Robert E. Fulton, Jnr, passed through Afghanistan and the Khyber Pass, 'the latter famed the world over as a danger spot. But Fulton found the guardian of the pass a meek, peaceful fellow whose greatest desire in life was to visit Hollywood and New York' (*Popular Mechanics Magazine* 1937: 238–9). This little article included a photo of Afghans performing a sword dance, and another of the Bala Hisar fortress in Kabul. I must have seen these as a child, as I frequently used to leaf through our bound volume of the magazine for 1937. But there was no mention of Afghanistan or the North West Frontier in Rowland Walker's *Stories of British History*, a patriotic book for children first published in 1928, even though there was surely a place for Lieutenant Eldred Pottinger, 'The Hero of Herat', in its pages! On the other hand, the Ealing comedy *Carry On Up the Khyber*, released in 1968, clearly assumed that British audiences would recognize the film's historical context.

When I first visited Afghanistan in 1965, travelling with friends in a battered old Ford Fairlaine Country Sedan, bound for Australia, I had little idea what to expect. I knew a couple of people who had been there, hitch hiking and travelling on local buses (this was some years before the advent of the so-called hippy trail), and heard from them the same reports that one hears even today: going to Afghanistan is like travelling back in time to the Middle Ages, it is *so* medieval. My 1965 encounter was relatively brief. Entering the country from Iran, we spent several days in the city of Herat, which made a profound impression, with its minarets, its Grand Mosque, the streets lined with little open-fronted shops selling jewellery, second-hand clothes from the USA (I bought a pair of battered Texan boots), groceries, anything and everything. It was in Herat that I first encountered Afghan music, blaring from the loudspeaker system in the central park in the early evening. There was a little teashop near the Grand Mosque where in the evening we found a man playing a long-necked lute that at the time I identified, incorrectly, as a 'rebec' and now know to have been a 3-stringed *dutâr*. He was accompanied by his friend beating out the rhythm on an upturned tin basin. I had a go on his lute and was puzzled as to how one could create such wonderful music on this seemingly simple instrument. The next day the *dutâr* was being played outside the teahouse, on the wooden platform (*takht*) placed there for customers to sit on while taking their tea, poured from small individual teapots. Again it was played with tin basin accompaniment, and a caged bird, probably a canary, sang along with the music.[7]

We planned to drive to India, but India was at war with Pakistan and we were advised that the border was closed. From Herat we drove along the brand new Soviet-built highway, almost devoid of traffic, to Kandahar, and thence into Pakistan via the Bolan Pass. Finally, after having given our wreck of a car to the Pakistani Automobile Association in Karachi, we made our way to Australia. Travelling through so many countries in that year, across the Middle East, Iran, Afghanistan, Pakistan, Sri Lanka, Australia, to Panama and through Central America and the USA, the encounter with Afghanistan was especially memorable. The geography was stunning, the material culture fascinating, and the people

---

[7]   By the time I began my fieldwork in 1973 such teahouse performances were banned in Herat.

very friendly and hospitable. It also seemed a very artistic society. This was most obvious in the highly decorated lorries one met on the road (see Blanc 1976 for lorry painting), and in many other examples of decorative arts, from the tile work of Herat's Grand Mosque to the painted murals in the teahouses. My interest in the music was further stimulated by the acquisition of an LP of Afghan music recorded by J.C. & S. Lubtchansky in 1956, released by the Musée de l'Homme as *Afghanistan et Iran*. Above all it was the city of Herat that lingered in my memory.

In 1970, following the spirit of Lyse Doucet's as yet unarticulated aphorism, I drove again through Afghanistan, once more en route for Australia, and spent a little more time in this special country, visiting Herat, Kandahar, Kabul and Mazar-e Sharif. I had just completed a PhD in Experimental Psychology at the University of Sussex for research on human spatial orientation and motor control, and was becoming interested in the psychology of music. I had also discovered Bruno Nettl's seminal *Theory and Method in Ethnomusicology* (Nettl 1964) in the Sussex University library, which led me to Mantle Hood's paper 'The challenge of bi-musicality' (Hood 1960), which argued that training in basic musicianship is fundamental to any kind of musical scholarship, and that the student of exotic music should learn to perform what is studied. In Mazar-e Sharif I made my first recordings of Afghan music, using a domestic audiocassette recorder, of a barber in his barber's shop playing the *tanbur*. At that time I had no idea about the close connection in Afghanistan between the occupations of barber/hairdresser and musician.

Before getting to Australia I spent seven months in Kathmandu, where I encountered a small group of young Nepali professional musicians who had received training in North Indian classical music. I started to take *tabla* lessons from Krishna Govinda KC, and later published what I had learned (Baily 1974). His partner in music, the *sitâr* player Narendra Bataju, taught me something of the basics of Hindustani music, starting with *Rāg Yeman*, well known as the ideal beginner's *rāg*. Both Krishna Govinda and Narendra were graduates of the Bhatkhande Music Institute in Lucknow, where Govinda studied with Ustad Ahmad Jan Thirikwa, and Narendra with Ustad Ilias Khan. The introduction to Hindustani music that I received from these two musicians proved to be of enormous value when working later in Afghanistan, where the same music theory is followed as in the Indian Subcontinent, though with some significant differences of detail. These two musicians, who had played together since boyhood in Nepal, moved to Paris in 1972. I visited them there many times and they continued to be important in my musical development. Narendra in particular helped me by listening to recorded performances from my Afghan field recordings, making comments on what he heard from the perspective of his Lucknow-based knowledge of Hindustani music. He also composed a number of classical instrumental pieces (*gat*s) for me to play on the *rubâb*.

On the basis of these musical encounters in Afghanistan and Nepal, I decided that ethnomusicological research was the kind of academic work I wished to pursue in the future, and putting together music and psychology seemed the way to do it. In 1972 I made contact with John Blacking, newly appointed to the Chair of Social Anthropology at The Queen's University of Belfast, and already recognized as a dynamic new voice on the international ethnomusicology scene. He understood the potential of my scientific specialization in human movement, motor control and the acquisition of sensori-motor skills, for he was already interested in the ergonomics of musical performance and the ways certain aspects of music structure are rooted in the body (Blacking 1973: 12–19). He encouraged me to undertake the research I was considering. When it came to selecting a region of the world in which to work I had little hesitation in choosing Afghanistan and its long-necked lutes. I liked what I knew of the country and its people; I liked their music and was eager to know more about it and to learn to play it.

In preparation for this project I and my wife Veronica Doubleday moved to Tehran, where it was easy to find work teaching English to Iranian students. Being in Tehran was also a great opportunity for learning about Persian art music. I enrolled in the Center for the Preservation and Propagation of Iranian Music, and had some lessons for the *sehtâr* from Daryush Tala'i and Jalal Zo'l-fonun, today both recognized as masters of that instrument. The Professor of Music at Tehran University, Hormoz Farhat, who had a PhD in Ethnomusicology from UCLA, kindly lent me a copy of his thesis. This gave me an excellent understanding of the principles underlying Persian music, with its modulations from one melodic mode to another in the course of performing a *dastgâh*, a type of modal suite.[8] There were also many concerts of Persian music in the Rudaki Hall for us to attend. This experience of Persian music was later very useful in understanding the music of Afghanistan, especially that of Herat. After eight months' working in Tehran I was successful in winning a post-doctoral award from the Social Science Research Council to carry out research in Herat on the emergence of a new type of long-necked lute, the 14-stringed *dutâr*, with Blacking in an advisory role. In 1973, accompanied by Veronica, I began my first year of ethnomusicological fieldwork in the city of Herat. So began our 40-year connection with the music culture of Afghanistan.

The Music Loving Amirs of Kabul

A number of authors writing in English have traced the succession of Amirs (rulers) of Kabul over the last 150 years in terms of political policies and events, but I want to look at the Amirs in another way, as patrons of music. Patronage by political elites has been of great importance in many places and at many times, and musical rivalry between courts has been an important element in the creation of new musical styles and genres and the emergence of virtuoso performers. This was certainly true of the regions neighbouring Afghanistan.

---

[8]   Professor Farhat's thesis was later published as *The Dastgâh Concept in Persian Music* (Farhat 1990).

The period of the British Raj (1857–1947) was the time when the separate stylistic schools (*gharânâs*) of Indian classical vocal music flourished and proliferated.

> Rulers and nobles no longer permitted to fight wars often squandered their incomes instead on their courts, including the musical establishments. There was an explosive development of Hindustani classical music and much rivalry and exchange amongst the many princely musical centers. (Powers 1979: 23)

Similar developments were taking place in neighbouring countries. For example, in the Qajar court of Tehran, during the late nineteenth century, the repertoire (*radif*) of classical Persian *dastgâh* music was formalized by the eminent master musician Agha Ali Akbar Farahani. The system of art music known as *shash maqâm* developed in the court of the Amirs of Bukhara, notably during the time of Amir Muzaffar, who ruled from 1860 to 1885. Likewise, court patronage in Kabul during the late nineteenth and early twentieth centuries led to the creation of distinctly Afghan art music.

Ahmad Sarmast's PhD thesis (Sarmast 2004) is a goldmine of information about the history of music of the various dynasties that have existed in the territory of Afghanistan over the centuries. From the 1860s we find a succession of Amirs on the throne of Kabul who were notable as music lovers and royal patrons of music: Sher Ali Khan, Abdur Rahman, Habibullah, Amanullah and Zahir Shah. There was much more progress and modernization in this period than is generally recognized by those who like to see Afghanistan in terms of the Great Game and 'The Wild Tribes'.[9]

Sher Ali Khan (1863–65, 1868–78) was a modernizer who is remembered for his attempts to 'institute progressive reform programmes. He founded a system of civil and military schools, the first regular newspaper in Afghanistan, established new towns, and built several factories and large public buildings. He introduced also the postal service' (Reshtia 1990: 277). In 1868 the British Indian government sought to establish friendly relations and win Afghanistan's support to counter further Russian expansion in Central Asia. In 1869 Sher Ali Khan was invited to attend a conference in Ambala, in today's Indian Punjab, to discuss the Russian threat. Ambala is close to Patiala, whose court is associated with one of the great traditions of North Indian vocal music (the Patiala *gharânâ*). After attending the conference Amir Sher Ali Khan invited to Kabul a number of singers, musicians and dancers from North India to serve as his court entertainers and to provide music lessons for 'princes and other members of the ruling dynasty' (Sarmast 2004: 179).

Sarmast lists the following performers at Sher Ali's court (ibid., p. 180; Baily 2011a: 12–13). I follow Sarmast in the spelling of their names.

---

[9]   Following the title of Pennell's *Among the Wild Tribes of the Afghan Frontier* (Pennell 1922).

Male
- Singers: Mia Samandar, Sayan Gund Kali Khan, Nata Khan, Mia Mahtab Khan
- *Tabla* players: Bar Pur, Gamu, Taleh-mand, Karim Bakhsh, Khuda Bakhsh
- *Sârangi* players: Qando Raji, Mohammad Akbar
- *Rubâb* player: Rang Ali

Female
- Singers: Mina, Gawhar
- Dancers: Anwari, Maltani, Gulshah
- *Daf* (frame-drum) player: Haji Begum

Sarmast (2004: 183) suggests that these were basically members of dance troupes of the *nautch* girl type, well known in India at the time, female dancers performing with the standard accompanying instruments, notably *sârangi* and *tabla*. *Khatak* dance had undergone significant development in the Lucknow court of Nawab Wajid Ali Shah in the mid-nineteenth century, and *nautch* performers took on at least some aspects of the new dance. It is quite possible that when local Indian rulers received Sher Ali Khan during his state visit in 1869 he was entertained with such dance performances and wanted to have something of the sort to grace his court in Kabul. The addition of Rang Ali the *rubâb* player to the list of musicians is intriguing, but Sher Ali Khan was something of a player of the *rubâb* himself (Nabi Misdaq, personal communication, 20 June 2008), and, as Sarmast noted, the musicians were there not just to entertain, but to provide music tuition for princes and other members of the ruling dynasty, which might have included the Amir himself.

But apart from their names we know little about the number and origins of these dance troupes, which probably came from different parts of India, including Kashmir. Sarmast (2004: chapter 7) provides a number of family trees showing how some of today's musicians in Kabul are related to those early court musicians. The *tabla* player Gamuddin came from Kasur, a town near Lahore, in present-day Pakistan, the burial-place of the Sufi poet Bullhe Shah, and a centre for classically trained hereditary musician families. Kasur is also said to be the ancestral home of singers who created the Patiala vocal *gharânâ*, which was later to become associated with the leading vocalists of Kabul, notably Ustad Sarahang. Gamuddin was an ancestor of Ustad Hashem Mahmoud and his brothers Asif and Arif, and was the maternal grandfather of Ustad Sarahang (1923–82).

When Amir Sher Ali Khan brought the first Indian musicians, singers and dancers to Kabul he gave them residences in a section of the old city adjacent to the Bala Hisar, the citadel which housed the royal palace, so they could be easily summoned to the *durbar* (royal court). In due course this part of the old city became famous as the musicians' quarter of Kabul, generally known as Kucheh Kharabat, which means 'Kharabat Alley'. The word *kharâbât* has a very interesting semantic field. It can mean a tavern, a pothouse, a gaming house, a brothel (ibid., p. 184). But in Sufi terminology *kharâbât* is an important and frequently used word that implies the desolation and destruction of the Sufi's self and will and actions and epithets, and his complete subjugation and subordination and obedience to God (Baily 2011a: 64–5). Thus the term is infused with ambiguity.

Over the years the Kharabat grew larger. By the mid-twentieth century several hundred musicians lived there, cheek by jowl, in small mud-brick and wooden two storey houses. Local Afghan hereditary musicians had joined the community of musicians whose ancestors came from outside Afghanistan. The denizens of the Kharabat constituted the most important musical resource in Afghanistan. Special codes of musicianly behaviour developed, which one might refer to as the protocols of the Kharabat, many of them derived from Indian practice. Central to these was the *ustâd–shâgerd* (teacher–student) relationship, cemented by the string-tying ceremony (*gormâni*) at a gathering of musicians, where the string tied around the pupil's wrist represents an unbreakable chain connecting teacher and disciple. This clearly derives from the *ghanda-bandan* of India (Neuman1980: 43–58). The *ustâd*s ran their own little private music schools. They taught youngsters from within the Kharabat, who learned through an apprenticeship system, in which they paid not with money but with service to their teacher. They also taught amateur musicians from outside the hereditary musician community, who paid for their lessons in cash and gifts.

After the Second Anglo-Afghan War of 1878–80, Sher Ali was succeeded by his nephew Abdur Rahman (1880–1901). This larger-than-life character, sometimes described as the 'Iron Amir', was known for a succession of ruthless campaigns to subdue the country, and is especially reviled by the Hazara people of central Afghanistan on that account (Mousavi 1998). He allowed the British to dictate his foreign relations, blocking contact with the Russians in return for subsidies and arms. His reign witnessed the destruction of many of the Timurid monuments of Herat, in 1885, to prevent them being used in any possible Russian assault on the city (Fraser-Tytler 1967: 165), and he acquiesced in the demarcation of the Durand Line (1893) separating Afghanistan from British India. His predilection for cruel punishments was noted by George Curzon (later Viceroy of India), who visited Kabul in 1894 and stated, 'This man of blood loved scents and colours and gardens and singing birds and flowers' (Schofield 2010: 104).

We get a rich picture of musical life at court and its environs in this period from the Amir's own memoirs, the *Tâj-ul-twârikh*, and from the published accounts of Dr John Gray, Abdur Rahman's personal physician, and Frank Martin, an engineer (Gray 1895, Martin 1907). Gray and Martin mention the brass band (the *Dasta-ye Muzik Huzur*, the 'Music Band of the Court'), probably trained by the Indian bandsman Zabto Khan (Sarmast 2004: 300). There were also military bagpipe bands, an idea probably borrowed from India, and the old-fashioned *naqqarakhâna* ensemble of shawms, long trumpets and kettledrums, housed above the gateway to the Bala Hisar and palace complex, which marked the hours of the day. Gray

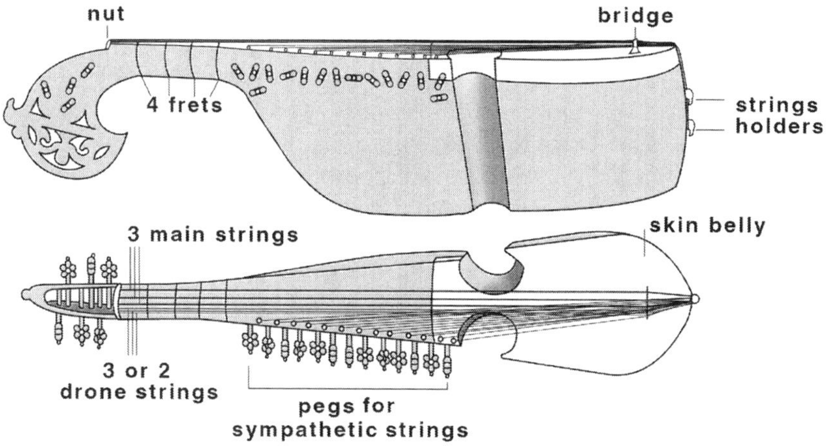

Figure 1.2   The Afghan *rubâb*

reports the performances of Indian dancing girls and of dancing boys, and mentions a western piano in the palace.

In his memoirs the Amir records that the musicians of his court were of '*Hindi* (Indian), *Irâni* (Persian) and *Afghan* (Pashtun) origin' (ibid., p. 188). Sarmast has been able to identify a number of the Indian (*Hindi*) court artistes by name. Amongst them were three male singers, Sattar Ju (father of Ustad Qassem), Atta Hussain (father of Ustad Ghulam Hussain) and Qurban Ali (son of Mia Samandar, one of Sher Ali's imports). The musicians of *Irâni* origin were not necessarily all from Iran but were probably performers of Khorasanian music from Herat and Mashhad. The musicians of *Afghan* origin were presumably Pashtuns or at least Pashto-speaking clients, and were probably singers or reciters of stories and epics who accompanied themselves on the Afghan *rubâb*. By his own account the Amir was 'a great patron of music and musicians, as well as a skilful *rabâb* and *kamâncha* player himself' (ibid., p. 187).[10]

The *rubâb* (often transliterated as *rabâb*) is the national instrument of Afghanistan, played by four of my *hamkârân*, who enter my tale in later chapters. It is a short-necked double-chambered plucked lute with sympathetic strings that give the *rubâb* its special sound. They are tuned to the notes of the melodic mode (*râg*) being deployed, and reinforce the sound of each note as it is struck (Figure 1.2).

The sympathetic strings produce a wash of sound, with complex interactions of the harmonics of each string, greatly enhancing the instrument's resonance. The *rubâb* is often highly decorated with intricate mother-of-pearl inlays. The name *rubâb* is said by some Afghans to be a combination of two words: *ruh*, meaning

---

[10]   *Kamancha* here probably refers to a spike fiddle with skin belly, like the Persian *kemâncheh* or Uzbek *ghaichak*.

'soul' and *bâb*, 'doorway', so the *rubâb* becomes 'the doorway to the soul'. Although etymologically questionable, this claim is a manifestation of the Sufi-infused culture that still prevails in Afghanistan despite 30 years of warfare and the cultural incursions of the Wahhabis. Many Afghans adhere to the Sufi doctrine that music is *qazâ-ye ruh*, 'food for the soul', or 'spiritual nourishment'. The *rubâb* also has a special connection with the Pashto speaking population of Afghanistan and it is not surprising that it should have been specifically patronized by the Amirs of Kabul. In the emerging Kabuli style of classical *ghazal* singing the *rubâb* became the predominant accompanying instrument, responding to and answering the singer's voice.

There are some interesting parallels here with the use of the long-necked lute, the *târ*, in the Qajar court at this time and the formulation of the *dastgâh* system (Baily 2008a). There were certainly musical contacts between Kabul and Tehran in this period, with evidence for Afghan musicians visiting Tehran and introducing certain Indian *râg*s into the *radif* (Pourjavady 2007). Another significant aspect of this period is that patronage of music extended beyond the court of the Amir: 'Kabuli nobles, aristocrats, clerks, artisan guilds, and others began to patronise music for weddings, and other gatherings and festivities' (Sarmast 2004: 220). There are parallels here with developments in Iran during the Constitutional Movement of 1906, when the first public musical performances took place.

In 1901 Abdur Rahman was succeeded by his son Habibullah. He lacked the forcible personality of his father and occupies less space in the anglophone history books, yet his reign was of great importance in several respects. He continued the modernizations of his father, especially road building, including the highway from Kabul to Herat via Ghazni and Kandahar, constructed Afghanistan's first hydro-electric generating plant, near Jalalabad, and saw to the building of a textile mill and many workshops in Kabul (Gregorian 1969: 190–91).

The modernization project was supported by the influential Afghan intellectual Mahmud Tarzi, who introduced Afghans to the modern world through his writings (Wide 2013). His father and large extended family had been exiled by Abdur Rahman and Mahmud Tarzi grew up from the age of 16 in Ottoman Syria. He was permitted to return to Afghanistan in 1902, when he formed a close friendship with Amir Habibullah. Tarzi had many ideas about the modernization of Afghanistan within an Islamic framework, emulating some of the changes that had taken place in Turkey, in turn inspired by influences from Europe. He became the centre of a small group of modernist Afghan intellectuals, sometimes called 'The Young Afghans' who were full of ideas about how to modernize Afghanistan within a Muslim framework. Tarzi started the influential newspaper *Siraj al-Akhbar*, which published many articles advocating the necessity of modernization in Afghanistan.[11] All this in spite of the fact that an Islamist faction

---

[11]   He translated four of Jules Verne's novels, including *Around the World in 80 Days* and *Twenty Thousand Leagues Under the Sea*, books that introduced Afghan readers to many recent innovations in European material culture, such as the submarine and the hydrogen balloon.

was strong in court circles at this time, and opposed in principle the westernization that modernization seemed to imply.

Like his father, Amir Habibullah had a keen interest in music (Sarmast 2004: 211), was a patron of music at court and an enthusiastic *rubâb* player. Habibullah also had Indian, Iranian and Afghan court musicians (ibid.) including two new singers who were in due course to became famous *ustâd*s, sons of earlier migrants: Qassem, the son of Sattar Ju from Kashmir, and Ghulam Hussain, son of Atta Hussain, origin unknown. Ustad Piyara Khan, from Lahore, was also associated with Kabul: he is credited with having brought the Patiala *gharânâ* of Hindustani vocal music to Habibullah's court. Piyara Khan was the teacher of the young Qassem, who started off as a *rubâb* player in the court of Abdur Rahman, and learned vocal music both from his father Sattar Ju and from Qurban Ali. As for the '*Irâni*' musicians, three of them were from Herat: the singers Haidar Namadmal and Haidar Pineh, both of whom also played the Iranian *târ*, and the *tabla* player Said Qureish. They performed in the Khorasanian style that was current before the formulation in Iran of the *radif* by Agha Ali Akbar Farahani. I had heard about these Herati musicians during my fieldwork in 1974 (Baily 1988a: 20). My understanding was that they had been invited to perform at the court for a national celebration, but not that they were permanently employed there.

According to Sarmast (2004: 212), Habibullah had a keen appreciation of Pashtun music and admired the art of Logar singers Gulbuddin Logari and Ali Gul Logari, who would appear to have been narrators, in speech or song, of Pashtun epics, with *rubâb* accompaniment. Habibullah banned the performances of dancing girls in court except in the harem of the royal women (ibid., p. 213) while it appears that performances of dancing boys continued. Indeed, the tradition of dancing boys flourished in connection with *Logari* instrumental music, which to this day is closely connected with solo dance. Dancing boys adopted elements from the now restricted dancing girls: the wearing of ankle bells, female dress and made-up faces (Sarmast, personal communication, 1 September 2012).

The new rules concerning dancing girls were to have important repercussions, for the Indian musicians, players of *tabla* and *sârangi* who were conversant with the melodic modes and metric cycles (*râg*s and *tâl*s). They were highly skilled in the performance of Hindustani music, and were now encouraged to concentrate their efforts on the provision of art music, rather than classical dance. It is at this point that we start to discern the presence of court singers of art music. Sarmast credits Qurban Ali, son of Mia Samandar (see above), with the introduction to Kabul of both *khyâl* and the Indian style of *ghazal* singing with Persian texts, when poems of a usually spiritual-mystical character were set to music, especially those by the Indo-Muslim poet Bedil (Sarmast, 2004: 219). The *ghazal* became the principal genre of Kabuli art music, as discussed below. At the same time, the *rubâb* was emerging as an instrument of solo classical performance, not just used for vocal accompaniment.

Habibullah ruled Afghanistan through the period of the First World War, when there was strong pressure from within Afghanistan to side with the Central

Powers and attack India. But during a visit to India in 1906 Habibullah had become of freemason in the Concordia Lodge, and he 'vowed to prove a faithful friend of England as long as England kept faith with him' (McMahon 2013). The Niedermayer–Hentig expedition of 1915–16 was dispatched to Afghanistan to try to persuade the Amir to support an attack on British India (Hopkirk 1994: chapters 8–10).[12] Habibullah managed to resist these pressures and to adhere to the policy of his father in allowing British India to control Afghanistan's foreign affairs. In 1919 Habibullah was assassinated while on a hunting expedition near Jalalabad. The assassins were never identified. The motivation may well have been to avenge Habibullah's stance of neutrality during the war. His third son, Amanullah, seized power in Kabul.

Amanullah's 10 years in power were characterized by a remarkable move towards further modernization and secularization, inspired in part by political events in Turkey following the demise of the Ottoman Empire and the establishment of the Republic of Turkey in 1923 by Ataturk. Mahmud Tarzi, whose daughter Soroya was married to Amanullah, was the driving force behind many of Amanullah's innovations and was also crucial in Afghanistan attaining complete independence from British India after the Third Anglo-Afghan War of 1919. There is no need to describe in detail the reforms instituted by Amanullah, many of which met with great resistance from the more conservative sections of society. Particularly controversial was the appearance of Queen Soroya and other female members of the royal family without their veils in quasi-public places. Amanullah assumed the title of King in 1926 and in 1927 he and Queen Soroya embarked on an extensive royal tour of Europe that was adversely reported in Afghanistan. Upon their return there was an uprising inspired by religious conservatives which ended with Amanullah's abdication. He went into exile in Italy, and remained in Europe until his death in 1960. There are suspicions that the British at the very least colluded in his downfall; it was rumoured that photographs taken in Europe of Amanullah and the unveiled Queen were spread amongst the tribes by the British (Misdaq 2006: 64).

Amanullah's reign was a very significant period in terms of music at court, a time when music assumed a new significance in this modernizing context. The leading vocalist at Amanullah's *durbar* (court) was Ustad Qassem, who was born in Kabul in 1883 and died in 1956, the son of the Kashmiri singer Sattar Ju who had been prominent in Abdur Rahman's court. When Amanullah took the throne, Ustad Qassem became his principal court singer. His fame rests principally on being the 'originator of the new Afghan music', or the 'Father of Afghan Music'. Besides being endowed with a wonderful voice he had an excellent knowledge of the practical and theoretical principles of Hindustani music supplemented by his own modifications and innovations. His song texts were derived from the Persian classical poetry of poets such as Bedil and Hafez, often Sufi in character. He also

---

[12]   The main achievement of the Niedermayer-Hentig expedition was to take of number of valuable photographs in Herat and Kabul (Niedermayer 1924).

sang in Pashto. He enjoyed the reputation of being an excellent *ghazal* singer, with a great fund of poetry at his command. And he also sang Afghan folk songs, in Dari and in Pashto, with certain additions derived from Hindustani music, such as short improvised passages. With these innovations he created a new kind of Afghan music that served as the basis of what was to become Kabuli vocal art music.

Ustad Qassem made a number of 78 rpm gramophone records for the Gramophone Company in India. In the Afghan List for June 1926, part of their Indian Native Catalogue published in Calcutta, we find no less than 40 78 rpm records under the name of 'Kassim Afghan'. The catalogue describes him as HRH King Amanullah's Court Singer.[13] After Amanullah secured Afghanistan's full independence from British control there were annual celebrations on Independence Day, with great festivities held in Kabul and other cities. Ustad Qassem became nationally famous at these celebrations for the *ghazal*s he performed expressing patriotic and nationalistic sentiments.

Notwithstanding his high status as the King's court singer and personal friend, indicated by his dressing in western clothes, such as lounge suit and tie, evening dress, or golfer's tweed plus-fours, Ustad Qassem lived amongst the other hereditary musicians in the Kucheh Kharabat. He ran a small music school in his house and trained many youngsters from the musician families living around him. The most famous of his vocal students, and the one who was later said to sound most like him, was Ustad Rahim Bakhsh. Several of his sons and grandsons (Yaqub, Yusuf, Musa, Essa, Wahid and Abdullah) also became professional musicians (see family tree, Sarmast 2004: 190). His grandson Wahid Qassemi is today one of the leading vocal stars of Afghan popular music.

The insurrection against Amanullah was led by Habibullah Kalikani, a Tajik from Kohistan, an area to the north of Kabul. Better known as Bacha Saqao, 'son of the water carrier', after his father's lowly occupation, he was branded a bandit and executed with his henchmen. This occurred when the inevitable Pashtun reaction against the usurper took place, led by another branch of the Mohammadzai royal family, Nadir Khan, and his three brothers, Hashim Khan, Shah Mahmud and Shah Wali. The short reign of Nadir Khan is seen as a further period of reform and modernization, and the formulation for the first time of a Constitution in 1933, in which the two official languages were defined as Pashto and Dari. Little mention of music is made of this period. In 1933 Nadir Khan was assassinated while making a school visit in Kabul, the result not of an uprising against his reforms but of a vendetta between two powerful families, the Musahiban, which included Nadir Khan and his brothers, and the Charkhis (Misdaq 2006: 285–6, Fraser-Tytler 1967: 245). Afghanistan now entered a most unusual political phase. Instead of fighting between themselves for power after the violent death of their sibling, the Musahiban brothers put Nadir Khan's son Zahir on the throne. Zahir Shah, as he then became, was 19 years of age.

---

[13]   Some of these records have been published on CD in the USA by Watan Music, in Falls Church, Virginia.

Zahir Shah had been educated in France and was a fluent French speaker. He was a keen sportsman, a good shot, a horseman, tennis player, and also a great music lover. Zahir Shah was in many ways like a constitutional monarch, a ceremonial figurehead who for much of his 40-year reign played little active role in politics. He was devoted to his many hobbies, including music and agriculture. For 20 years Afghanistan was run by his two highly competent uncles, Hashim Khan, Prime Minister 1929–46, and Shah Mahmud, Prime Minister 1946–53. The Musahiban brothers continued to promote and consolidate the reforms instituted by Nadir Khan and a new nationalist trend became discernable in Afghanistan. According to Reshtia (personal communication, 21 April 1985), 'The nationalist movement was a deliberate initiative which originated in 1935–36'. Gregorian (1969) gives an account of the arguments put forward by nationalist writers of the time. They recognized that one of Afghanistan's problems was its ethnic diversity, and the nationalists were preoccupied with establishing a common history, religious background, and ethnic origin for all the peoples of Afghanistan, claiming that they were descended from the same Aryan stock. The Pashto language was given great importance in this nationalist ideology. It was claimed that Pashto was the purest and oldest Aryan language and that 'the Avesta and the earliest Vedas were the greatest masterpieces of Afghan and Pashto literature' (Gregorian 1969: 347).

> Many urged that Afghanistan's folklore and traditional music be collected, and called for the development of a new literature reflecting both the nation's historical legacy and its present social realities, needs and aspirations. Poets and writers were exhorted to see themselves as vehicles of social change and their role as the awakening of the Afghan people. (ibid., p. 349)

Zahir Shah was a keen player of the *sitâr*, and received tuition from the Kharabati musician Sirajuddin. Many of India's great musicians were invited to perform at the court. His daughter, Princess Mariam, told me the names of some of the visitors (personal communication, 2012). He favoured *sitâr* players, notably Ustad Vilayat Khan, who came to Kabul many times, also Pandit Ravi Shankar and Ustad Rais Khan. He also invited singers from Pakistan, such as Salaamat Ali Khan and his brother Nazarkat Ali Khan. Musicians from Kabul also performed at court, but he does not seem to have had a principal court singer comparable in status to Ustad Qassem. It would appear that the era of court patronage was coming to an end; in the 1940s the radio station, Radio Kabul, was taking over as the centre of musical patronage and creativity.

The Amirs oversaw and patronized the development of a distinct Afghan art music that brought together Indian, Khorasanian and Pashtun music elements. The Kabuli *ghazal* style embodies features of all three: to mention the most obvious, the *ghazal* musical form comes from India, the interpolated poetry in free rhythm from Khorasan, the frenetic instrumental sections and dramatic rhythmic cadences from Pashtun music. By the 1930s the *ghazal* and genres of Kabuli instrumental art music such as the *lâriya* (overture) and the *naghma-ye klâsik* (classical instrumental piece) were fully formed and ready to be carried to other Afghan cities, such as Herat. A more detailed account of these developments and the case for regarding them as constituting a distinctive *Afghan* art music are discussed with reference to the Kabuli singer Ustad Amir Mohammad in Baily (2011a).

Radio Afghanistan

The relationship between music and radio broadcasting in Afghanistan is a fascinating and complicated story, yet to be told in full.[14] Here I can do no more than outline some of the principal strands in that story. In a country that had little in the way of conservatories or schools of music, university music departments, arts councils, national sound archives, or organizations protecting composers' and musicians' rights, and where music was not part of the school curriculum, the radio station in Kabul played a crucial role as the national centre for musical activity and creativity. As well as functioning as the national broadcasting station it served in part as an informal conservatory, providing permanent posts for musicians and composers, and it housed record and tape archives. Radio Afghanistan ran occasional courses for amateur musicians, and provided a context in which musicians could improve their skills through working with more experienced colleagues. It was a bastion of modernism, and its establishment led to considerable upgrading in the status of musicians and singers, men and women, amateur and professional, some of whom came to enjoy 'star' status.

Radio broadcasting in Afghanistan was initiated in 1925 during the reign of Amanullah; a typical gesture of modernization of the time. It had a limited range and impact, with an estimated 1,000 receiving sets in Kabul by 1928. The radio station was destroyed in the following year during the uprising against the King. A new radio station was set up in the 1930s with technical aid from Germany, experimental transmissions began in 1939 and Radio Kabul was officially opened in 1940. During the Second World War broadcasting was seriously hampered by difficulties in obtaining new equipment or spare parts and an effective broadcasting service that could be received in most parts of the country was not established until the mid-1940s. Ownership of radio receivers was very limited and to ensure the dissemination of radio broadcasts, receiver appliances in a number of cities were linked to loudspeaker systems in their central parks and main streets. They broadcast the news, music, and other programmes, to a predominantly male audience in those public spaces. This project was launched in 1940 and completed by 1945 in the main provincial towns (Reshtia, personal communication, 21 April 1985).[15] The buildings of Radio Kabul were located on the edge of the old city,

---

[14] But see Slobin (1974); Baily (1981, 1988a, 2007a); Sakata (1983); Madadi (1996); Sarmast (2004).

[15] Sayed Qassem Reshtia had a distinguished career as a writer and diplomat. For a period in the 1940s he was Director of Radio Kabul.

near the Pul-e Bagh-e Umumi, and within easy reach of the Kucheh Kharabat, the musicians' quarter, from where many of its musician employees were recruited.

Radio broadcasting opened up new possibilities for communication between Kabul and the rest of the country. According to Restia (ibid.) the stated aims of the radio station were to spread the message of the Holy Quran, to reflect the national spirit, to perpetuate the treasures of Afghan folklore, and to contribute to public education. The government saw radio as the best and quickest way to communicate to and inform the population of its policies and development programmes. It may well be that music on air was seen as a way of attracting an audience that could then be informed about local news and government edicts and policies. Music may also have been deliberately used to promote nationalism, modernity and secularism.

A significant figure in the early days of Radio Kabul was Ustad Abdul Ghafur Breshna (1907–74). Breshna was a multi-talented artist: a painter, composer, singer, he wrote radio dramas, and was a teacher at the Art School. He was one of a group of Afghan students sent by Amanullah to Germany in 1921, where he studied painting, lithography and typography. He returned to Afghanistan in 1929 and taught at the School of Arts and Crafts, where he later became Director and introduced new styles of painting. He was Managing Director of the state-owned Printing and Publishing House of Afghanistan (1939–43). From 1943–53 he was Music Director and later Director of Radio Kabul and it was in that capacity that he took the controversial step of introducing women singers to the radio station. One of the first such singers he promoted was Parwin, who started singing on air in 1951. Sakata (1983: 98, 2013: 51) describes her early career.

In the extensive notes that accompany the CD *Mahwash. Radio Kaboul. Hommage aux compositeurs afghan*, Hossein Arman states that in the early days there were three ensembles at the radio station: one with traditional Afghan and Indian instruments; a folk music band; and a western reed and brass band that was seconded from the Afghan army (Lecomte 2003).

The first mentioned of the three ensembles was made up of musicians from the Kucheh Kharabat and was known as the *Arkestar Klâsik Radio Afghanistan* (Classical Orchestra of Radio Afghanistan).[16] A photo from 1943 in the *Radio Kaboul* notes shows the following members: Ustad Ghulam Hussain, vocal and *'armonia*; Mohammad Omar, *rubâb*; Mahrajuddin, *sitâr*; Din Mohammad, *sârangi*; Fakir Hassan, *sârangi*, Chacha Mahmud, *tabla*; Mohammad Rahim, *tânpurâ*.[17] The *rubâb* was the only Afghan instrument in the ensemble, the rest were instruments of Hindustani music. Working for the radio station was an attractive prospect for many hereditary musicians based in the Kharabat, offering a regular and somewhat prestigious official job that allowed time for private performances and teaching outside work hours. The knowledge and expertise of these musicians were important for organizing other ensembles and large orchestras at the radio

[16] *Arkestar* is Sarmast's preferred translation and transliteration of 'orchestra'.
[17] Sarmast (2004: 316) gives a slightly different list of names from Arman.

station, and these men played a key role in training a new generation of amateur musicians, mainly singers. For example, the classical singer Ustad Ghulam Hussain, father of Ustad Sarahang, was employed as a staff member, with the official position of *montazem*, 'arranger'. He was responsible for the recording of new songs, and choosing what should be broadcast. He helped many young vocalists, including the Herati singer Abdul Wahab Madadi, whose singing he coached. 'He was always singing to himself, he was a genius, like Ustad Qassem, he was the Afghan Mozart. I worked under him for ten years, I learned a lot from him. He was very nice; other *ustâd*s were not so helpful. He used to say, "Madadi, bring me poetry and I'll compose new tunes for you to sing"' (Madadi personal communication, 31 July 2012).

The second ensemble from the early days of Radio Kabul was the band of Ustad Durai Logari, from the Logar Valley. Like other areas close to Kabul, such as Parwan, Wardak, and Shomali, this is a mixed Pashto–Dari speaking area. The *Logari* style is a blend of Pashtun and Tajik elements, and remains extremely popular. The typical *Logari* ensemble consists of singer-*'armonia* player, with *rubâb*, *sarinda* and *dohol*. The musical style is predominantly Pashtun, using the three common melodic modes of Pashtun music – *Pâri*, *Kesturi* and *Bairami* – and is characterized by short up-tempo instrumental sections, with strong rhythmic cadences leading to dramatic breaks. Song texts are either in Dari or Pashto. The *Logari* style is associated with solo dance; the dancer is required to freeze in a dramatic pose when the breaks occur in the music. Today *Logari* is one of the main genres of dance music, both in Afghanistan and in the Afghan diaspora.

The third ensemble mentioned by Arman was the *Arkestar-e Jâz* (Jazz Orchestra). The term *jâz* here refers not to North American jazz music, but simply to the use of European instrumentation. The history of this type of ensemble goes back to the military reed and brass bands of the time of Amir Abdur Rahman. The first school of music was established in Kabul in 1924 as part of the Military College. At that time the Afghan army was trained by Turkish military instructors and it is probable that the teachers of military music were also from Turkey. This school of military music closed at the time of Amanullah's abdication, to reopen in 1934 as the *Maktab-e Musiqi* (School of Music). Two of the instructors were Khalid Rajab Beg and Farruk Effendi. In about 1937 another Turk, Mukhtar Beg, a conductor and string specialist, joined them. The young bandsmen were largely recruited from orphanages, so not subject to parental discouragement from becoming musicians. The intention was to train them to establish military music ensembles in garrisons in provincial cities such as Kandahar, Mazar and Herat.

By the 1940s there were several *arkestar-e jâz* ensembles in Kabul, attached to the Ministry of Defence, the Directorate of the Press and the Municipality of Kabul. The function of the latter was to provide musical entertainment in public places of the capital, while the *arkestar* of the Directorate of the Press played on the radio. The original members of this radio ensemble, sometimes known as *Arkestar Shomara Dovom* (Orchestra Number Two) were: Ustad Salim Sarmast, leader of the ensemble, mandolin and trumpet; Faqir Mohammad Nangiyaly, trumpet;

Ghulam Sakhi, accordion; Nala, flute; Juma Khan, saxophone; and Mohammad Ali, drum kit (Madadi 1996: 235).

Another western orchestra in this period was attached to the Municipal Theatre, the *Kabul Nanderi*, to accompany singers who performed between scenes. Their songs of love, comedy and satire, accompanied by an *arkestar-e jâz*, were known as *pish pardaha* (before the acts). Sarmast (2004: 321) identifies five genres of song performed in the theatre: (1) Dari and Pashto folk songs; (2) Hindi film songs with new texts in Dari or Pashto; (3) Iranian popular songs, presumably learned from 78 rpm discs; (4) imitations of European popular songs or dance tunes; and (5) Afghan composed songs in the new *tarz* style that was becoming a fully recognized and widely practised genre of popular music. We can assume that all five types of music were also performed on the radio, and in this context it is the new *tarz* style that is particularly significant in terms of creativity and originality.

The word *tarz* has several meanings – style, method, melody – and here applies to the newly developed song form characterized by verse, refrain and a melodically distinct instrumental section.[18] From the late 1940s a large number of popular songs of the *tarz* type were composed in order to create a distinctly Afghan music suitable for radio broadcasting (Baily 1988a: 30). These were performed by the first group of Afghan amateur radio singers, accompanied by the newly founded *Arkestar-e Jâz* at Radio Kabul. Later on, a number of singers such as Hafizullah Khyal and Jalil Zaland, who were on the payroll of the radio station, were contracted to compose a certain number of songs every month.

In 1957 a new ensemble was established, the *Arkestar Kiliwâli Radio Kabul* (The Folk Ensemble of Radio Kabul), also known as the *Arkestar Mili Radio Kabul*. Led by Ustad Mohammad Omar, the *rubâb* player, it consisted of musical instruments considered to be 'Afghan'. The instrumentation consisted of three *rabâbs*, two *tanburs*, a *dutâr*, two *sarindas*, *tula*, *dohol* and *zirbaghali*; the ensemble did not include the *'armonia* or *tabla*, both imports from India in the nineteenth century. The *Arkestar Mili Radio Kabul* made a number of trips to give concerts abroad, in the USSR, Iran and India.

The dynamism of this period is shown by Karim Herawi's reconfiguration of the *dutâr*. Karim was from Herat, joined the radio station in 1957 and became a member of the new folk music ensemble. The Herati *dutâr* he brought with him was a relatively simple instrument with three strings. Working at Radio Kabul he was prompted to redesign the instrument, to make it larger and to add sympathetic strings with pegs along the side of the neck, like the *tanbur* or the *rubâb*. In due course news of the new instrument reached Herat and the 14-stringed *dutâr* became one of the principal instruments of Herati music making. The transformation of the *dutâr* was the subject of my research in 1973 (see Baily 1976).

In 1960 a new radio station building was opened in Ansari Wat, on the outskirts of Kabul, although the old building of Radio Kabul continued in use, mainly as

---

[18] I never heard the word *tarz* meaning a genre of modern popular music in Herat. My use of it here reflects my confidence in Sarmast's account.

a rehearsal space. With more powerful transmitters giving a new international outreach, the name of the radio station was changed to Radio Afghanistan. Until the 1950s broadcasts from Radio Kabul were live, which imposed unaccustomed time restrictions, and performances might be less than perfect. Tape recorders were introduced in the 1950s, but most music broadcasting continued to be live. When the new Radio Afghanistan building opened, music was usually broadcast from tape, ensuring a higher standard of output and more control of content. Only a few artists, such as Ustad Sarahang and Ustad Rahim Bakhsh, were permitted to perform live on air. Over the years an important tape archive of music was built up, catalogued by Madadi after his period of training in Cologne in 1964 (described in Chapter 4), using a card index system, which allowed for speedy access and retrieval. The tapes were well curated, with five or six songs per tape and blank leader separating the individual tracks. The survival of the archive in the Taliban era is discussed in Chapter 5. The music of Radio Kabul in this period is well documented in the *Ethnic Folkways* LP FE4361, recorded at Radio Kabul and published in 1961.

In 1970 a new orchestra was established, the *Arkestar-e Bozorg Radio Afghanistan* (The Big Orchestra of Radio Afghanistan), also known as the *Arkestar-e Siohasht Nafari* (Orchestra of Thirty-eight Persons), though it frequently operated with fewer than the full complement of musicians. The usage of musical forces was also fluid. For example, in 1976 the *Arkestar-e Bozorg* I saw in rehearsal with a singer consisted of: two *rubâb*s, two *tanbur*s, mandolin, Spanish guitar, *tulak* (cross-blown wooden Afghan flute), Boehm flute, piccolo, two tenor saxophones, clarinet, piano, string bass (plucked), *tabla, sitâr*, and *delrubâ* (Baily 1981: 110). This was in fact a combination of the *Arkestar-e Klâsik Radio Afghanistan*, the *Arkestar-e Kiliwâli Radio* and the *Arkestar-e Jâz*, though these ensembles continued to have their separate identities.

The *Arkestar-e Bozorg* was led by Ustad Salim Sarmast, who also served as composer and arranger for the orchestra. Many of the folk songs of Afghanistan were collected by staff members and performed by radio singers with this orchestra, in accord with one of the stated aims of radio broadcasting, 'to perpetuate the treasures of Afghan folklore'. Members of staff made occasional trips to other parts of Afghanistan to collect local folk songs to be re-arranged and broadcast by regular radio singers. For example, Madadi made a visit to his hometown of Herat to record local singers of Herati songs, using an Uher tape recorder. A few of the singers were then invited to Kabul to record their songs for the radio station. Amongst Madadi's discoveries was *Mullah Mohammad Jân*, recorded by Majgan and his wife Soroya Majgan. Today this is one of the best-known songs from Afghanistan, and remains very poplar and much sung throughout the Afghan diaspora.

Radio Kabul/Radio Afghanistan was owned and run by the Afghan Government, originally through the Directorate of the Press and the Municipality of Kabul, and later through the Ministry of Information and Culture. Everything was subject to censorship, both in political content and aesthetic quality. In the past, as today, the radio broadcast songs with a rather restricted range of texts: notably love songs, especially songs of unrequited love, and classical poetry, mostly in Persian, some Pashto too, often of a Sufi mystical nature. There was very little in song about the harsh realities of everyday working life.

As already noted, the radio station was a bastion of modernism. Bringing music to the people led to considerable upgrading in the status of singers and musicians. Some came to acquire 'star' status, something probably adopted from Indian popular culture, especially from the Hindi movies of the time, which were shown in Kabul's cinemas. Singers such as Nashenas and Madadi, discussed in later parts of this monograph, demonstrate a transition from amateur to professional in the face of family resistance. The new respectability conferred by radio was most remarkably shown by the way it allowed a number of women singers to achieve fame. Hitherto, women who sang in public (as in the theatre) were associated in popular imagination with questionable morality. Now, a number of women from highly respectable families came forward. One of the first was the above-mentioned Parwin, and undoubtedly the best known was Farida Mahwash, who worked as a secretary at the radio station. Her singing career began in the 1960s, and in 1976 she was given the honorific title of *Ustâd* (master musician) by the Afghan government. She remains active today as a singer, based in California. Mahwash was an occasional singer with the Arman family's Geneva-based *Ensemble Kaboul* for several years after 2001, and made a breakthrough with them on the world music scene. Together they were honoured with a BBC Radio 3 Award for World Music in 2003.

The singer Ahmad Zahir is the best example of achieved stardom. He came from an elite Mohammadzai family and his father, Dr Zahir, was for a short time Prime Minister in the 1960s. The family was wealthy and cosmopolitan. Ahmad Zahir represented the most westernized form of Afghan popular music at the time (1960s–70s). When not accompanying himself on the *'armonia* or piano accordion, he played an electric organ and was accompanied by instruments such as trumpet, electric guitar and trap drum set, instruments not available to the average amateur enthusiast. In certain ways he modelled himself on Elvis Presley, and is sometimes referred to as 'the Afghan Elvis'. He cultivated the Presley image in terms of hairstyle and sideboards. He had the advantage of being able to employ some of the best poets and composers in Kabul, like the much-admired Nai Nawaz and Shah Wali Taranasaz. Ahmad Zahir died in mysterious circumstances in 1979. His funeral cortege was followed by many hundreds of grief-stricken women fans weeping and wailing. His recordings, re-released on numerous CDs, remain very popular, both in Afghanistan and in the diaspora. In 2011 I found there to be an FM radio station in Kabul that broadcast only the songs of Ahmad Zahir.[19]

From its inception in the 1940s the radio station started to take over from the royal court as the main patron of musicians and institutional sponsor of

---

[19] Several clips juxtaposing Ahmad Zahir and Elvis Presley singing songs such as *It's now or never* can readily be found on YouTube.

new developments in music, employing many of the important musicians in the country. It played a crucial role as the national centre for musical activity, as well as functioning as the national broadcasting station, with all the demands for scheduling and time keeping that role demanded. In 1981 I proposed the representation shown in Figure 1.3 for the circulation of popular music.

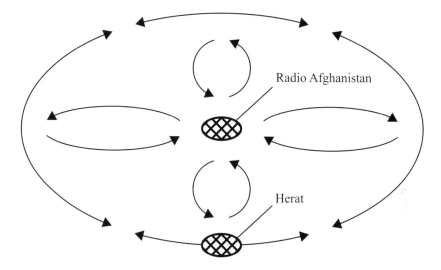

Figure 1.3   The circulation of popular music in the 1970s between Radio Afghanistan and the periphery

This shows the two-way flow of music as information between the centre and the periphery of the urban network, viewed from the perspective of the provincial city of Herat in the 1970s. Moving from the centre to the periphery, we see that new popular songs were learned from Radio Afghanistan and recreated in Herat, played by small local ensembles – professional and amateur – that typically consisted of a singer accompanied by *'armonia*, *rubâb*, *dutâr* and *tabla*. In the 1970s the audiocassette was just becoming common, and cassettes imported from Kabul were also a source of new songs in Herat. But the radio provided the quickest access to the latest hits.

At the same time, when moving from the periphery to the centre, we have a process of Herati songs (many but not all of them traditional songs of unknown authorship – that is, 'folk songs') being turned into popular radio songs performed with radio ensembles. Madadi, from Herat, recorded a large number of such songs: when I visited the radio archive in 1976, I found he had well over 100 songs there, many originating from Herat. Iran also served as a source of new popular songs, which were often transmitted to Kabul by Herati musicians who listened to Iranian radio or had access to Iranian popular music cassettes. The regional musics of other parts of Afghanistan were likewise absorbed into the radio station's repertory.

There was also direct communication between different parts of the periphery. In Herat, for example, items of repertoire from Mazar-e Sharif in the north, and from the Logar Valley in the south, were very popular. These borrowings were in part the result of visits by musicians to other parts of the country. The singer Bolbol Herawi, with Rahim Khushnawaz (*rubâb*), Gada Mohammad (*dutâr*) and Naim Khushnawaz (*tabla*), all from Herat, had spent some time as a band in Mazar-e Sharif in about 1971; Salaam Logari (vocal and '*armonia*) and his band played at the spring country fairs in Herat in 1974 (Baily 1982). In the 1970s many *Ramazân* concerts in Herat brought in musicians performing popular music from Kabul, such as Zaland and Khyal in 1974, and Afsana, Shamsuddin Masrur and Aziz Ghaznawi in 1977.

Fieldwork in Herat in the 1970s

> If anyone asks you which is the most beautiful of cities, tell them the truth, that it is Herat. If the world were as the ocean, Khorasan would be like an oyster shell in which Herat shines like a pearl.[20]

In the 1970s my wife Veronica Doubleday and I had the good fortune to live for more than two years in the city of Herat, in western Afghanistan, when I was a Post-Doctoral Research Fellow in the Queen's University of Belfast, then at the height of 'the troubles'.[21] We arrived in Herat a week before the coup of Mohammad Daud against his cousin and brother-in-law King Zahir, and spent several weeks in Kabul waiting to ascertain whether I would be given permission to conduct the planned ethnomusicological fieldwork. During this pause I started to learn the *rubâb*, from Ustad Mohammad Omar, the doyen of *rubâb* players in the late twentieth century, whose name comes up repeatedly in my story.[22]

The research consisted of two one-year periods of fieldwork, with a six weeks' visit interposed between them. The first year (November 1973 to October 1974) focused on the recent transformations undergone by the Herati *dutâr* – the local long-necked lute – from a 2-stringed instrument of rural amateurs to a 14-stringed

---

[20]   I thank Bijan Omrani for his personal communication of 25 January 2011 concerning this saying about Herat, attributed to the eighteenth-century poet Lutf Ali Beg of Isfahan. Perhaps the most lyrical accounts of Herat's Timurid architecture are to be found in Robert Byron's *The Road to Oxiana* (Byron 1937).

[21]   My very first visit to Belfast, 21 July 1972, to meet with John Blacking, coincided with 'Bloody Friday'; 19 car bombs in 65 minutes, 9 people killed, 130 injured (Baily 1994a: 7). It is ironic that in those days Afghanistan was at peace and Ulster in terrorist turmoil.

[22]   All Afghan *rubâb* players acknowledge Ustad Mohammad Omar as a brilliant master musician; this early training was crucial in my personal development as a player of this wonderful instrument.

instrument of urban professionals. This research involved a comparison between the *dutâr* and the *rubâb* in terms of 'the ergonomics of performance'. Although I had no academic background in ethnomusicology, my training in experimental psychology proved to be very useful in this systematic approach to music making. Blacking was supposed to join me for two or three weeks, but was never able to find the time. Nevertheless, he was very good at sending me advice through a series of letters (Baily 1994a). The final stages of this research involved lengthy recorded interviews with 10 *dutâr* players, covering a wide range of topics. This part of the research was facilitated by Safar Sarmed, who had recently graduated in engineering from the Afghan Institute of Technology in Kabul. He spoke excellent English and had an affable manner; he helped me greatly. A number of publications resulted from this first year's work.[23] The six weeks' visit in the summer of 1975 was made to renew contacts and check data already collected. This was a very productive visit, showing how much can be achieved in a relatively short time once you have established good relations with the people you work with.

The second year of fieldwork (September 1976 to September 1977) was devoted to the much more diffuse issue of the anthropology of music in Herat, looking at a wide range of musical activities: urban and rural; amateur and professional; solo and ensemble; secular and sacred. Veronica and I benefited from being in the ethnomusicological-anthropological milieu of the Queen's University of Belfast. We were by now quite fluent in the Herati dialect of Dari, had a good understanding of Herati culture and codes of behaviour, and were acquainted with dozens of musicians and singers. At this stage Veronica started her own research on women's music in Herat, a domain inaccessible to me.[24] Living in Herat at that time was a wonderful experience, and also very hard work, especially in the matter of keeping up with writing field notes. This time we drove to Herat in a Land Rover and were able to take large supplies of equipment and stationary, including two typewriters, many reams of A4 paper, and carbon paper to make two copies of everything we typed. It was also very useful to have a motor vehicle in Herat, allowing me to visit areas outside the city.

In our fieldwork in the 1970s we used the standard research techniques: attending social gatherings such as marriage celebrations, spring country fairs and *Ramazân* concerts, as well as small informal parties; making audio recordings of music both 'in context' and 'out of context'; recording interviews and conversations, usually in Dari. Veronica acted as our photographer, and I also had a basic Super 8 ciné camera, primarily to film the hand movements of *dutâr* players, but later to document music making in its many social contexts. I devised a test of sound perception, recording verbal responses to a long series of sounds, from natural

---

[23]   For example, Baily (1976, 1979, 1985b, 2001a).

[24]   Our major publications from this period are two monographs, Veronica's *Three Women of Herat* and my *Music of Afghanistan: Professional musicians in the city of Herat*, both published in 1988.

sounds like running water, thunder, wind and crackling fire, to animals, birds, babies, speech, poetry, unaccompanied singing to purely instrumental music (Baily 1996). Learning to perform was very important. I studied the 14-stringed *dutâr* principally with Gada Mohammad, and the *rubâb* with Amir Jan Khushnawaz, while Veronica learned many songs from the professional woman singer Zainab Herawi and for a short time even became a member of Zainab's band.

Musicians in Herat

In the music culture of Afghanistan an important distinction is made between professional (*kesbi*) and amateur (*shauqi*) status for musicians, a feature of Afghan music first noticed by Sakata and later by Slobin in the 1960s (see Sakata 1976 and Slobin 1976). The term *kesb* refers to an occupation or profession, while a *shauq* is a hobby, a passionate interest. With reference to music the distinction is based on two criteria: economic support – the *kesbi* plays to make a living, the *shauqi* from a love of music; and recruitment – the *kesbi* is a hereditary musician brought up in that role from an early age, while the *shauqi* is a (usually) self-taught enthusiast.

This apparently straightforward dichotomy did not actually fit the facts, for there were many musicians in Afghanistan who were originally *shauqi* but became *kesbi*, coming to depend on music for their livelihood. In Herat this was particularly true of *dutâr* players, like my teacher Gada Mohammad, who started as an amateur and came to play in the best bands of hereditary musicians. There was no specific term for the amateur who became professional in this way; he had an ambiguous status, he was *kesbi* by occupation but *shauqi* by recruitment. Amateur-turned-professional musicians liked to emphasize that they did not come from those low-class families who played music as an inherited profession, while the hereditary musicians criticized the *dutâr* players they employed in their bands for being self-taught and ignorant of music theory. There was plenty of scope for disagreement about the differences between *shauqi* and *kesbi*. Committed *shauqi*s would never accept payment for playing: to offer payment would be an insult. Some thought a non-monetary gift would be appropriate, others would accept money but would not agree a sum in advance (Baily 1979).

The archetypal hereditary musicians in Herat were players of the *sornâ* (shawm) and *dohol* (double-headed frame drum), instruments of rural music making used to stage processions and to play for group dancing by men at village weddings. All players of these two instruments (often referred to collectively as *sâzdohol*) were closely associated with the occupation of barber. A few barbers also worked as actors (*magad*) in the Herati *seil* (folk drama), also a feature of village life. Barbers in Herat, and in other parts of Afghanistan, have a very low place in society. In Herat they called themselves *Gharibzâda*, a word meaning 'foreigner' that points to their possible origin as a separate ethnic group, while Heratis in general referred to them as *Jat*, a highly pejorative term (Baily 1988a: 102). The connection between the occupations of musician and barber was not confined to these rural *sâzdohol* players in Herat Province; many urban musicians in Afghanistan also had connections with the hairdressing business, including musicians in the Kharabat.[25]

There were two extended families of hereditary musicians in Herat, performers of Kabuli art and popular music, vocal with *'armonia, tabla, rubâb, dutâr* and occasionally other instruments such as the *delrubâ*. These were the Khushnawaz and the Golpasand families. Both could be referred to as *sâzanda* (professional musician) or more politely as *honarmand* (artist). There were some important differences between them. In the Khushnawaz family only male members had a role as musician. Head of the family, the singer Amir Jan Khushnawaz, had been the apprentice (*shâgerd*) of Ustad Nabi Gol, the Kabuli musician who introduced the new Kabuli art music to Herat in the 1930s. In the Golpasand family both men and women worked as professional musicians, though not in mixed ensembles. The singer Ali Ahmad Delahang led the principal men's band. There were several women's bands, each consisted of a lead singer who also played *'armonia*, accompanied by women playing *tabla* and *dâira* (frame drum), and they performed mainly at women's wedding parties. The Khushnawaz family considered themselves a cut above the Golpasands, though male members of the two families had frequent occasions to play together. The Golpasands had a connection with barbering and owned a hairdressing salon near the street where they had their residences, while the Khushnawaz family were not associated with the hair cutting business. The fact that women from the Golpasand family worked as musicians brought the family into further disrepute. Their work necessitated contact with men with whom they had no family relationship, who came to hire them, convey them to the wedding party, and as members of the bridegroom's family might hover about in the background at the women's gathering.

Veronica and I worked with both families. She was adopted as a *shâgerd* by Zainab Herawi, the leading woman singer in Herat, and in due course became an occasional member of her teacher's band, going out to play at women's wedding celebrations. These experiences gave her extraordinary insight into the world of working women musicians and their low social standing in Herati society. Her experiences are described in *Three Women of Herat* (Doubleday 1988). My interactions with the Khushnawaz family were restricted to contact with the men of the family, while Veronica enjoyed full access to the women's quarters in their home.

Amateur musicians came from a wide variety of backgrounds, and included singers, singer-*'armonia* players, and players of the *dutâr, rubâb, tanbur, tabla, doholak, zirbaghali* and other instruments. The *dâira* was the principal instrument played by women and played by very few men, at least in public. Unlike Kabul, the instrumentarium of Herat consisted of 'traditional' Afghan instruments. Apart from the military band in the local barracks and the band attached to the

---

[25] Musicians have a low status in many societies. Merriam (1964) identified three characteristics of the 'musician paradigm': high importance, low status and a licence to deviate. This certainly fits with traditional trends in Afghan culture.

Municipality, European instruments were hardly known at that time. Amongst the amateurs there were certainly 'musical families' that had a long-standing interest in playing music and provided models for aspiring young amateurs to copy in a process of 'self-paced self-instruction through imitation' in learning to perform (Doubleday and Baily 1995).

The Annual Cycle of Music

John Blacking, celebrated for his seminal work on Venda music in South Africa in the 1950s, advocated that one needed to spend a whole year in the field in order to understand what he termed 'the annual cycle of music'. The idea of an annual cycle is somewhat inappropriate when applied to Muslim cultures, where the solar calendar determining the seasons is out of phase with the lunar calendar of religious observances that consequently occur 10 to 12 days earlier each year. Looking at the annual cycle in terms of the solar calendar alone, we note that in the winter, from early November to the end of February, Herat was quiet musically. It was cold, often with snow on the ground, with little heating in most houses, conditions not conducive for holding social gatherings. Things picked up musically with the coming of spring.

In Afghanistan, as in Iran and Central Asian countries, the spring equinox, usually 21 March in the solar calendar, is celebrated as *Now Ruz*, 'New Year'. Mazar-e Sharif, in northern Afghanistan, housing the tomb of Hazrat Ali in an ornate Timurid mausoleum, is the site of the *Mela Gol-e Sorkh*, the 'Tulip Festival', that continues intermittently for 40 days after *Now Ruz*. Mazar was the destination of thousands of pilgrims at that time. Similar celebrations over 40 days were held in Herat, though on a smaller scale, when there were regular country fairs (*mela*s), with tented teahouses, bands of musicians, and many other entertainments (Baily 1988a: 136–40). The Herati *mela* bands were predominantly composed of amateur-turned-professional *dutâr* players, performing almost exclusively a vernacular popular music, with special emphasis on songs and tunes from Mazar, the centre of *Now Ruz* celebrations.

Summer heralded the wedding season; especially after the harvest when people were less busy and had money to spend. Most live music performance in Herat took place in connection with wedding celebrations. These were usually held outdoors, in gardens or inner courtyards of private houses, with separate parties for men and women, ideally in adjoining houses. In the city a band of *sazanda* male musicians would provide a programme of music lasting for from six to eight hours, that would include *ghazal*s, possibly a classical *tarâna* or two, popular songs from Radio Afghanistan and Iran, a few local Herati songs, music for solo and group dancing, and music for comedy routines. The women's wedding party, in an adjoining courtyard, would be entertained by one of Herat's groups of professional women musicians from the Golpasand family, singing and playing *'armonia, tabla* and *dâira*. Their engagement would last for 24 hours, starting around 6.00pm in the evening, with a few hours' break for sleep at the compound or house where the women's party was taking place, and continuing next day till about 6.00pm. Their work demanded great stamina and required a degree of interchange of musical roles as lead singer or *tabla* player, not to mention time off to feed the babies they would usually take with them. Music was also played to celebrate the birth of a child and male circumcision, but not in connection with death, when music was considered to be completely inappropriate. In the villages, wedding music for the men's party was played by the *sornâ* and *dohol*, while the women provided their own music, singing and playing the *dâira*.

Another venue for performance, run by the local office of the Ministry for Information and Culture, was the Herat theatre (*Herât Nanderi*), with its troupe of actors, playwrights, directors and musicians, which presented nightly dramas throughout the year, except in the depth of winter. Music was provided between scenes (like the *pish pardaha* in Kabul). There was a strong emphasis on comedy in those productions, and the theatre boasted some famous Herati comedians. And there were private music parties of many kinds, such as women's gatherings in the build-up to the big wedding celebration (*'arusi*), dinner parties (*mehmâni*), after-dinner parties (*shau nishini*), and simple get-togethers of music enthusiasts for the sake of having fun (*shauq*). These private parties presented an ideal performance context for a kind of chamber music never intended for the western-type concert platform.

Musical performance was also affected by the religious (lunar) calendar. For the Shia population, *Muharram*, the period of mourning for the martyrdom of Hazrat Hussain and his family at the Battle of Kerbala, was a time when music was restricted. Many Sunnis, out of respect for their Shia neighbours, also observed this abstinence from music. In theory the period of mourning lasts for two months (the lunar month of *Muharram* followed by that of *Safar*); in practice it is the first 10 days of the month of *Muharram* that are particularly significant, culminating with the day of the actual battle, *Ashora* (the tenth), commemorated with mourning ceremonies. In contrast to *Muharram*, *Ramazân* (Ramadan), the month of fasting, was particularly rich in musical performance, with half a dozen restaurants and cafés in Herat offering nightly performances, often with bands of musicians from Kabul hired for the month. Between 1973 and 1977 we were in Herat for at least part of the five consecutive months of fasting. Ustad Rahim Bakhsh, Haji Hamahang, Aziz Ghaznawi, Shamsuddin Masrur, Zaland, Khyal, and other less famous singers from Radio Afghanistan appeared at one time or another while we were there. These were concerts for a listening audience who paid an entrance fee. The programme of songs was to some extent shaped by written requests sent up by members of the audience and the ability and readiness to oblige were necessary attributes of a successful singer.

Music and Religion

Given the central role that Islamic attitudes against music came to have in the years following my fieldwork in Herat – ways of thinking that determined the life of music and the lives of musicians – reference needs to be made to the comparatively relaxed views held by many people in the 1970s. We return to the issue of the lawfulness of music in later chapters; indeed it is a recurrent theme throughout this monograph. Here I describe the situation as I found it in pre-conflict Herat.

The controversy about music has coloured Islam from the time of Prophet Mohammad. Although the Quran does not make any explicit statements about music, a number of Quranic verses have been variously interpreted as sanctioning or condemning music (Farmer 1929; Robson 1938). On the negative side, music was thought to be overly engrossing, with the added danger of leading people to neglect or simply forget to say their prayers at the right time. In the popular imagination music was associated with other activities that were more explicitly proscribed by Islam, such as lascivious dancing, illicit sexual relations and the drinking of alcohol. On the positive side there were *hadith*s (Actions or Sayings of The Prophet) showing that Prophet Mohammad sanctioned musical performance on certain occasions (Baily 1988a: 148–9). Music was an area of uncertainty and mild controversy. Because I worked mainly with musicians I heard much more about the positive side of the discourse. It was generally accepted that from the mullahs' point of view music was sinful, but people did not necessarily agree the mullahs were correct. Many musicians told me how they were censured and criticized in the past, and there continued to be reservations about music as a profession. But things had changed in the last few years, 'Who thinks about such things today?' as one musician put it. Radio Kabul brought about changes in public opinion, familiarized listeners with the everyday experience of music, and displayed a model of more respectable musician status. The technology and style of presentation of the prestigious modern mass medium lent music a new kind of acceptability, especially during the 'decade of democracy' in the 1960s. In any case, some mullahs had modified their ideas, because, as they said, 'The times have changed' (ibid., p. 152).

In 1977 I made a special study of religious singing. During *Muharram* in 1977 I attended and recorded a number of Shia mourning ceremonies. These are intensely emotional gatherings, with solo and group singing, chest beating and self-flagellation with scourges. It was hard not to be moved by the rousing account of the battle, when members of the gathering broke down in tears one by one. These commemorations included both solo and congregational singing. I also attended a number of gatherings of Sufis for the performance of *zikr*, the 'Recollection of God', through the group recitation of certain esoteric phrases, perhaps the best-known being *Allah Hu*, 'God is He'. The Herat Valley is famous as a historical centre of Sufism and is the site of many *ziyârat*s, the tombs of Sufi saints, some in good structural condition, others in a ruinous state. Herat is sometimes referred to as *Khâk-e Auliyâ*, 'Dust of the Saints', 'a land impregnated with the memories of past generations of saints, scholars and poets' (Bruce Wannell, personal communication, 1986). At the time of my fieldwork the Qadiri and Naqshbandi Sufi orders were active in a number of *khânaqâh*s (places for the performance of Sufi ritual), where *zikr* was practised on a regular basis. Sufi poetry was well known and highly regarded.[26] Music was often described as *qazâ-ye ruh*, 'food for the soul', an idea widely expressed in Sufism (Baily 1988a: 152). Ideas held by Heratis about the positive values of music were also found in Sufi ideology, though they were not necessarily borrowed directly. Sufism was the crystallization of ideas that had a wide social currency and which were manifest in various aspects of poplar religion (such as the cult of saints). One link between music and the mystical systems of thought that constitute Sufism was provided by musicians in Kabul, where many *sâzanda* were adherents of the Chishti Sufi Order, which uses the instruments and structures (melodic modes and metrical cycles) of secular music in its spiritual concerts (*samâ'*).

My work on religious singing was greatly assisted by Abdul Wahed Saljuqi, from the illustrious Saljuqi extended family of theologians and scholars, who worked as the English teacher in one of Herat's two Theological Colleges. Through him I had access to Maulawi Nurahmad, the teacher of *ilm-e tajwid*, the 'science of the correct pronunciation of the Holy Quran' and his students. I never experienced any difficulties with the men of religion with whom I had contact; they were always welcoming and courteous. My most important work with Abdul Wahed was in the village of Kawarzan, some miles from the city, the site of the *khânaqâh* of Agha Abdul Ali, otherwise known as Agha Diwana (The Crazy Agha). This dynamic and somewhat eccentric Sufi *pir* made me very welcome on a number of visits, and allowed, even encouraged, me to record freely the performance of Qadiri *zikr*. I returned to Kawarzan 17 years later, after the Soviet occupation and civil war that had devastated much of Afghanistan, and Agha Diwana was back from exile in Iran.

---

[26] See Baily (2011a) for a collection of spiritual *ghazal*s sung by Ustad Amir Mohammad recorded in Herat in the 1970s.

Chapter 2
The *Jihâd* (Holy War) Era

The War Against the Communist Government Begins

On 27 April 1978 President Daud was overthrown in a violent coup staged by the communist People's Democratic Party of Afghanistan (PDPA). In a well-coordinated attack by Afghan troops whose officers were clandestine members of the PDPA, Daud and his family were massacred in the Arg, the Presidential Palace, formerly the Royal Palace built by Amir Abdur Rahman. The series of events leading up to the coup is complicated and well beyond the scope of this monograph.[1] Here I simply highlight some significant moments as I see them in relation to my own story. I perhaps give undue attention to the rise of the PDPA and the communist revolution of 1978 but I consider that an understanding of subsequent events merits a consideration of the political background. I am almost completely dependent on secondary sources, and these give rather different accounts, compare, for example Halliday (1978) and Misdaq (2006).

In 1963 King Zahir, then approaching his 60th year, shook off the control of Afghanistan by a succession of prime ministers – his uncles Hashim Khan and Shah Mahmud and his brother-in-law Mohammad Daud – and attempted to rule for himself. King Zahir promulgated a new constitution in 1964 (replacing that of 1931), which promised to transform Afghanistan into a constitutional monarchy along Western European lines. This permitted free speech, a free press and the formation of political parties, though the latter proposal was never fully ratified. Misdaq (2006: 106) refers to this as 'the decade of democracy'. As a result of liberalization there was a flurry of political activity that saw the establishment of numerous political parties covering a wide range of interests, including nationalism, Islamism and socialism. Misdaq (ibid., p. 80) lists eight of these parties and states there were over 30 newspapers and periodicals expressing the views of various pressure groups. Amongst the parties were two pro-Soviet communist factions that together formed the PDPA. They were known by the names of the periodicals they published, *Khalq* (The Masses) and *Parcham* (The Banner, or The Flag). Membership of the Khalq party, led by Nur Mohammad Taraki, was mainly Pashtun, and largely rural based, while the members of Parcham, led by Babrak Karmal, were mainly non-Pashtuns, more urbanized, and with family connections to the urban elite (ibid., pp. 101, 104, 105). In the wider context of enduring inter-

---

[1]   Many authors have dealt with the history of this period, amongst them Anwar (1988), Braithwaite (2011), Halliday (1978), Hyman (1984), Loyn (2009), Misdaq (2006), Schofield (2010), Steele (2011).

ethnic rivalries it is not insignificant that Khalq was largely a party of Pashto speakers, and Parcham of Dari speakers. The PDPA was the development of earlier leftist movements: *Jawanon-e Afghân* (Young Afghans) of the 1920s, and the *Wish Zalmyân* (Awakened Youth) movement of 1947 (ibid., p. 98). At the same time, two Maoist parties came into being, both opposed to the PDPA. This antagonism between the pro-Soviet and pro-Chinese communists reflected the difficult relations between USSR and China in this period (Lo 2008).

From the outset there was intense rivalry between the two pro-Soviet factions, despite the fact that in 1965 they came together to form the PDPA. The rivalry was in part the result of personal animosities, and in part due to differences in opinion as to how communism should be introduced to transform Afghanistan. The Khalqis advocated violent revolution; the Parchamis, with their links to the elite, favoured a more gradual approach and were ready to work with the existing regime to achieve their aims. Furthermore, the two factions also expressed different ethnic interests, Pashtun and Tajik. Both Taraki and Karmal were KGB agents, and closely connected with the USSR.

In the election of 1965 four members of the PDPA were elected to the *Wolesey Jirga*, the 'Lower House', all from the Parcham faction; in the election of 1969 only two were elected, Hafizullah Amin, from Khalq, and Babrak Karmal from Parcham. The proceedings of the Lower House, whose deliberations were broadcast live by Radio Afghanistan, were sometimes disrupted by the Parcham members, with interruptions and filibustering, and there were frequent student demonstrations against the government. In one incident members of the Lower House broke the chairs in the debating chamber and used the broken pieces to beat the Parchamis, severely injuring Babrak Karmal (ibid., p. 102). In 1967 the PDPA formally split into its two factions, and the Parchamis became a separate party, with its own weekly paper, *Parcham*. This was closed down by the government in 1969, on the eve of the general election.[2]

During the 'decade of democracy', with its new approach on freedom of speech and freedom of political expression, an Islamist movement was emerging at the other end of the political spectrum. The establishment of the Faculty of Theology in Kabul University in 1951 was an important stage in this development (ibid., p. 145). Several graduates of this faculty went on to further religious study in important centres outside Afghanistan, such as Al-Ahzar University in Cairo. Some of these returned graduates, including Burhanuddin Rabbani, Sebghatullah Mujadidi and Abdur Rasul Sayyaf, taught at the university and organized an Islamist group (*shura*) there, which in due course attracted other students such as Gulbuddin Hekmatyar and Ahmad Shah Massoud, drawn from Kabul University, the Institute of Technology, and from high schools. The five individuals mentioned above were later to become important *mujahideen* leaders. In 1965 the students established the

---

[2]   *Khalq*, the paper of the Khalq faction, had been published briefly in 1966, and was closed down after the sixth issue for being 'anti-Islamic, anti-constitutional and anti-monarchical' (Dupree 1973: 608, cited in Misdaq 2006: 105).

Sâzmân-e Jawânân Musulmân (Organisation of Muslim Youth). In 1972, after the arrest of several Islamists, the university teachers secretly set up the *Jam'iat Islâmi*, the 'Islamic Society', with Rabbani, a lecturer in theology, as its head.

In 1973 King Zahir was deposed by his cousin and brother-in-law Mohammad Daud, who had served as Prime Minister from 1953 to 1963, and who had close links with the military from the time he was Prime Minister. He had the tacit support of the Parchamis (ibid., p. 149). There was an immediate crackdown on political parties and freedom of expression. The privately owned newspapers, journals and magazines published during the so-called decade of democracy were closed, as were privately owned theatres such as the *Behzâd Nanderi* in Herat. Daud chaired a cabinet and a central committee, and both included a number of Parchamis, Babrak Karmal amongst them. Many other Parchamis were appointed as provincial governors and to high office in the ministries in Kabul (ibid., p. 83). The Parchamis were acceptable because of their moderate views about working with non-communists; as hard-liners the Khalqis, were excluded. Seeking alternative ways to exercise power, the Khalqis cultivated close links with officers in the army and air force, which proved to be of crucial importance in Taraki's coup in 1978.

When Daud became President a number of the Islamists, knowing that his government included some PDPA members or sympathizers, sought refuge in Pakistan, fearing they would be arrested. They were welcomed by the Pakistani authorities, who saw them as a way of hitting back at Daud for his continued espousal of the Pashtunistan issue.[3] They were given military training by the Inter-Services Intelligence (ISI), the Pakistani secret service, and a number were sent into Afghanistan in 1975 to stir up anti-government insurrections (ibid., p. 149). In this they were unsuccessful. Around 200 of their supporters were arrested and later executed. Others returned to Pakistan, where they were to become leaders of the principal *mujahideen* parties, including Rabbani, Massoud and Hekmatyar.

Whereas King Zahir had maintained a degree of balance between the US and USSR in matters of aid, under Daud Afghanistan moved closer to the USSR. The new republic received large financial loans, sent Afghans to the USSR for training programmes, and organized cultural exchanges. In due course Daud realized that he had become too closely connected with the Soviet Union, and tried to draw back, but it was too late. Rumours of a planned PDPA coup reached him. The arrest of prominent PDPA member led to the military coup by Taraki on 27 April 1978, known as the *Saur* Revolution after the month in which it occurred.

For three months the Khalqis and the Parchamis shared power, but disagreements surfaced and the solution was for high-ranking Parchamis to be sent abroad into 'diplomatic exile' as ambassadors, to both communist and non-communist countries. Karmal was sent to Prague as ambassador to Czechoslovakia (ibid., pp. 119, 319 note 3). According to the prominent Marxist intellectual Fred Halliday:

---

[3]   This was the demand that the Pashtuns of northern Pakistan should have their own autonomous state, Pashtunistan. The issue was the cause of severe political problems between Pakistan and Afghanistan in the 1950s and 1960s.

[The new Khalqi government] committed itself to land reform, to equality of the nationalities, to emancipating women, to a solution of the nomadic question.[4] So it was that at a time and in a place suspected by few, and in a country renowned only for colonial war and narcotic plentitude [here presumably referring to Afghanistan as a destination for young tourists], a revolutionary process of some description had begun. (Halliday 1978: 4)

The new communist ideology was unacceptable to most of the people of Afghanistan, particularly in the rural areas, where the majority of the population lived. There was resistance from the outset in many parts of the countryside, resulting in a wave of repression in which thousands of people were arrested and in many cases executed. Radek Sikorski, who travelled clandestinely to Herat in 1987, reports lengthy interviews with individuals on both sides of the developing conflict (Sikorski 1989: 180–83). He recounts a conversation with a former communist official who worked in Herat in the early communist period, describing the objectives and methods of the new regime in transforming the villages in the Herat valley:

> Our programme was clear: land to the peasants, food for the hungry, free education for all. We knew that the mullahs in the villages would scheme against us, so we issued our decrees swiftly so that the masses could see where their real interests lay. All estates above thirty jeribs [six hectares] of good land were to be expropriated and the surplus divided among the landless. All debts and mortgages (by which the rich had the poor in their pockets) were annulled. We wanted to create a class of independent peasants which would owe its emancipation to us. (ibid., p. 182)

It was in Herat that the first significant uprising against the new regime took place, starting on 15 March 1979 (24 *Hoot* 1357 according to the Afghan calendar). A mob of villagers marched to the city and for several days took control, with attacks on all who were identified as supporters of the regime. A large number of Afghan troops mutinied and fought with the rebels, led by Ismail Khan, who was an officer in the Herat garrison and went on to become the principal *mujahideen* commander in western Afghanistan. Thousands of Afghan civilians were killed in the uprising, which came to an end 12 days later, after bombing raids by the Afghan air force. The Soviet response to this and other lesser uprisings in Paktia, Paktika, Kunar and Kapisa Provinces was to provide the Afghan military with modern arms, vehicles and helicopters, and technicians to service the machines and train the Afghan military in their use. The Soviets were there to support the Afghan

---

[4]   The 'nomad problem' arose in part from the free movement of nomadic peoples back and forth across the Afghanistan–Pakistan border. There were also long-standing disputes between the (Pashtun) nomads and the Hazaras over sheep grazing rights in the mountains of Hazarajat (Misdaq, personal communication, 6 December 2011).

government in its fight with the developing Islamist insurgency and some Soviet special units were also deployed (Braithwaite 2011: 56–7). Government reprisals led to many non-Islamists seeking refuge in Pakistan. When news got back that the refugees were well received by their neighbour to the south, the numbers started growing. The migration of 3.5 million refugees to Pakistan had begun.

Having dispatched the Parcham leader, Babrak Kamal, into diplomatic exile, the Khalqis opened an internal schism between the founding figure of Taraki, and his able second in command, Hafizullah Amin. They came from very different backgrounds. Nur Ahmad Taraki, a Ghilzai Pashtun, was from a humble rural background. He spent some years as a young man in Bombay working as a clerk in an Afghan business, and it was there that he came in contact with the Communist Party of India, and became interested in Marxism. He later worked in Kabul as an interpreter, having acquired a good command of English while in India and became well known as a writer and poet. Hafizullah Amin was from a more educated background, and was a graduate of Kabul University. He took a master's degree in Columbia University in New York, and later started a PhD there, but was recalled to Afghanistan because of his political views. It was Amin in particular who took care to cultivate close relations with members of the armed forces, who were to the fore in the revolution against Daud Khan.

Taraki tried unsuccessfully to check Amin's rise to power. In September 1979 Taraki visited Cuba, stopping off in Moscow on his way home for meetings with Brezhnev and other Soviet leaders to discuss the situation and win their support in his plan to send Amin into diplomatic exile. He returned to find a very tense situation in Kabul in response to rumours of plots to eliminate Amin. There was an unsuccessful attempt to kill Amin when he visited Taraki in the Palace of the People (the former Arg) on 14 September, thereupon Amin ordered his troops to surround the palace, disarm the guard and arrest Taraki (Braithwaite 2011: 66). On 16 September the Party Plenum and the Revolutionary Council of the PDPA met and resolved to expel Taraki from the Party and elect Amin to the posts now vacated: General Secretary of the Party and Chairmanship of the Revolutionary Council (ibid., p. 68). Taraki was assassinated several days later by Amin's agents, being bound and smothered with a cushion – a rather quaint method of execution that usually leaves no obvious external trace of violence. Braithwaite (ibid., pp. 72–3) gives an authoritative account of what he terms an intrigue worthy of Shakespeare's *Richard III.* Amin, who had forever extolled the virtues of his mentor, Taraki, and often referred to him in public as 'the great leader', the 'star of the east', 'the great thinker' or by other similar sycophantic epithets (Anwar 1988: 114), ended up having him murdered.[5]

---

[5] I am reminded of Sa'di's story of the master wrestler who was challenged by his favourite student; with the difference that here the master defeated his student with the one throw he had refrained from teaching him. Sa'di concludes his Story with the couplet: 'None learn of me the science of the bow, Who makes me not their target in the end' (Eastwick 1974: 61–2).

Amin's period of power was short-lived, a mere 104 days (Misdaq 2006: 130). The Soviets were alarmed by the situation that was developing in Afghanistan and did not approve of Amin's extreme methods, which bore some similarities to those of the Pol Pot regime in Cambodia. It is ironic that both Taraki and Amin repeatedly pleaded with the USSR to send reinforcements to support the government's war against the insurgents, and finally when the USSR did send in the troops, ostensibly to protect Amin, it was to eliminate him, with a dramatic battle fought on 27 December 1979. The Soviets replaced him with Babrak Karmal, the leader of the Parcham faction of PDPA, then living in exile in the USSR. Braithwaite (2011: chapter 4) gives a detailed and fascinating account of these events. The large-scale invasion of Soviet troops by land and air began on the same day. By the spring of 1980 there were approximately 81,000 Soviet troops in Afghanistan; rising to a maximum of about 109,000 by the mid-1980s (ibid., pp. 122–3).

The western response to the *Saur* Revolution, in what was still the Cold War era, naturally varied. The political Right saw it as a resumption of the Great Game, with the descendants of Imperial Russia in conflict with the successors of the British. The Russians were assumed by some to be on their way to gain access to 'warm water ports' on the Indian Ocean, and to pose a threat to western access to oil reserves in the Middle East (Misdaq 2006: 155). The Left saw it as another success for the spread of Marxism, with Afghanistan joining Cuba, Angola and Ethiopia (Halliday 1978). According to Braithwaite (ibid., p. 46), the Soviet Union was anxious to support a new communist regime brought about by revolution, but could not understand what was going on in Kabul, and the factionalism within the PDPA. Because of the close links between many prominent PDPA members with the USSR, illustrated by the fact that Taraki and Karmal were both KGB agents, the USSR was closely involved in trying to influence interactions between prominent players amongst the Afghans. Moreover, there was nervousness about Islamism spreading into Central Asia, especially to Soviet Republics like Uzbekistan and Tajikistan. In the early stages of the invasion the Soviets drew heavily on troops from these countries, thinking that their commonalities in terms of language and other aspects of culture would be an advantage. But they were soon replaced with non-Central Asian troops for fear of contagion by Islamist ideology (Anwar 1988: 207).[6]

The Organization of Islamist Resistance

After the Soviet invasion the war got underway in earnest; it now became a *jihâd*, a holy war, not just against Afghan communists, who were at least compatriots, but against a foreign invader, and a *kafir* (non-Muslim) invader at that. There was a big

---

[6]   That these fears were well-founded is shown by reports that in 2011 there are Islamist IMU bases in northern Afghanistan that are used for mounting attacks in Uzbekistan and Tajikistan. See: http://www.rferl.org/content/in_afghanistan_imu_taliban_alliance_chips_away_at_the_stone/24230127.html.

difference between the situation in urban and rural areas. While the government had control of the cities, especially Kabul, they did not control the hinterland, where the majority of the population was located. Thousands of Afghan men, young, middle-aged, even old, joined one or other of the many quasi-autonomous *mujahideen* groups.

Seven Islamist *mujahideen* parties were recognized by the Pakistan government. Misqaq (2006: 158, 302–5) lists them in two groups, fundamentalist and progressive.

- Fundamentalist parties:
  - *Hezb-e Islâmi Hekmatyâr* (Party of Islam), led by Gulbuddin Hekmatyar, a Ghilzai Pashtun.
  - *Hezb-e Islâmi Khâlis* (Party of Islam), led by Mohammad Yonus Khales, a Khogyani Pashtun.
  - *Itehâd-e Islâmi* (Unity of Islam), led by Abdur Rasul Sayyaf, a Ghilzai Pashtun.
  - *Jam'iat-e Islâmi* (Islamic Association), led by Burhanuddin Rabbani, a Tajik from Badakhshan.

- Progressive parties:
  - *Harakat-e Enqalâb-e Islâmi* (Revolutionary Islamic Movement), led by Mohammad Nabi Mohammadi, a Ghilzai Pashtun.
  - *Jabh-e Nejât-e Meli* (National Liberation Front), led by Sebghatullah Mujadidi, a Sufi Pir of the Naqshbandi Order and of distant Arab ancestry.
  - *Mahaz-e Meli Islâmi Afghânistân* (National Islamic Front of Afghanistan), led by Sayed Ahmad Gailani, a Sufi Pir of the Qaderi Order and of distant Arab ancestry.[7]

The seven parties had their separate headquarters in Peshawar, and each had its own militia or small army. The West was initially slow in offering military aid to the *mujahideen*, thinking that they had little chance of effective resistance. But over time this changed. A number of individuals were determined to bring what was happening to the attention of western democracies, and to call for military aid for the parties in Pakistan. In terms of armaments, the West favoured supplying Soviet arms manufactured outside the USSR; Afghans were already familiar with the use of such weapons, and also this disguised their source (Misdaq 2006: 159). These armaments were supplied via the ISI, who controlled their distribution; some parties received more help than others. Hekmatyar's *Hezb-e Islâmi* was

---

[7] There are confusing similarities in the names of some of these parties and it is not surprising to find them commonly referred to by the name of their leader. For example, *Hezb-e Islami Khalis* (Party of Islam), led by Mohammad Yonus Khales, broke away from Hekmatyar. The two parties are often known as *Hezb-e Hekmatyâr* and *Hezb-e Khâlis*.

regarded as particularly effective on the battlefield and received a disproportionate quantity of munitions.

At the same time, there was great financial support from other Muslim nations, especially Saudi Arabia. This is also the period when the Afghan *mujahideen* attracted recruits from outside, such as Saudi Arabia, Egypt and Libya. *Mujahideen* leaders in general remained in the safety of Pakistan but one notable exception was Ahmad Shah Massoud, a commander of Rabbani's *Jam'iat-e Islâmi*, who for much of the war was based in Afghanistan's Panjshir Valley. He was lionized by the West as a Che Ghevera type of young revolutionary, and his headgear, the woolen *pakol* hat, became a fashion item in the West.[8]

In addition to the seven parties recognized by the Pakistan government there were three Shia parties, based in Iran:

- *Hezb-e Wahdat* (Party of Unity), led by Abdul Ali Mazari, a Hazara.
- *Harakat-e-Islâmi Afghânistân* (Islamic Movement of Afghanistan), led by Qizilbash Sheikh Asef Mohseni.
- *Shorai Enqelab-e Etefâq-e Afghânistân* (United Revolutionary Party of Afghanistan), led by Sayed Beheshti.

Refugees from Afghanistan began arriving in Pakistan in the late 1970s and grew to a steady stream following the Soviet invasion of 1979, eventually numbering, it is estimated, about 3.5 million persons (Centlivres and Centlivres-Demont 1988: 71–2). Iran in turn hosted another 1.5 million. The majority of refugees in Pakistan were housed in camps set up in the North-West Frontier Province, Baluchistan and along the tribal area bordering Afghanistan, with financial assistance from the United Nations High Commissioner for Refugees (UNHCR). Life in the camps was certainly harsh but most families received adequate provisions from the Pakistani Government and medical facilities and schooling were available in some degree. Tents were gradually replaced by more durable structures, and the camps (so-called Afghan Refugee Villages) began to assume a permanent aspect, like very large villages (ibid., p. 75). The Afghan refugees considered themselves to be *mohajir*, following the example of Prophet Mohammad's migration (*hijra*) to Medina in 622 C.E. (ibid., p. 74). They regarded themselves as temporary guests, expecting to return to Afghanistan, just as Mohammad had done when he reconquered Mecca. The term 'exile' is more appropriate than 'refugee' for the Afghans, who regarded their migration as a tactical manoeuvre.

---

[8]   Sandy Gall helped to make Massoud famous, through making three intrepid expeditions into Afghanistan to meet him, which resulted in several books and television programmes. Gall felt it necessary to publicize the war and win support for the *mujahideen* (Gall 1988: 13–14).

Music in Kabul under Communist Rule

Notwithstanding the many books published in English about Afghanistan over the last 30–40 years, very little has been written about urban cultural life in Afghanistan during this period. We have plenty of information about the minutiae of political events, the double-dealings, the ever-changing political alliances, the reign of terror, the assassinations, and the war in all its brutality, but we hear nothing about the arts. What was going on in Kabul and other cities all this time? According to Dr Faridullah Bezhan, of the Monash Asia Institute in Australia, who lived in Kabul throughout the 1980s and was a lecturer in Kabul University, this was a period of considerable creativity in the field of literature (Bezhan, personal communication, 28 April 2009). Many young writers and poets stepped forward, and their works were published. There were poetry circles that met regularly to allow young poets to read their work, and have it discussed critically by their peers.

How did music fare in all this? Again, very little information is available and no systematic study has been made hitherto. The succession of communist governments supported music, which they regarded as integral to the type of secular society they aspired to establish. The authorities were supportive of regional folk music traditions, which were seen as being closer to 'the people' than the art music of Kabul, associated with the former royal court. Radio and television artists who complied with the new regime were treated well; they had good salaries, received medical care, and in some cases were allocated apartments and even motorcars. Many were ready to sing songs in praise of the new regime; others were not and felt it expedient to leave the country. They joined the exodus away from war and insecurity as Afghans crossed the borders into neighbouring countries.

The communists came to power shortly after the opening of the television station in Kabul, when Radio Afghanistan became transformed to Radio Television Afghanistan (RTA). The building, studios, equipment and transmitters were donated by Japan as part of an aid programme initiated in the time of Daud Khan. Television was a state-of-the-art medium and had an important role in broadcasting musical performances and promoting new artists. In due course local RTA stations were established in some provincial cities, such as Herat.

Radio and television broadcasting remained under the control of the Ministry for Information and Culture, as had been the case of radio from its inception in the 1940s. The Ministry exercised tight control over what was broadcast. Some video recordings of performances recorded at the time are commercially available (though how that has come about is unclear). The imaginative sets and the high quality of programme making are noteworthy. A number of young singers had the opportunity to appear on television, and in many cases their performances are very westernized, continuing the lead set by Ahmad Zahir. Videos of the time show new-looking electric guitars and bass guitars, keyboards and drum kits. According to Madadi, who was Head of the Music Department of RTA for much of this period, the instruments were owned by RTA and kept in a special rehearsal studio where young musicians could have access to them. It would appear that there was a strong influence here from the popular music of the Soviet Republics of Tajikistan and Uzbekistan, which was highly westernized.

Two famous bands of young musicians emerged at this time at RTA, *Goroh-e Bârân* (Rain Band), led by Farhad Darya, and *Saman* (Jasmine), led by Wahid Qassemi (a grandson of Ustad Qassem). Farhad Darya remained in Kabul until 1989, and in 1988 was teaching western music in Kabul University. Today he and Wahid Qassemi are superstars of the new Afghan music, based in the US (Darya) and Canada (Qassemi). The 1980s does seem to have been a time for younger singers and musicians to have an opportunity to develop their musical talents, perhaps symbolizing the 'rebirth' of Afghanistan under a new political system.

Raja Anwar's book *The Tragedy of Afghanistan* provides a few valuable insights into the role of music in the early days of communist rule.[9] He describes how in 1979 Taraki obtained a *fatwa* from a sympathetic religious establishment 'which declared that *jihad* against religious reactionaries who followed in the footsteps of the *Akhwan-ul-Muslimi* [the fundamentalist Muslim Brotherhood of Egypt] had full religious sanction' (Anwar 1989: 149–50). In other words, the communists declared a holy war against those who had themselves declared holy war upon the government. Anwar continues:

> The official media were also directed to use the *fatwa* to attack the Mullahs and their campaign. On TV (whose transmissions did not go beyond Kabul [at that time]), it was made the basis of skits, songs and plays. One chorus broadcast regularly by both TV and radio had the refrain:
>
> Lannat bar tu aye Akhwan-ul-Shaitan
> (May the curse of God be upon you, you brothers of Satan). (ibid., p, 150)

Concerts were also held in support of the Taraki regime. Anwar describes one memorable performance:

> On the evening of 14 September [1979], a concert of Afghan folk music was in progress on the lawns of Afghan Music, an academy next to the Indonesian embassy and barely a kilometre away from the presidential palace. Such evenings were regularly organized by the Khalq government to propagate Party programmes and achievements. As was customary, the stage was profusely decorated with large photographs of the 'great leader'. Popular artists, including Qamar Gul, Gul Zaman, Bakhat Zarmina, Master Fazal Ghani, Ahmad Wali and Hangama, were busy singing the praises of the Revolution and the Party. The well-known comic, Haji Kamran, who was acting as master of ceremonies, was dutifully leading the crowd into chants of 'Long Live Taraki' and 'Long Live Amin whenever a new performer appeared on the stage. At about 6.30 p.m.,

---

[9]   Raja Anwar is a Pakistani journalist and writer and was adviser to Zulfikar Ali Bhutto. He fled to Afghanistan after Bhutto was overthrown by Zia-ul-Haq in 1977.

when the concert was at its climax, tanks from the 4th Armoured Corps moved into the city, taking positions in front of important buildings and occupying major squares. The rumble of the tanks on the roads so unnerved the organizers of the concert and the artists that they ran away helter-skelter, leaving even their musical instruments behind. (ibid., p. 172)

Hafizullah Amin's coup to depose President Taraki had just begun. Two of Amin's supporters, Taroon and Nawab, who were killed in the coup were later commemorated: 'special songs were commissioned for radio and TV extolling their "great deeds"' (ibid., p. 171). Anwar noted that a recording of Ravi Shankar performing *Râg Mallhâr* on the *sitar* was often played over the air when a change of regime came about; it was so used when Daud came to power, and when Taraki and Amin were toppled. *Râg Mallhâr* is believed to bring rain (ibid., p. 100) and also has cooling and pacifying effects.

The *International Herald Tribune* for 6 February 1986 ran an article about one private engagement party in Kabul:

There was disco dancing, an ear-splitting band, proud parents and the nervous young couple – all the elements of an engagement party anywhere in the world. Then there were a few extras: the armed soldiers at the entrance to the gloomy hotel, the slick band leader singing 'Our Heroic Party', and the portrait of Afghanistan's president, Babrak Karmal, gazing over the crowded ballroom. ... At the party for Roya and Kamran, the future student bride and groom, Kabul's young men eagerly went through their disco paces – with other young men. Although they have long given up the Moslem custom of covering up their eyes and legs, the women stayed in a corner by themselves, swaying to the deafening music. 'Yes, this is quite modern, it is not an arranged marriage', shouted the bride-to-be's father, Colonel Nur Ahmad, over the din. 'Nowadays, young people meet first and then consult their parents about marriage', said the colonel, who said he taught military subjects at Kabul University ... Zaffar Shah, lead singer of the band at the engagement party, said his five-piece group was booked for functions like this most nights. Besides Western music and tunes from Indian movies, the band's repertoire includes patriotic songs about the Communist Party and against the counterrevolutionaries, as Kabul calls the Moslem rebels. 'I always try to topple the counterrevolutionaries in my poems and songs', the singer told government officials acting as interpreters for visiting foreign journalists.

An indication of the state of music in this time is provided by training in Indian classical music provided through the Indian Embassy in Kabul. Several excellent musicians were employed to run these courses. One was the *sarod* player Ustad Irfan Khan, who lived in Kabul for three years, where he taught *sitâr*. One of his students was Ehsan Irfan (he adopted the name of his teacher as his surname), whom I met in Peshawar in 2000, and again in Kabul in 2002, and 2011, when he was employed as a *sitâr* teacher at the Afghanistan National Institute of Music. Another of Ustad Irfan Khan's *shâgerd*s is Khalil Gudaz, who emigrated to Australia and who I met several times there in 2009 (see Chapter 6).

Film School Days

Having described at some length what was happening inside Afghanistan during the *jihâd* period I now return to my personal narrative, which takes me next to the National Film and Television School (NFTS), in Beaconsfield, England. In 1983 the Royal Anthropological Institute advertised two one-year anthropological film-training fellowships, funded by the Leverhulme Trust, and tenable at the NFTS. At the time I was a Lecturer in Ethnomusicology in The Queen's University of Belfast. I was one of many who applied for a film training fellowship: three films I had edited in Belfast from my Herat footage no doubt led to my being successful.[10] My fellow anthropologist/trainee was Dr Paul Henley, who in 1987 became Director of the Granada Centre for Visual Anthropology at Manchester University, a position he held until 2014.

Working at the NFTS was a transformative experience. Established in 1971, it is housed in the old Beaconsfield Studios, halfway between London and Oxford. It has large stages and many cutting rooms, and a small, comfortable and well-equipped cinema, where we spent many hours watching documentary classics and, later, our own films as they progressed from cut to cut in the editing process. The School's Director was Colin Young, who had in 1966 established an ethnographic film training programme at UCLA that produced a number of well-known anthropological filmmakers such as David and Judith MacDougall, David Hancock and Herb DiGioia, who was Head of Documentary Film at the NFTS when I started my work there as a trainee filmmaker.[11]

Colin Young was the driving force behind a new style of documentary filmmaking that had developed at UCLA, known as observational cinema. Young's chapter in *Principles of Visual Anthropology* (1975) is very helpful in explaining the aspirations of this documentary film style. Henley (2014) describes how it grew out of, yet differed from, the direct cinema of Robert Drew and his associates in the 1960s, with their use of new lightweight equipment to allow filmmakers mobility, to literally follow the action with the hand-held camera. But there were significant differences. Direct cinema, designed initially for US television audiences, was very much engaged with following dramatic crises, while observational cinema is more concerned with the detailed observation of everyday life. 'The details of our films must be a substitute for dramatic tension, and the film's authenticity must

---

[10]   *The Annual Cycle of Music in Herat, The City of Herat* and *The Shrines of Herat* (Baily 1982, 1983a, 1983b).

[11]   Herb DiGioia and David Hancock had worked in Afghanistan with anthropologist Louis Dupree, making a series of films, the best known being *Naim and Jabar* (1974).

be a substitute for artificial excitement' (Young 1975: 74). There is an emphasis on 'being allowed to experience the event and make our own analysis' (ibid., p. 70), where the audience can make up its own mind on the basis of the evidence shown, rather than what it is told: 'the difference between TELLING a story and SHOWING us something' (ibid., p. 69). The idea that making a film was a way of doing ethnographic fieldwork was inspiring. I enjoyed the feeling of being embedded in an avant-garde movement that had broken new ground in ways made possible by the invention of synchronized lightweight 16 mm cameras and portable battery-operated open reel tape recorders.

After the first term at the NFTS it was time to plan my major film project. In the course of making a series of programmes about Afghan music for the BBC World Service Pashto Service with Nabi Misdaq, then a Producer for that Service, it dawned on me that it should be possible to make a film about Afghan musicians in exile in Peshawar, Pakistan. I hoped to find some of the musicians I had formerly known in Afghanistan. I had also heard that cassettes of *mujahideen* nationalist songs could be found in the Peshawar bazaar. I had read about a wave of new poetry about the war (Moin 1985), which might have musical implications.

Nationalist songs were certainly part of Afghan culture; an example of a song celebrating the annihilation of the British army retreating from Kabul in 1842 is to be found in André Singer's film *Khyber* (1979), made around the time of the communist coup. Two musicians sat on top of a hill with *'armonia* and *tabla* and according to the subtitles, their song (in Pashto) went:

Keep your hands off
For you cannot succeed
This is the land of the Afghans
And we will not be fooled any more

Child of Imperialism
Stay silent and don't play with fire

For I am the Afghan
And I made the British flee
I was the thunder over their heads
And my hands destroyed them

So get out British
For you cannot escape
This is the land of the Afghans
And we will not be fooled any more

Similarly, *A Valley Against an Empire* (Bony and de Pontfilly 1983), a French television film about Ahmad Shah Massoud's *mujahideen* army in the Panshir Valley, ends with a resistance song from a man sitting on top of a burnt-out tank accompanying himself with a *dambura* (a type of long-necked lute). I was therefore interested in finding out how musicians were faring as refugees. Were they able to continue in that profession? What effects, if any, did the political situation have on music making? Was a new kind of political music coming into existence? How was the long-standing condemnation of music by orthodox Islam affected by the present situation?

Wayne Derrick, then in his final year as a documentary director and camera student at the NFTS, agreed to come with me to do the camera work, while I would conduct preliminary research, direct the film and act as sound recordist. Wayne had a special interest and commitment to the school's type of documentary filmmaking, and has a particular flair for the long sequence-shot with a hand-held camera. Some good examples are to be found in our film, *Amir* (Baily 1985a). He is from Texas, and was formerly a keen singer, guitarist and song writer, useful attributes for the work we were about to undertake.

I went ahead to Pakistan to carry out research for the film, taking the Nagra tape recorder and a good supply of tapes with me. I stayed at the Afghanaid staff house in University Town, and Wayne later joined me there. Peshawar at the time was full of ambitious and adventurous young journalists and photographers excited by this exotic war and the possibilities it provided for them to make their reputations. Their centre of social activity was the American Club. However, their endeavours were not entirely laudable. Writing about the club as he experienced it in 1989, Robert Darr wrote:

> The American Club was populated by a peculiar group of colorful ex-patriots: journalists, aid workers, would-be spies, and political operatives. The strongest presence at the club was a clique of journalists who covered the Afghan war with a markedly pro-American intervention bias ... They portrayed the Afghan fighters as noble warriors fighting solely to liberate their country from brutal Soviet invaders and their puppet Marxist government.
>
> This certainly was true in a general sense. The irrepressible Afghan will to drive out the invader was both heart-wrenching and inspiring to witness throughout the early years of that conflict. Yet a shadow was falling across this bright picture of bravery, a pall of sectarian and interethnic warfare and the emergence of those with a literalist, militant interpretation of Islam. Theft, murder, drug smuggling, and the oppressive reign of petty warlords also darkened this image of the struggle for freedom. Yet none of these issues were adequately addressed by the press. The Peshawar clique was partly responsible for this inattention to detail. Its members were fully engaged in describing a simple military struggle. For many of these journalists and politically-motivated aid workers, the Afghan Mujahideen were doing what the Cold War had been unable to do: bring down the 'Evil Empire'. (Darr 2006: 235–6)

I only visited the American Club once or twice but I heard plenty about the war and the *mujahideen* from Alastair Fairweather, Acting Field Officer of Afghanaid in Peshawar, and from others staying there. For a more critical view of things I had several meetings with Professor Bahauddin Majrooh, Director of the Afghan Information Center (AIC), who was assassinated in 1988 in Peshawar. However, I was not so interested in the complexities of the relationships between the seven rival *mujahideen* parties; I was there for the music. Afghanaid ran a tailoring project, employing tailors in a particular camp to make school uniforms that were then distributed to Afghan children. That part of Afghanaid's work was overseen by Wali Jan Sultani. He took me round in the first few days, looking for audiocassettes and for musicians.

Within a few days of my arrival I discovered that political ideology and music were strongly interconnected, and I found out that there were unforeseen problems with my film project. In a meeting with Nassim Jawad, working for an Austrian non-governmental organization (NGO) and who had spent six months living in a camp so as to experience camp life directly, I learned that the camps were run according to strict religious rules. This provided a situation in which the Islamist parties were able to impose a rigidly orthodox regime. Hekmatyar had a powerful place in this respect; many camps were under his control or that of his representatives.[12]

Music was forbidden in the camps by the mullahs and by party officials. Men had to grow their beards and were not permitted to wear western clothes. The camps were maintained in a perpetual state of mourning, justified by the constant influx of new arrivals who had lost relatives in the fighting. Refugees were allowed to own radios so that they could listen to news programmes but they were not supposed to listen to music on their radios (though no doubt some did). Refugee musicians who were forced by circumstance to live in the camps hid their identities. I realized that it was going to be difficult to find musicians in the camps. On the other hand, there were active musicians living in the city of Peshawar, where the parties did not have such tight control. Nassim mentioned Peshawar's Dubgari Road as a place where musicians might be found.[13]

I went in search of audiocassettes that related to the war. Peshawar had a thriving cassette industry but to my surprise the cassettes in the bazaar were mostly of love songs; cassettes about the war were not easy to find. With Sultani's help I tracked down several. One was of Haikal, an Afghan Pashto

---

[12] Women suffered more from the rigours of camp life than men, who were at least free to spend time in the local bazaar, even if they had little if any money to spend there. *Purdah* (the seclusion of women) was strongly enforced in the camps. Individual families were often separated from their former local village communities, within which women had considerable freedom of movement, and in the camps women were in many cases confined to their tents, hardly able to get outside at all.

[13] This ban on music in the refugee camps contrasts with conditions in some other places with refugee populations, where music making has been encouraged to relieve boredom and provide a creative outlet, see for example papers by Kaiser (2006) and Van Aken (2006), and the collaborative CD project *Giving Voice to Hope. Music of Liberian Refugees*, between the University of Alberta and the Buduburam Liberian refugee camp, http://tinyurl.com/ott3w3.

singer who had performed on Radio Afghanistan and was now based in Peshawar, accompanied by *'armonia*, *rubâb* and *tabla*. This contained a 40-minute epic about a particular *mujahideen* group operating in the north of Afghanistan. At one point Haikal declaimed:

> It was in the dark of night when the *mujahed*s were fighting
> It was difficult to tell between friend and foe
> In the morning it was time for the third attack
> '*Allah O Akbar*' could be heard amongst the bombardment
>
> The *mujahideen* advanced into the district
> And they were happy for the blood they shed in martyrdom
> When they made their third attack on the town

Following the vocal line describing the *mujahideen* advance there was a prolonged interlude of imitated gunfire played on the *tabla* drums. This imitation of gunfire seemed to be one of the few musical innovations of the war! I have to admit I was rather dismissive of this development at the time. Many years later, listening to Aaron Copland's *Billy the Kid* (Philips CD 422 307–2) I discovered a striking gun battle in music that has caused me to revaluate the artistic sensibility in this use of *tabla* by Haikal's band and regard it in a much more positive light.

It was not clear who these cassettes were aimed at – certainly not people living in the camps, who would not be permitted to play them. Presumably there was some market amongst the many thousands of Afghans living outside the camps. And it seems that such cassettes were bought by some *mujahideen* fighters and taken to the war in Afghanistan. In Simon Broughton's BBC film *Breaking the Silence*, shot shortly after the defeat of the Taliban government, a former *mujahid* explained the importance of such recordings to the men engaged in the fighting:

> Although it was a holy war, we still listened to music. We were not narrow minded. Music was our entertainment. Here is an example of what we used to listen to [turns on tape recorder]. There was the sound of weapons firing. These tapes calmed us down when we were fighting. When we sat with our friends, this was our entertainment. (Broughton 2002, 14′ 08″ from start)

This may seem paradoxical, given the Islamist attitude against music and musicians, but as already mentioned, there were seven recognized *mujahideen* parties in Pakistan and they varied greatly in their degree of fundamentalism. This informant must have been from one of the more open-minded groups, such as Sayed Ahmad Gailani's NIFA party.

I visited Radio Peshawar several times, and found the Head of Music, Nawab Ali, extremely helpful. He sent for members of staff to come and explain and demonstrate things for me to record. He allowed me to attend a recording session of the weekly radio music programme *Hujra*, and later arranged for me to have copies of several of these programmes on tape. It was in Peshawar in 1985 that I had my first opportunity to learn about Pashtun music. In Nawab Ali's office I heard about several different regional styles of Pashtun music: *Yusufzai*, *Khattak*, *Waziri* and *Afridi*, based on the names of certain tribes. The dominant style in Peshawar area was *Yusufzai*. Vocal genres included *tappa*, *charbeita*, *badla*, *lobah*, *santara* and *nimakay*, and instrumental dance pieces like *sakhanay*, *shân* and *shadola*. I learned about the low rank of the musician in Peshawari society, and the close link between the hereditary occupations of barber and musician. Both came from a minority known as *Dom*; although Pashto was their mother tongue they were not considered to be part of Pashtun tribal society.

On my second visit to the radio station Nawab Ali sent for the Afghan singer Shah Wali Khan, the most popular of the Afghan singers in Peshawar at the time, and a star of local radio and television. When Shah Wali arrived I immediately recognized him as the singer in the film *Khyber*, a fact he confirmed. 'I have a *rubâb* player in my band from Herat', he said, 'his name is Amir Jan'. I was puzzled, I did not recall such a person, the only Amir Jan I knew was Amir Jan Khushnawaz, and he was dead. Shah Wali then drove me in his car to Dubgari Road. We went upstairs to his suite of rooms above a furniture shop, to be greeted by someone I did know from Herat. He embraced me passionately, kissing my neck, and burst into tears.

Profile: Amir Jan Herati (Rubâb Player)

There are several Amirs in my life, it gets a little confusing for the reader. Apart from the music loving Amirs of Kabul, there is Amir Jan Khushnawaz, senior member of the Khushnawaz family in Herat, father of Rahim, and my main *rubâb* teacher in 1976–77. There is Ustad Amir Mohammad, the singer from Kabul who was so popular in Herat in the 1970s, the subject of my monograph *Songs from Kabul* (Baily 2011a), and Amir Khusrau, the Sufi saint who is important to Afghan historical identity. The Amir I met again in Peshawar in 1985 was often known as Amirak in Herat, a rather pejorative name meaning 'Little Amir'.[14] Here I elect to call him simply Amir, or sometimes Amir Jan Herati, meaning 'Amir from Herat', to distinguish him from the others (Figure 2.1).

In Herat I first got to know him when he was in his early 20s. He had recently finished his military service and was earning his living as a professional singer and *'armonia* player. He was not central to my interests at the time for he was not a musician who was in demand to play at prestigious wedding parties in Herat. He was in that second tier of urban musicians, mostly men who had started out as amateurs and who for one reason or another had turned to music as their economic

---

[14] The Heratis had a predilection for giving people nicknames. There was, for example, Haidar Dandan, 'Haidar the Tooth', so-called because he was a dentist; Bacha Bini, 'Son of Nose', whose grandfather had a false nose; Karim Lang, 'Lame Karim'; and Amin Bacha Matari, 'Amin, Son of the Stick Wielding Fighter'.

Figure 2.1   Amir Jan Herati, Peshawar 1985. © The RAI

mainstay. I remember him as a stylish dresser, wearing elaborately embroidered shirts and expensive silk turbans. Sometimes he would sport a hippy-style silk bandana tied round his head. He was very articulate, a wonderful raconteur in the stylized manner of talking found amongst certain men of the Herati 'underworld' of gamblers, *charas* (hashish) smokers, dancing boys, *kâkas* (well-dressed petty criminals with attitude) and some musicians.[15] I usually saw him performing at spring country fairs (*melas*), in *dutâr* bands, with *tabla* or *zirbaghali*. The *mela* was not a prestigious type of venue, not a place where one would expect to find a band of hereditary professional musicians. It is noteworthy that while the Khushnawaz, Golpasand and Ustad Amir Mohammad ensembles were relatively

---

[15]   The *dutâr* player Amin-e Diwaneh (Amin the Madman) personified this kind of musician role (Baily 1988b).

stable, the personnel of the bands Amir played in seemed to change from week to week during the two months of the *mela* season (Baily 1988a: 136–9). There were endless disputes about the sharing out of the money. Often, singer-*'armonia* players like Amir argued they should receive two shares (*taksim*) of the money because they were doing two jobs, singing and playing *'armonia*.

I got to know Amir better during my second year in Herat. By this time Veronica had started her lessons with the professional woman singer Zainab Herawi and was spending lots of time in her teacher's house.[16] It transpired that Amir was a nephew of Zainab's husband, Khalifa Shekar, a barber with a hairdressing salon in a *hamum* (public bathhouse). Amir lived in his uncle's family home, located in the heart of the area occupied by the Golpasand extended family, generally known as *Sar Tapa*, 'Top of the Hill', on account of it being built on high ground. Although this was Amir's home he was rarely there in the daytime, and often not at night either, according to Veronica's report. He was extremely friendly with Ezatullah Mujadidi, from the wealthy and powerful Mujadidi family,[17] who was a keen amateur musician and ran the Sunrise Hotel, which served more as his personal guest house for his friends and for music sessions rather than as a genuine business enterprise. It also allowed him to fraternize with tourists.

In 1977 Amir, his uncle Khalifa Shekar, Veronica and I drove in our Land Rover to Shendand, a town on the main road to Kandahar that was an important base for Afghanistan's small air force. The presence of servicemen in the base no doubt also created a demand for barbers, and Shendand was the home of a number of barber-musician families. The men used to make long journeys to remote rural areas to service the nomads, cutting hair, shaving beards, performing circumcisions, providing *sâzdohol* music and performing folk drama (*seil*) for wedding parties. Amir's maternal uncle was Haji Amin, a comedian who achieved fame in the theatres of Kabul.

Visiting Shendand encouraged Amir to tell us more about his personal history. He was born in the remote village of Pai Koh (Foot of the Mountain), near Shendand. His parents died when he was very young and he was brought up by a paternal uncle. But when Amir was about 12 he was packed off to Herat with a sack of wheat to sell and told to find his uncle Khalifa Shekar, who would look after him from then on. Amir managed to find Shekar and moved into the home with Zainab and their young children. It was in this social milieu that Amir became a musician, not through formal training but by exposure to music, observation,

---

[16]   These women musicians were amongst the few working-women, who were financially independent. She was one of Veronica's *Three Women of Herat* (1988), under the pseudonym of Shirin.

[17]   His relative, the Naqshbandi Sufi Pir Sebghatullah Mujadidi, was leader of the National Liberation Front, one of the more moderate of the seven *mujahideen* parties, and Prime Minister for six months in 1992. Ezatullah Mujadidi later achieved fame as a musician in the USA, under the name of Aziz Herawi. He changed his name to avoid embarrassing his religious relatives.

imitation and participation. While young enough to attend women's wedding parties, he sometimes went out with Zainab's band, playing *tabla*. Though connected to the Golpasand clan, and from the same barber-musician background, he was not a blood relative. Zainab was not a blood relative either, but she had been recruited into a Golpasand women's band because she was a good singer and came from a local *Gharibzâda* family in Deh Tappeh, near Herat city (Doubleday 1988: part III). Amir had not been treated well by the male Golpasand musicians, who did not let him play with them, denied him musical training, and used to tease him about his ignorance of classical music and inability to sing *ghazal*. His repertoire consisted of Herati songs and current popular songs from the radio.[18]

On one occasion I went with Amir and several other friends to Mir Daud, a local beauty spot, for a day out. We listened to a tape of Indian music (*santur* and guitar) on the two-in-one radio-cassette machine I had brought along, and Amir started telling stories about great musicians of Kabul and India and Sufi saints and their shrines. I recorded his discourse on a second tape machine. Back in Belfast, listening to this wonderful recording, with the music in the background, I regretted that I had not done more with Amir; he was such a good raconteur. He was 'the one who got away'. And now here he was in Peshawar, vulnerable, out of his milieu, far from friends and relations. No wonder that when we met in Peshawar he had greeted me as a long-lost brother. I connected him with the past. As he often said to me, 'When I see your face I see Herat.' The feeling was reciprocal. Amir was the ideal protagonist for the portrait film I had in mind. He was highly articulate and a great story-teller, had an attractive personality, and was quite a good musician, on occasion capable of the sublime.

When I knew Amir in Herat he was a singer and *'armonia* player. Now he was playing *rubâb* in the band of Shah Wali, a popular singer from Afghanistan who had become a local star of Pakistani radio and television. I was surprised to find him in such company, especially as a *rubâb* player, an instrument I had hardly ever heard him play before. In contrast to his humble origins, he was now a member of the top Afghan band in Peshawar. In the film *Amir* he recounts briefly how he met Shah Wali in Peshawar:

> Then I met Shah Wali. He embraced me and said: 'You are my brother from Herat'. We went to a shrine together. There he said, 'What can I do to help you? I have a room, use it, don't go anywhere else'. At first I didn't tell him I was a musician. One day he made me sing and I played the *rubâb*.[19]

I was never quite sure what Shah Wali saw in Amir. Certainly he was a social asset: he had charm and tact with patrons, was ready to ingratiate himself with them and to act the humble sidekick. Perhaps coming from Herat he had better

---

[18]   Social ranking amongst professional musicians was determined in part by an individual's knowledge of music theory and terminology (Baily 1988a: 121).

[19]   *Amir* – 8' 09" (Baily 1985a).

manners and more social graces than many Afghans. He was always smartly turned out, with hand-embroidered and freshly ironed clothes. When patrons came to hire the band Shah Wali would consult Amir about the terms offered, the distances to be travelled, and the comforts promised, for above all Amir was an experienced professional musician, the veteran of hundreds of engagements, and knew how to get on well with people and create a good ambiance at a wedding or private party.

On one occasion four Pakistanis from the town of Pishin, near Quetta, came to Shah Wali to discuss booking the band for a four-day and -night event over the coming *'Eid* celebrations. This was a commercial enterprise; they were planning to sell tickets to the general public. After a lot of discussion about the organization of the programme, morning, afternoon and evening, travel and accommodation, the question was put about the fee. Shah Wali said he needed to discuss this with Amir. They left the room for five minutes to discuss the matter; on their return Shah Wali named his price as 40,000 rupees. The concert organizers immediately agreed to that sum. After they had gone Amir complained to Shah Wali about the payment. Shah Wali said to Amir, 'That's the price you suggested.' Amir responded, 'No, that was my suggestion for the last price, you should have asked for 80,000 rupees. Then we could have seen how they responded, and gone down accordingly.' From this I realized that Shah Wali was very keen to get Amir's advice on such matters, and that Amir was a good hustler, perhaps the outcome of his many arguments with his fellow musicians in Herat about rates of pay.

Afghan Music in Peshawar in 1985

The blind cannot remain here
This is the homeland of the sighted
My homeland is the country of the angels
The blind cannot remain here
My homeland is the country of the angels

I had not gone to Peshawar to make a systematic study of Afghan music in that city, but to shoot a film. Much of what I learned about the music scene came from spending so much time with Amir and Shah Wali Khan. But of course I also learned a good deal about the broader picture. Afghan musicians started moving to Pakistan soon after the communist coup of 1978. I met several who had been in Peshawar from those early days. Nearly all the refugee musicians I encountered were from Laghman, near the city of Jalalabad. They were not Pashtuns, but *Dom*s (barbers and musicians) of Pashtuns, whose first language was Pashto. My friend Amir, from the distant city of Herat, where Pashto was seldom heard, was an exception. The Afghan musicians in exile in Peshawar encountered and adopted a rather different kind of business arrangement to that which operated in Afghanistan. The business centres for professional musicians in Peshawar were

Dubgari Road and the Qessakhani bazaar, once a centre for storytellers. In these areas bands of musicians rented rooms, or even suites of rooms, above the open-fronted shops so that prospective patrons could come and visit them, to hire them for wedding parties or other kinds of gathering for men. These rooms were called in Pashto *deyrah*, and in Dari *daftar*, words that can be glossed as 'office'. Until recently these upstairs rooms also have been venues for dancing girls, as one finds in Lahore. The *deyrah* system of Peshawar was different from arrangements in Kucheh Kharabat in Kabul, where musicians operated from their own houses rather than from separate business premises.

Those Afghan refugee musicians who wished to continue with the profession hired business premises alongside the local Peshawari musicians. Relations between the refugees and the local musicians were generally cordial. The Peshawari musicians must have been aware that the Afghans were taking their work but I never observed or even heard of conflicts between them. The Afghan musicians were canny enough to play the system through accommodating to the local *ustâd-shâgerd* relationships. They were careful to show respect to the Peshawaris, and were ready to take lessons from them, as I witnessed on a number of such occasions. Shah Wali learned some pieces from Ustad Nawab Khan, an elderly singer and *'armonia* player. I also benefited from these teaching sessions and was able to learn several compositions to play on the *rubâb*.[20]

Shah Wali was born in about 1950, and was from Tagau, near Jalalabad.[21] He was a talented youngster and sang on Radio Afghanistan as a boy. He became well known in the Tagau area and was later employed full-time by RTA as a second-level artist. He remained at the radio station during Taraki and Hafizullah Amin times and left after Babrak Kamal came to power, when he refused the request to record some political songs. He and his family flew to Jalalabad, and then travelled to the border on foot. He and his brother Wali went first to find somewhere to live and to investigate the work situation. Shah Wali was already well known in Peshawar from a cassette recorded some time earlier for the *Afghan Music* label. He also had some contact with Sayed Ahmad Gailani, leader of the moderate NIFA party, who helped him find work at Pakistan TV in Peshawar, which led to his becoming so popular in Pakistan.

Shaukat Ali, a Programme Producer at Pakistan TV in Peshawar told me about the popularity of Afghan music in Peshawar at this time. There was a difference in style, he said: Afghan music was more interesting rhythmically and used different *tabla* rhythms, and in playing *Logari* dance music the rhythmic cadences and breaks were more distinct. Shah Wali was one of only four local 'A' grade artists (a classification used to determine status and rates of pay). He commented that Shah Wali did not have a strong voice, or even a very distinctive voice, but that he was very musical. His style was more classical than that of local Peshawari singers, he knew lots of *râg*s and he played the *'armonia* very well. He was right

---

[20] See *Amir* – 13' 03" – where Ustaz Bakhtiar gives Master Ali Haidar a lesson.
[21] In 1985 he told me he was 35 years old.

for television performance, where the weakness of his voice did not matter. To that I might add, having seen some TV footage of Shah Wali in action, that he came across as a dynamic, charismatic and very good-looking performer. Afghan music was popular in Peshawar at that time but the local audience was not interested in songs about the *jihâd*, and such material was not broadcast.

In 1985 Shah Wali's band consisted of Shah Wali himself, vocal and *'armonia*, his younger brother Wali, also vocal and *'armonia*, Mena Gol on *tabla*, Amir on *rubâb*, and a Peshawari clarinet player called Mustafa. I never discovered whether Mustafa was in the band in order to make it more inclusive by adding a local Peshawari musician, or because the clarinet was an important part of the Peshawari sound. Perhaps both considerations applied. Before Amir joined the band Shah Wali had the Peshawari *rubâb* player Ustaz Bakhtiar in his band, but the somewhat elderly Bakhtiar did not like going on long trips to distant places to perform. Perhaps Bakhtiar was useful because of his contacts with the Peshawar television station.[22] After making a cassette recording with Amir on *rubâb*, Shah Wali decided to have Amir join the band as a regular member.

Of the various *deyrah*s that I visited, Shah Wali's was particularly well appointed, a place where wealthy patrons could be entertained in comfort. It consisted of three rooms, with a latrine on the roof. Although the *deyrah* served mainly as an office, on occasion the musicians might sleep there after a late gig, and a visitor could stay there for a night or two. In that sense it was also like a guest room. A lot of bookings came up at short notice, and the musicians needed to be around in the late afternoon and early evening in case patrons came to hire them, though some engagements were booked well in advance. On one occasion Shah Wali took me to a big reception in the cantonment (military area) for Fazl Haq, the Military Governor of Peshawar. Shah Wali was announced over the PA system as a television artist and I noticed that his was the only band playing. On another occasion Shah Wali complained that he had had to cancel a programme on television because he was requested by the Police Commissionaire to play at a police function and the police had refused to pay Shah Wali the 5,000 rupees he was going to get from the TV station. From this one gets a sense of how he was obliged to keep the local authorities sweet.

As musicians, the main source of income for Shah Wali and his band came from playing at Pakistani (rather than Afghan) wedding parties, and they travelled large distances to make a living. 'We go up to the border, or to Waziristan, to places where Shah Wali is known, to Swat, to Lahore, to Karachi – our compatriots are there, too', Amir told us in the film.[23] At a wedding they would provide the usual love songs in Pashto that were considered appropriate for such festivities,

---

[22] Ustaz Bakhtiar was the most interesting of the Peshawari musicians I met. He had two styles of *rubâb* playing, which he called *sarod bâj* and *rubâb bâj*. *Bâj* here means style. On one occasion Bakhtiar invited me to a *gormâni* in Dubgari. His student was a girl of about 15, from a *tawaif* (dancing girl) background I assume.

[23] *Amir* – 24' 44" (Baily 1985a).

rather than political songs. They recorded commercial cassettes in a studio, or personalized cassettes for any patron to send to a friend, and this could be done in the comfort of the back room of the *dayrah*. Shah Wali's status was enhanced by his ownership of a motorcar. He told me that a wealthy Pakistani patron had given this car to him after a music party that must have thrilled the patron. He handed Shah Wali his car keys and told him to collect the car the next day! On another occasion Amir complained that Shah Wali should have sold the car and divided the proceeds amongst the band rather than keep it for himself.

Shah Wali could also be generous. On one occasion he took me to an Afghan wedding in the area of Akundabad where Amir, Mena, and other musicians lived in very poor housing. The musicians were performing free of charge, as an act of charity for the impoverished families. As usual, they had microphones and a PA system. A few minutes after the music started there was a loud banging on the door of the courtyard where the performance was taking place, and two mullahs were admitted. I was recording the music at the time and so caught the following exchange on tape:

> **Mullah:** We have come as refugees from Afghanistan, we left everything behind but we should not leave behind our honour and customs. Don't play that thing because God and the Prophet will be offended. You play these things on happy occasions like weddings and circumcisions but it's not right to play here, we've come as refugees and if other people hear us [they'll say] it's just not right to hear such merry making. Turn it down! Because other people may be offended and your party may turn sour. I can tell you this thing is forbidden because it is *sorud* [music]. Now you've come here, all of you together, you must cut the loudspeaker altogether. If you play too loud the whole neighbourhood will stay up late and they will miss their [morning] prayers. And then God will ask you on Judgement Day why were you playing that game, and so putting the whole community to such inconvenience?

> **Shah Wali:** The best thing would have been if you had discussed this amongst yourselves before inviting me. I am a radio and television singer, wherever I go this thing goes with me …

> **Mullah:** Allright, we understand it is a happy occasion, we're not going to stop you but cut the speakers off completely.

> **Shah Wali:** Okay.

> **Mullah:** … although God and the Prophet have forbidden this thing.

> **Shah Wali:** Well Sir, it is the custom.

Mullah: Any wedding that has got you in it is not going to be a good wedding because the angels are not going to come and visit. Cut the speakers!

Musician [Amir]: Haji Sahib, it's finished, it's the end, the subject is dead, and we are going to start our concert. These people you refer to are our neighbours, they are not strangers, what are you talking about? ... And if you feel like that about it, you go along to the radio station and the television station and tell them to stop playing music ... . (Baily 2001a: 29–30)

In the end the wedding continued with the sound system switched off, so the mullahs had their way. This incident illustrates several themes in the censorship of music by Afghans. It shows the direct interference by mullahs in a performance of music, the idea that music is inappropriate, implicitly (though not stated outright) because people are in a state of mourning, that listening to music will cause people to neglect their prayers, and highlights tension over the matter of amplification (ibid., p. 30).

On another occasion Shah Wali took me to a relatively lavish Pakistani wedding in Malakand, about 30 miles from Peshawar, depicted in the film *Amir*. This wedding was very different from those I had experienced in Herat in the 1970s. The performance was shorter, about two hours, with a break for tea. Shah Wali and his brother did not perform long sets of continuous performance; instead, songs were separated by short pauses. There was no *takht-e dâmâd* (bridegroom's throne ceremony) and no dancing of the *attan* (the national dance), though there was some uninhibited solo dancing towards the end. Unusually for a wedding performance, Shah Wali sang two songs that referred to the war. The second of these received rapturous applause from the audience. It transpired that this was originally a song about Pashtunistan, with poetry by the famous Pashtun poet Malang Jan, which Shah Wali had altered a little, changing 'Pashtunistan' to 'Afghanistan'. It articulates in a very direct manner some key Pashtun values.

> The blind cannot remain here
> This is the homeland of the sighted
> My homeland is the country of the angels
> The blind cannot remain here
> My homeland is the country of the angels
>
> Here every Pashtun is standing up for his honour and grace
> He is standing up to protect his homeland with honour and courage
> Those who are prepared to die for their homeland
> Are the defenders of their homeland
> My homeland is the country of the angels
> The blind cannot remain here
> Afghanistan is the homeland of the angels
> Afghanistan is the homeland of the warriors

As the cries of the warriors are full of zeal for freedom
Similarly every maiden is modest and full of zeal
The Pashtun way of life binds one to the homeland
My homeland is the country of the angels
The blind cannot remain here
My homeland is the country of the angels
As these rocks and mountains are witnesses
The enemy remains thwarted
Rashid, this is the homeland of the lions
My country is the homeland of the angels
The blind cannot remain here
My country is the homeland of the angels[24]

Perhaps the most notable aspect of the evening was the frequent firing of guns: pistols, rifles, Kalashnikovs and ancient blunderbusses. A number of guests were armed, with ammunition belts around their shoulders. I noted three blunderbusses (*dâhanpor*) leaning against the wall in a corner of the courtyard. These were later brought out and carried off and fired from a distance outside the courtyard, producing loud explosions, like bombs. Then they were brought back into the courtyard by two men who discharged one in front of the musicians, then threatened to let another off in front of a row of important guests facing the bandstand, but they were bought off with some folding money. They then threatened the musicians with the same, but walked off. In the sky there were periodically flaming kites. During the very last song an unfortunate incident occurred. Shah Wali stopped playing, turned round and without apparent reason slapped Amir across the face. Amir was very quiet on the way home. Later he told me that Shah Wali was annoyed with him for chatting with the *tabla* player and sharing a joke while they played.

Fortunately, the next day one of the band's patrons arrived in Peshawar from Lahore, and this created a diversion. The patron was Mohammad Shahabuddin Khan, whose father had been the Nawab (ruler) of the small princely state of Dir, on the border with Afghanistan. The state of Dir was abolished in 1969, and the Nawab, Mohammad Shah Khusrau Khan, was exiled. His son was also banned from visiting Dir. He would come periodically to stay at Dean's Hotel in Peshawar, a famous relic of the British Raj, where his father's former subjects would come to visit. I assume he still owned land and property in Dir. Shah Wali and Amir always referred to their patron as the Nawab Sahib-e Dir, and I shall follow their usage (although it is strictly incorrect).

Amongst other things the Nawab was a great music lover and amateur singer and *'armonia* player. He brought with him the first electronic keyboard I had seen in those parts, a small Casiotone MT-70, which Shah Wali referred to as the Nawab's 'organization'. The Nawab had helped Shah Wali and Amir in various

---

[24]   *Amir* – 30′ 32″ (ibid.).

ways, for example, by giving them instruments, a fine *'armonia* and two *rubâb*s, one of which Amir lent to me during my stay in Peshawar. He was also good at mediation and reconciliation, and whatever the difficulty was between Shah Wali and Amir, he healed the rift, at least for a while.

The Film *Amir: An Afghan refugee musician's life in Peshawar, Pakistan*

Amir Jan provided me with perfect access to the Afghan music scene in Peshawar. For three weeks after meeting him I spent much time in Shah Wali's *deyrah* in Dubgari with Amir and other musicians, and went out with Shah Wali's band to observe it at various engagements. My ability to play the *rubâb* was a great asset in interacting with the musicians, and the fact that I could claim to be the student of the revered Ustad Mohammad Omar gave me special status. I was often called upon to perform at informal gatherings of Afghan musicians. From the Afghan point of view this gift distinguished me from other western filmmakers and journalists in Peshawar at the time. Not only did I know a lot about their music, but I could also play it. The time I had spent honing my musical skills in Belfast was by no means time wasted.

Wayne Derrick arrived from the UK with the camera equipment. I travelled to Islamabad to meet him and take us through the tortuous customs formalities to get the film equipment into the country. By this time I had a good idea about the range of activities we might expect to encounter in our work in Peshawar. Although when working in the observational cinema style one should film things as they happen, without provoking or in any way controlling them, this ideal proved sometimes difficult to achieve. Familiarity with the subject would inevitably suggest types of scene to be sought out, which might be passively awaited or more actively provoked. The film we made was in no sense scripted in advance. We spent a lot of time with the musicians in Dubgari Road and followed Shah Wali's band when they went to the mountains for a holiday during *Ramazân*, the month of fasting. Although he spoke no Dari, Wayne fitted into the scene very comfortably. Like me, he wore Afghan clothes, *piran o tâmbân*, long shirt and baggy trousers when we were 'at work', he enjoyed the music and he enjoyed the company. When we were filming I was able to communicate with him by facial expression when necessary about where to point the camera.

There is no doubt that filming imposed considerable strains on relations amongst the musicians, notably between Amir and Shah Wali. The members of the band were by no means naïve about filmmaking. They had often seen themselves on Peshawar TV and were familiar with Hindi and Urdu movies. They occasionally hired a VCR and monitor to watch films in the *deyrah*. Shah Wali had composed the music for a film in Pakistan, and had performed in at least one western documentary (André Singer's *Khyber*). In the musicians' experience filmmakers worked at high pressure, but we did not conform to that expectation. Instead we spent our time taking part in the life of Dubgari and only reaching for the camera

Figure 2.2   From left to right: Amir Jan, John Baily and Wali Jan in Shah Wali
               Khan's *deyra*, Peshawar 1985. © Wayne Derrick

and tape recorder when something interesting started happening. Amir was happy
with this arrangement but it clearly began to irritate Shah Wali. From his point of
view, I realized, we should have been making a film about him, the famous singer,
not someone who was his henchman and menial, a mere accompanist. Amir gave
us access to Shah Wali, and Shah Wali did not necessarily appreciate it.

Wayne and I returned to the UK and I began editing the film at the NFTS, with
its many editing suites equipped with Steenbeck editing tables for cutting 16 mm
film. One of the great assets of the NFTS was the availability of editing facilities
and the way in which we students were able to retain such a suite for more or less
as long as we needed it. This contrasted with conditions in the industry itself,
where time is money and editors work under great pressure to get things done as
quickly as possible. In any event, editing the film proved relatively unproblematic;
the final cut was not so far removed from the first rough cut.

I discovered the joys of working at the editing table and of track laying. Clearly
it was a portrait film about my friend Amir, and I think I had decided on the title
for the film even before I started editing. There were a few cuts that proved tricky
to get right, but solutions were found. Periodically, Amir sent me audiocassettes he
recorded with the latest news and towards the end of the editing process I received
ill tidings from Peshawar. A cassette arrived to say that after another falling out
with Shah Wali, Amir had been sacked and was out of the band. The first public
screening of the film was at the RAI Ethnographic Film Festival in London
in 1985. I felt it necessary to insert an inter-title at the end of the film, before the

credits, to say that Amir had lost his job. However, a few days later I received another cassette from Amir saying that he had been re-instated. I removed the disconcerting inter-title and finished the editing and sub-titling as soon as I could, before a fresh inflow of bad news might be received.

The film *Amir* has been very well received and shown at many ethnographic film festivals, including the Margaret Mead and Nuoro. It won a special *prix de jury* at the *Bilan du film Ethnographique* in Paris, and a prize from the American Anthropological Association. It was favourably reviewed by Hugo Zemp, the doyen of ethnomusicological film (Zemp 1988), by Mark Slobin (Slobin 1988) and discussed by Peter Loizos his book on ethnographic film (Loizos 1993: 85–8). In 2011 *Amir* was selected as one of the outstanding films to have been shown in the 30 years of the Jean Rouch Film Festival. On the basis of this the RAI agreed to make a new, digital, print from the negative, and the subtitling had to be re-done, which allowed for a few mistakes to be rectified. It is the original 1985 version that comes with the accompanying DVD.

The success of *Amir* as an 'arthouse anthropological documentary' was no doubt due to the fact that it embodied many of the principles of observational cinema as I learned about them at the NFTS (Baily 1989a). There was no pre-scripted storyboard, filmmaking was used as a form of research in its own right (Figure 2.2). We followed events rather than created them. Amir himself initiated the visit to the Sufi shrine of Rahman Baba, which forms the most powerful part of the film.[25] Apart from 90 seconds of commentary in English at the beginning of the film, spoken in the first person by me, there was no use of voice-over, and minimal use of captions to explain locations or other matters. Speech and song (in Dari and Pashto) were sub-titled. Wayne Derrick hand-held the camera throughout, making some exceptional sequence shots. The film was reflexive, exposing the filmmaking process with a long shot of the sound recordist (Baily) at work, and at another point one musician explains to another, 'This is a film for the cinema. They'll show it in England.'[26]

Amir has a strong narrative coherence. For much of the first half-hour we see the musicians in the workplace; life as a refugee musician does not seem too bad. But after the wedding scene, where songs about the war are sung by Shah Wali, the film takes a much more serious turn, dealing with death and destruction, leading up to Amir's 'moment of truth' at the Sufi shrine, where he reveals his deep upset about being an exile. There is no story as such, but a journey into Amir's life: material, musical and emotional. In the process, a number of aspects of the situation are revealed: the material condition of refugees not living in camps; the music business and the lives of working musicians; aspects of Pashtun culture as highlighted in Shah Wali's political songs; the importance of Sufi shrines; and the atmosphere of a Pashtun wedding celebration with the firing of guns. A final factor for the film's success was surely the rhythmically upbeat Afghan music, which

[25] *Amir* – 39' 30" (ibid.).
[26] *Amir* – 18' 09" (ibid.).

is readily enjoyed by a western audience. In editing *Amir* I was conscious of the need to present Amir, and other musicians, in a positive light to counteract popular prejudices against musicians. I wanted to show him at prayer, even though this is such a cliché in films about the Muslim world. As for his tears at the shrine, he had no objection to this depiction, which expressed how he felt. The study guide to the film (Baily 1990) provides more information about the editing of *Amir*.

I remained in touch with Amir via the audiocassettes we exchanged for several years, and he reappears at various points of my tale. He benefited greatly from the film and the contacts it provided, particularly with Bruce Wannell, who proved to be a generous patron. Bruce, an aesthete and music lover, arrived in Peshawar towards the end of the shoot to take over running the Afghanaid projects. The morning after his arrival I got up early, to find him sitting in the small garden outside the Afghanaid house, with a copy of Hafiz (in Persian, of course) in one hand and a rose in the other, lifted up so that he could enjoy its fragrance with the poetry. For some years Bruce remained in Pakistan and looked after Amir's interests, organizing music sessions for him and introducing him to other expatriates who engaged him for parties. Thus the film was in certain ways the making of Amir as a successful musician.

These were some of the best days of Amir's life, mixing with foreigners, being invited to play in the homes of diplomats and being well remunerated. Later he visited Switzerland and Japan to give concerts as a *rubâb* player and he has participated in at least two commercial recordings. At the time of writing he still lives in Peshawar. Although he has visited Herat several times, he does not seem inclined to return to live there. His five children were born, brought up and educated in Pakistan, making it difficult for them to go and live in Herat. I have seen him many times since 1985; whenever I go to Kabul he somehow finds out and comes to pay his respects.

Chapter 3
The *Mujahideen* Parties Come to Power

Coalition and Chaos

In 1985, the year of my visit to Peshawar, American policy towards Afghanistan underwent a profound change. As Victoria Schofield explains:

> President Ronald Reagan issued a 'directive' to use 'all available means' to force the Soviets to withdraw [from Afghanistan]. Pakistan, under the dictatorship of General Zia-ul Haq, became the conduit for a massive injection of sophisticated weaponry to the mujaheddin [sic], administered through the Inter-Services Intelligence agency (ISI), Pakistan's military secret service. (Schofield 2010: 323)

The sophisticated weaponry provided by the USA included the Stinger surface-to-air missiles that were very effectively used by the *mujahideen*, with an estimated 50 per cent hit rate (Misdaq 2006: 165). According to Misdaq: 'Fighters like Mullah Yar Muhammad in Kandahar, and Mullah Abdul Salaam, nicknamed "Mullah Rocketi" became nationally known as highly skilled in firing these missiles' (ibid.). Stingers were used against bomber aircraft and helicopter gunships and were claimed to have made a decisive change in the conflict. Between1981 and 1985 the annual US military aid to the *mujahideen* increased from $30 million to approximately $280 million (Schofield 2010: 323).

US Congressman Charlie Wilson was one of the most effective facilitators in executing the Reagan doctrine. From 1984 he developed a close working relationship with Gulbuddin Hekmatyar, seen as the most competent of the seven *mujahideen* leaders based in Pakistan. A number of revealing anecdotes about Wilson can be found in David Loyn's well-indexed *Butcher & Bolt* (Loyn 2009). It is hard to imagine the two men interacting, the hard drinking womanizer on one hand, and the fanatical Islamist on the other. However, they continued to do business, 'Hekmatyar had become used to the whisky-drinking Texan having a different girl with him every time he came to town [Peshawar], and he was not going to complain' (ibid., p. 180).[1] But Hekmatyar must have hated Wilson's behaviour, which would have confirmed all his prejudices about western values and culture. These differences notwithstanding, 600 million dollars out of the total of 3 billion that the US spent on the war were channelled through Wilson to Hekmatyar (ibid., p. 204).

---

[1] Hollywood's version of this adventure is *Charlie Wilson's War*, released in 2007 and described as both a drama and a comedy. An Afghan audience might well not see the humour.

Significant changes were taking place in the internal politics of Afghanistan. The USSR had lost confidence in the ability of President Babrak Karmal to bring about a negotiated end to the war and arranged to replace him with Dr Najibullah, a founder member of the Parcham faction of the PDPA in the 1960s. Under Karmal he had been Director of KHAD (*Khedamat-e Amniyat-e Daulati*), the Afghan national security network, equivalent to the Soviet KGB. In moves orchestrated by the USSR, Najibullah was made General Secretary of the PDPA in May 1986, and in November 1986 Babrak Karmal was removed to the USSR, ostensibly for medical treatment. In January 1987 Najibullah, as PDPA General Secretary, instituted a programme of national reconciliation and ordered the drafting of a new constitution that was ratified by a *Loya Jirga* in November of that year. In this, Islam was upheld as the state religion, Afghanistan was declared to be a multi-party democracy and Najibullah was elected President of the newly named Republic of Afghanistan (under the earlier communist regimes it had been called the Democratic Republic of Afghanistan).

At the same time, profound changes were taking place in the USSR under Mikhail Gorbachev. This was the era of *glasnost* (openness) and *perestroika* (restructuring), the movement for reform of the Soviet political and economic system that led to the breakup of the USSR. Gorbachev undertook the withdrawal of Soviet forces, which in 1988 numbered about 100,000 men (Braithwaite 2011: 283). On 15 February 1989 the last Soviet troops withdrew across the River Oxus, leaving Najibullah and his restructured regime to stand alone, though still in receipt of munitions, goods of all kinds, and money from the USSR. Against the expectations of many, his government endured until 1992, surviving a failed attempted coup by his Defence Minister Shahnawaz Tanai in 1990 in collaboration with Hekmatyar, and the set-piece battle for Jalalabad, a disaster for the *mujahideen*, who were estimated to have lost 20,000 men.

In 1991 with the breakup of the USSR, Soviet aid came to an end. Inexorably, the *mujahideen* took control of rural areas. Dostam's *Jowzjâni* Uzbek militia seized control of Mazar-e Sharif, and Naderi's Ismaili Shia militia took the Salang Tunnel, together cutting Kabul's supply line from the north. The writing was on the wall; it was time for those who had remained in Kabul to leave, faced with the coming of a very different regime, that of the victorious *mujahideen*. On 15 April 1992 Najibullah announced that he would resign (as distinct from his actual resignation), and soon after he tried with UN assistance to leave Kabul to join his family in India, but was turned back at the airport. He took refuge in the UN compound in Kabul, where he remained for the next four years.

The departure of Najibullah, though incomplete, marked a dramatic change in the political situation and the start of a period of extreme instability in Kabul. Whereas in earlier stages of the war the capital had been relatively safe from direct attack by the *mujahideen*, it now became the centre of conflict in a fast moving and bewildering series of shifting alliances that ended with the destruction of much of the city and the death of many thousands of its citizens. There was armed conflict between five rival factions: Rabbani and Massoud's *Jam'iat-e Islâmi*, Hekmatyar's

Hezb-e Islâmi, Sayyaf's *Itehâd-e Islâmi*, Mazari's *Hezb-e Wahdat* and Dostam's *Jowzjâni*. The first three were amongst the seven *mujahideen* parties recognized by Pakistan; Mazari's *mujahideen* party, largely Hazara (and Shia) in membership, was backed by Iran, while Dostam's Uzbek militia had previously supported the communists and had no overt religious affiliation.

Initially Kabul fell into the hands of an alliance between *Jam'iat-e Islâmi*, *Hezb-e Wahdat* and *Jowzjâni*. Hekmatyar, never at ease with Rabbani, joined with remnants of the Afghan army that were PDPA Khalq supporters. By the end of 1992 fighting had broken out between *Jam'iat-e Islâmi* and *Hezb-e Wahdat* for control of the southwestern areas largely inhabited by Hazaras. *Jowzjâni* made an alliance with *Hezb-e Islâmi*, and fought against *Jam'iat-e Islâmi* for control of central Kabul. Three-quarters of the population of Kabul were forced to move to safer areas of the city, or to refugee camps in Jalalabad.

Jolyon Leslie provides a graphic first-hand account of the exodus of thousands by night from the modern Microrayan complex in eastern Kabul, after being warned of an impending rocket attack by the newly formed Hakmatyar-Dostam alliance:[2]

> those of us who lived along the route were woken by the muffled sounds of the exodus and looked out to see a line of flickering kerosene lamps lighting the way for a huge column of families, clutching their possessions, walking or pushing wheelbarrows or bicycles. The only sounds above the fearful shuffle of thousands of frozen feet were the occasional cry of a baby, or bleating of a sheep. Doors soon began to open along the route, inviting those who were exhausted to rest, drink tea and tell their stories before heading on their way.
>
> Few of those who witnessed scenes such as this can forget that such episodes were caused by men who, less than a decade later, have been rewarded with ministerial posts in an internationally-backed administration, on the basis of sacrifices they allege to have made in liberating their people. (Johnson and Leslie 2004: 6)

The tragedy of Afghanistan is nowhere more evident than in the failure of the victorious insurgents to work together. Tales of the barbaric cruelties inflicted by Afghans upon fellow Afghans in Kabul at this time are almost beyond belief in their hideousness. After so many years of conflict, so many dead, so many injured, why could they not have overcome their differences? Ahmad Shah Massoud, the darling of the West, was the one person who might have succeeded. He had social capital, he had been in Afghanistan throughout the war, unlike

---

[2]   The term microrayan means in Russian a 'microdistrict', a residential area with kindergardens, schools, playgrounds, groceries and other shops, cafeterias and clubs. The microrayans of Kabul were built in the 1960s and were regarded as desirable middle-class housing. In the 1970s a number of musicians, including some from the Kharabat, were living in such districts.

those others who amassed their fortunes in Peshawar. Yet when it came to the crucial moment, he failed. Problems surfaced quickly. The plan was to have a rotating Presidency, and for the first six months Mujadidi held this position. He was in turn replaced by Rabbani, but when the latter's six months tenure came to an end he refused to give up his position, and he retained it until the fall of the Coalition to the Taliban in 1996.

Massoud's forces were based in the Bala Hisar, on the southeastern edge of the old city, and close to the Kucheh Kharabat, the musicians' quarter. Hekmatyar was well equipped with Scud missiles and used them frequently to attack Massoud's positions, and most of the houses in the Kharabat ended up being destroyed, with many people from the musician families killed. It is not known whether the Kharabat was deliberately targeted, but Hekmatyar may have been happy to witness the relentless destruction of that centre of liberalism and loose living. In the dying days of the Rabbani period, in 1996, Hekmatyar was appointed Prime Minister in a new coalition government, but soon after Kabul was to fall to the Taliban.

Little is known about the state of music in Kabul during the Coalition period. The testimony of musicians I met in Peshawar in 1992 reveals a strong oppression of music in the early days of the Coalition. In due course President Rabbani set up an Office for the Propagation of Virtue and the Prevention of Vice, although certain members of the government like Massoud did not support such strong measures to control the populace. When Hekmatyar became President in 1996, he closed Kabul's cinemas and banned music on radio and television. According to a report on July 15 1996 in the Pakistani newspaper *The Muslim*, a government spokesman had said:

> no music or musical instruments should be heard on radio or television ... any sort of music being played on air was illegal because it has a negative effect of peoples' [sic] psyches.

According to this report, Abdul Hafiz Mansoor, head of the state press agency Bakhtar commented:

> The government of President Burhanuddin Rabbani tried to shut down cinemas and ban music when it came to power four years ago [that is, in 1992], but it proved to be an unrealistic ideal which only lasted a few weeks ... It's difficult and potentially dangerous to take away a few simple pleasures from people who live in a ruined city with no electricity, [or] running water and which comes under constant rocket attack. (ibid.)

In this period I made three visits to reconnect with Afghan musicians, two to Pakistan (1991, 1992), and one to Herat (1994).

Islamabad 1991

> We do not drink wine for the sake of getting pleasantly drunk
> We drink wine to wash our self clean of all hypocrisy
>
> (Bedil)

In 1991 I received an invitation from the office of the UNHCR in Islamabad to participate in a project to produce a recording of Afghan music to celebrate the organization's 40th anniversary. The invitation came from Philippe Labreveux, a member of the UNHCR staff in Pakistan. UNHCR had done remarkable work for 10 years in Pakistan, helping to settle millions of Afghan exiles in refugee camps. The idea was to mark UNHCR's 40th anniversary by recording and releasing a CD of the famous Afghan singer Nashenas. I had never met Nashenas, but I knew him to be a Pashtun singer of high reputation. My role was to be honorary musical director and Bruce Wannell had been brought in as poetry consultant. Bruce, the former Field Director of Afghanaid was still living in Peshawar, and is someone with a profound and extensive knowledge of Persian classical poetry, Naturally, I accepted this invitation, and suggested that Amir Jan, the *rubâb* player and the Kabuli *tabla* player Ustad Arif Mahmoud should be included in the accompanying ensemble. I regarded this as an opportunity to make some recordings in the classical *ghazal* style of Kabul, a genre I knew well from performances in Herat by Kabuli singers such as Amir Mohammad, Ustad Rahim Bakhsh and Haji Hamahang. I arrived at Islamabad Airport on 24 May 1991 and went to meet Nashenas with Bruce and Philippe that afternoon to discuss the poetry and the music for the recordings.

Profile: Nashenas (Scholar, Civil Servant and Radio Singer)

At our first meeting Nashenas handed me a short document he had written about himself. The following brief account of his life is based on this memoir.

Mohammad Sadiq Fitrat was born on 28 December 1935 in the city of Kandahar. His family was from the Pashtun elite, members of the Kakar tribe. From 1940 to 1947 he resided with his family in various cities in India and present-day Pakistan, where his father was the representative of the Afghan National Bank. It was here that he learned Urdu, and this long exposure at an impressionable age to the culture of British India must have had important musical influences. He graduated in Political Economics from the Faculty of Law and Political Science of Kabul University in 1959, and then began a long-term career with the Ministry of Information and Culture. Initially he was employed by Radio Kabul (as it then was) as Director of Foreign Programmes. In 1962 he was sent to Moscow to study Russian in order to become an official interpreter, returning in 1966 to his position at Radio Afghanistan. In 1968 he was sent to Moscow University for post-graduate study and was awarded a PhD in Pashto linguistics in 1970.

Back in Kabul, Nashenas, or Dr Fitrat as he was sometimes called, was employed as a member of the History Department of the Ministry of Information and Culture. His singing career started in the 1950s. He was a self-taught musician who used to practise at home late at night, sitting with his *'armonia* under a blanket to deaden the sound of his singing, so that his father sleeping below should not know what he was up to. When as a university student he started singing for Radio Kabul it was under the pseudonym of Nashenas, which means 'Unknown', in order to hide his identity from his family. It was several years before he felt able to reveal to his father that he was the by then famous radio singer Nashenas. He was voted the most popular singer on radio in 1961, 1969, 1981 and again in 1984. In 1966 he visited Iran with an Afghan music group to give concerts in Tehran, Isfahan and Persepolis. From 1971 to 1973 he was sent to India to learn more about Indian classical music, and acquired a good knowledge of Indian *rāg*s in the process. He performed on stage, radio and television while in India in order to make Afghan music better known. He claims to have recorded some 400 songs for radio, television and cassette companies over the years, and to have composed the music for approximately 260 songs. Nevertheless, Nashenas is proud of the fact that he never made his living from singing. Music was for him a true *shauq*, a hobby pursued with passionate fervour.

On his return from India in 1973 he resumed work in the History Department of the Ministry for Information and Culture, and was then appointed Head of the Music and Literature Department of Radio Afghanistan, and was a member of various other literary bodies. After a brief spell as Director General of Radio Afghanistan, and following the *Saur* Revolution of 27 April 1978, he was reappointed Head of the Music and Literature Department of Radio Afghanistan. However, because he refused to join the PDPA, and because he refused to sing songs in support of the regime, he was soon downgraded to being a member of the Board of Fine Arts in the radio station, with no specific responsibilities. In 1985 he was sent as Second Secretary of Cultural Affairs to the Afghan Embassy in Moscow. He wrote in his memoir: 'I was the *only non*-party Afghan diplomat throughout all Afghan embassies in the world. The reason for sending me for such a mission was *to prevent my escape to any other country ...*' (his emphasis). Returning to Kabul in 1989 he had further difficulties with the PDPA. As somebody with a training in political economy he did not agree with PDPA economic policy over the last 12 years. He requested retirement but this was refused. On 5 October 1990 he and his wife and three children escaped from Kabul, arriving in Peshawar three days later. I have no doubt that Nashenas realized that with the withdrawal of the Soviet army it was only a matter of time before the last communist government would fall to the *mujahideen*. Indeed, by the time of our meeting the *mujahideen* had just captured Khost, the first step in their conquest of Afghanistan.

This was the man with whom I had come to work.

Working with Nashenas

Nashenas, then aged about 56, turned out to be a tall, thin, balding man, with a nervous manner, who talked very fast in excellent English. He and his family were living in a modern apartment under armed guard provided by the ISI. He lost little time in explaining to us his fearful predicament. On one side the Afghan Government was angered by his escape. Anticipating such a move, President Najibullah had personally reminded him that there were many KHAD agents in Pakistan and that he would be killed if he left. On the other side, the *mujahideen* parties targeted him because he had remained for 12 years working for the communist government in Kabul. 'I was threatened to be killed by both sides', he told us. He had applied to the USA for political asylum but this had been refused because of his long association with the communist regime, even though he had not been a party member. His children were unable to go to school in Pakistan for fear of being kidnapped. I could well understand why the UNHCR was anxious to help him out of his dire predicament.

In due course our conversation turned to the recordings we had come to make. My idea was that we should record Nashenas singing classical poetry, in the form of Persian and Pashto *ghazal*s. Nashenas was obviously very well versed in the poetry of these languages, and he and Bruce engaged in long conversations in Persian about the poetry he would sing, with Bruce making many suggestions of poets to be quoted and couplets to be included. Nashenas put a great deal of preparation into the choice of poetry, both the *ghazal*s and the interpolated couplets he would add to them (like picking a bouquet of roses, with a flower from here and a flower from there, as the Afghan *ghazal* singers are wont to say) and he normally made copious hand-written notes for his song texts.

Differences of opinion soon emerged regarding the music. My plan was for Nashenas to sing in the traditional Kabuli *ghazal* style, but Nashenas wanted a more modern approach. He had very recently been in Lahore (courtesy of the ISI, I suppose) and had recorded 38 songs in Persian, Pashto and Urdu, with an ensemble that included a western violin section and an acoustic guitar playing simple chord sequences. He played us some of these recordings, which were very much in the *filmi* style of India and Pakistan. Indeed, he claimed to be the 'Afghan Saigal', after Kundan Lal Saigal 1904–47, regarded as the first superstar of the Hindi film industry. This was the modern style in which he wanted to record, while my plan was that the recordings should use instruments traditionally associated with Afghanistan, such as *rubâb*, *sârangi* and *tabla*. In the event a compromise was reached: we would use traditional instruments but the musical form was more the Kabul radio popular song (*tarz*) style rather than the *ghazal* style, a difference most obvious in the use of separately composed instrumental sections.[3]

---

[3] In the popular radio song form units of text alternate with instrumental sections (*naghma*) that have a melody distinct from those used for the verse and refrain sections.

The next day the three Afghan musicians arrived for the recording sessions: Amir Jan Herati (*rubâb*), Lala Seid Gol (*sarinda*) and Ustad Arif Mahmoud (*tabla*), younger brother of Ustad Hashem and Ustad Asif Mahmoud, from one of Kabul's leading hereditary musician families. Their meeting with Nashenas immediately revealed some of the difficulties to come. Nashenas was a member of the Afghan elite, highly educated, an authority on Persian and Pashto poetry, with a PhD from the USSR, who had held high office within the Ministry of Information and Culture. Moreover, he had been one of the most popular singers on Afghan radio. Now he was being asked to work with low status uneducated hereditary musicians. In the studio he quickly formed a low opinion of Amir's abilities as a *rubâb* player, and the *sarinda* was too much of a folk instrument for his liking, being strongly associated with the local music of the Logar Valley. Only Ustad Arif could be said to match the abilities of the musicians Nashenas would have recorded with in Kabul. After an awkward lunch in an Iranian restaurant we made our way to Lok Virsa, the National Institute of Folk and Traditional Heritage of Pakistan, where we met three Pakistani musicians who had been engaged for the recording: Alla Rakha, a very good *sârangi* player originally from Delhi, Ustaz Bakhtiar, the *rubâb* player from Peshawar with whom I had had contact in 1985, and Irshad Ali, who had come to play the *tânpurâ* drone so important in the classical music of India and Pakistan. We then ran through a number of the songs Nashenas planned to record.

The following day we returned with Nashenas to Lok Virsa, where the recordings were to be made. We discussed the work with the Institute's Director Uxi Mufti, who agreed that at my request we should also make some instrumental recordings of Amir Jan playing *rubâb*, and we then went to visit the recording studio. Though capacious, with an eight-channel mixer, it transpired that the recording machine itself was a two-track quarter-inch reel-to-reel Revox, not exactly state of the art equipment.

Next morning we gathered at the studio for the first recording session. The *tânpurâ* player brought with him a suitcase full of small percussion instruments, rattles of various shapes and sizes, dancer's ankle bells, clickers and whistles, which Bruce referred to as the 'musician's toy box' and suggested that Irshad Ali had come to do some snake charming. Things got off to a bad start. The melody of the first *ghazal* turned out to be too difficult for Amir and Seid Gol, who were asked by Nashenas not to play. A little later he also laid off Bakhtiar, so his performance was with just *sârangi*, *tabla* and *tânpurâ*. The second *ghazal* used the whole ensemble. Nashenas wanted the sound of dancing bells, and Irshad Ali produced from his box of tricks a set of bells that I played during the instrumental sections. The next *ghazal* raised problems for the two *rubâb* players. There was a particular instrumental phrase that Nashenas wanted them to play and Amir, slow as ever to learn anything new, simply could not get it. After a break for lunch Amir finally managed to play the piece and we recorded it. Nashenas then recorded two

---

In the *ghazal* song form the instrumental sections (*duni*) are repetitions of the melody used for the refrain.

Figure 3.1   Nashenas in the Lok Virsa studio with his songbooks, Islamabad 1991

filmi songs from the repertory of Saigal, but these were never released. By now Nashenas was getting tired and growing a little hoarse. We finished at 3.30pm and he left for home. After the main session Amir recorded, with *sarinda* and *tabla*, some instrumental pieces for his own UNHCR CD.

The next day things started off rather better in the studio. Nashenas seemed more relaxed. He recorded two *ghazals* without Amir and Seid Gol. The next song, a *chahârbeiti* rather than a *ghazal*, required the whole ensemble. The *rubâb* players had difficulties in learning the instrumental section and again Amir just could not get it. Nashenas remained patient, but a dispute arose between Amir and Bakhtiar and Amir grew angry and stalked off. The piece was recorded without him. Hoping to conciliate Amir I suggested to Nashenas that he should record the famous *Jân-e Kharâbâtam*, which I knew Amir could deal with. Nashenas had not prepared for this but good-naturedly agreed and leafed through his songbooks to select the couplets he deemed appropriate. I persuade Amir to come back and he took the usual inordinate length of time to get his *rubâb* tuned, now to a new mode. Nashenas asked Bakhtiar not to play, and he then recorded the song. Bruce, ever the considerate host, turned up with a fine pizza lunch and a large carpet for us to sit on, and Amir and Bakhtiar made up their quarrel. After lunch Nashenas recorded three more *ghazals*, without the *rubâbs* or *sarinda*. Further recordings were made over the next two days, with Nashenas singing and then Amir Jan playing instrumental *rubâb* pieces after the end of the sessions. By this time our studio work had come to an end (Figure 3.1).

Next day Bruce and I visited Nashenas and had a productive session in which we decided on the selection of items and their sequencing, bearing in mind considerations such as poetry, *râg*, *tâl*, instrumentation and tempo. Eventually the artistic direction of the final cassette was very much the collaboration between the three of us.

The UNHCR Cassettes

The outcome of the recordings was not quite what I had hoped for; we had not recreated the *ghazal* sound of the Kharabat. In part this was because only Ustad Arif was really competent in that type of music, the other musicians less so. And in the performances Nashenas did not stick to the Kabuli *ghazal* format, with the use of fast instrumental sections reiterating the melody of the refrains. Instead, he adopted independent instrumental sections (*naghma*) more typical of popular music. A further factor preventing this from being a classic example of Kabuli *ghazal* was the lack of *rubâb* support. As described in Chapter 1, the *rubâb* is the principal accompanying instrument in the Kabuli *ghazal* style, and neither Amir Jan nor Bakhtiar was adequately familiar with that style of accompaniment. On the other hand, the music was quite classical in spirit and the *sârangi* playing was excellent. Bruce was more satisfied with the poetry than I was with the music. The original intention was to have the recordings released on CD in Europe, with a substantial booklet with transcriptions, transliterations and translations of the poetry. That never happened, perhaps because of the poor audio quality of the studio recordings, and the sheer size of the poetry project. In due course Lok Virsa released a double audiocassette, one cassette being the Nashenas recordings, and the other Amir Jan's recordings, with a small booklet. The cover used a striking photograph of white pigeons at the shrine in Balkh, taken by Marie Rose Nicod of Switzerland (Nicod 1985: 100).

The Nashenas cassette had poetry by Rumi, Bedil, Humam, Khushal Khattak, Hamid Mashukhel, Foroughi Bistami and Hafez. My personal favourite on the cassette is Track 5, a *ghazal* by the Indo-Afghan poet Bedil, performed without the *rubâb*s or *sarinda*. The translation is by Bruce Wannell.

> I am a wine-worshipper of creation. I am intoxicated with eternity.
> Counting the beads of my rosary has never stimulated me;
> From now on, I shall sit by the wine barrel and count grapes.
>
> I am a wine-worshipper of creation. I am intoxicated with eternity.
> Like the bead of the grape, I was carrying a glass of lover's wine in my breast.
>
> Stop reckoning sales and profits! Cut off your longings!
> Drink wine! Enjoy yourself. I habitually do just the same!

I dedicate myself to whoever, under the circling blue heavens,
Is free from worldly longings

We do not drink wine for the sake of getting pleasantly drunk
We drink wine to wash our self clean of all hypocrisy.

If stones shall weep at my state, it is fitting. For, if I live without you, I am
dead before my appointed time.

Shame kills me that I still draw breath without you –
Let this be shame enough for me while I live.

My exalted message needs a subtle understanding: the ways of my
Thought are not easy – I am as a mountain with hard passes.

I had so much to say, stored in the treasury of knowledge and art;
But in the general silence, I clearly saw how futile were my many words.

If the common people applaud you, do not be deceived by your
accomplishments. What you thought were praises in their mouths, are,
As far as we are concerned, mere curses!

My ocean-like nature, Bedil, is full of dancing waves of meaning.
If I start a verse, I have all at once an ode.

It is not clear how UNHCR benefited from the project, but Nashenas and his family certainly did. Some weeks after the recordings Nashenas was granted political asylum by the UK and moved to London, where he still lives. Since 1991 he has kept a comparatively low profile, with occasional public concerts in the USA, Canada and Germany, but rarely in the UK. Despite his claims that he was never a member of the PDPA, his long association with the communist regime in Kabul led to him being reviled by some in the Afghan diaspora. If it had been Philippe Labreveux's hope from the start to help Nashenas be given asylum in the West, then he succeeded. A few months later Philippe was able to repeat the exercise by making a cassette of recordings of the celebrated woman singer Farida Mahwash. Like Nashenas, she had recently escaped from Afghanistan, and was living in fear of her life. Philippe managed to arrange political asylum for her in the USA, where she lives today, the Diva of Afghan song and a star of the world music scene.

Peshawar 1992

O God, why is there war in our land?
O God, my heart is tired of this venture
O God, bring peace to this country
Where its people are tired of war
(Unidentified poet)

Having re-established contact with Amir Jan through the UNHCR project, I decided to make a follow-up visit the following year. The political situation in Afghanistan had changed dramatically. Najibullah's government had fallen in April 1992, and an uneasy alliance of *mujahideen* parties had taken over in Kabul. I arrived in Islamabad on 4 September 1992 for a two-week visit. My goal was to get to Peshawar and find out what was going on in the Afghan musician scene. I stayed with Bruce Wannell in his house in the modern city of Islamabad. Amir Jan came over to conduct me to Peshawar and from him I began to hear about the rocketing of Kabul and the exodus of Kabul's musicians to Pakistan, mostly to Peshawar and Quetta.

The following evening there was a music party at the UN Social Club arranged by Bruce to benefit Amir, who was both singing and playing *rubâb*. He was the only professional musician there; the rest were *shauqi*s, like myself. There I had the good fortune to meet Martin Barber, who was Acting Director of the United Nations Office for the Coordination of Humanitarian and Economic Assistance Programmes relating to Afghanistan (UNOCHA) in Islamabad. He offered me a quick visit to Herat on a UN flight to make a report on the state of Herat's culture, especially music. In the event there was not enough time to make the trip, especially as the availability of the return flight from Herat could not be guaranteed. Nevertheless, this was a very important contact with UNOCHA that enabled me to get to make an extended visit to Herat two years later.

Amir and I travelled by Flying Coach to Peshawar, I spent a sleepless night at his one-room house in Akhundabad, close to where he was living in 1985, causing domestic disruption because of having to keep his wife out of sight. The next day I moved to the colonial comforts of Dean's Hotel, where the Nawab of Dir used to stay on his visits to Peshawar, a place well known to Amir and his father-in-law Sattar Khan. Although this visit to Peshawar was short, it turned out to be very busy and productive in terms of research, largely thanks to the help of Sattar Khan, Amir's father-in-law.

Profile: Sattar Khan (Tabla Player and Singer)

During this visit I spent a lot of time in the company of Sattar Khan. In 1985 I had known him primarily as a *tabla* player; we had played *rubâb* and *tabla* together on various occasions, and had made several audio recordings with my Nagra. I discovered he was the *tabla* player on the Haikal cassette I had bought in

Peshawar in 1985, notable for its highly percussive drumming that sounded like imitations of gunfire. He confirmed that that was what he had been doing on the recording, and played further imitations of several weapons for me.

When I met him in 1985 he had joined the band of the Afghan singer Master Ali Haidar, wanting to play a more sophisticated style of music.[4] Now, in 1992, I found him working as an instrument maker and repairman. He had a workshop on the roof of a four-storey commercial block in the Kabari Bazaar, in the heart of the old city. In this building there were 20 or so rooms, all the business premises of bands of Afghan musicians. Sattar Khan's workshop shared the roof space with three latrines for the use of the occupants of the building and their visitors. In this room, which he termed (in Dari) his *dukân*, 'shop', rather than *karkhâna*, 'workshop', Sattar conducted his main occupation of making and fitting the heads of *tabla* drums. This is a highly skilled craft that involves compounding and applying the round black patches on the drums' heads that allow the player to make a range of drum sounds. He repaired and made other instruments, too, such as a large *tânpurâ* with the body carved from a block of wood rather than using the usual large gourd. This instrument was used in some of the music sessions that took place in Sattar's room while I was there. The presence of the *tânpurâ* declared a commitment to the art music of the Indian Subcontinent.

Although I visited a number of musicians' rooms, and attended and made audio recordings of various music sessions in them, I spent much of my time in Sattar's workshop, for the simple reason that he received a regular stream of Afghan musician visitors. It was a great opportunity to engage with them. I just sat there and was able to record their conversations, with each other and with me. Through this I developed a close relationship with Sattar Khan, who had a very different personality from that of his son-in-law Amir Jan. Where Amir was articulate, loud and sometimes outspoken, Sattar was quiet and modest, rather an introvert by Afghan musician standards. He was a tall good-looking man, from a barber-musician family in Laghman, close to the city of Jalalabad (Figure 3.2). His father was a cook, and there were *tabla* players on his mother's side. His younger brother worked in Peshawar as a barber, and also played the *sornâ*, the low status instrument played exclusively by barbers in Afghanistan, mainly for rural weddings.

Reflecting on the relationship between Sattar and Amir, I see that musically they were highly compatible. While both of them were vocalists, they formed an ideal instrumental duo, *rubâb* (or *dutâr*) and *tabla* (or *doholak*). They could play together at home, and perform for others outside. Both men gained from Amir's marriage to Sattar's young daughter, which could be viewed as an aspect of 'male bonding'. Amir the orphan gained a family, similar to his own in terms of being

---

[4] There are several scenes in *Amir* (Baily 1985a) in which we can see Sattar Khan; talking about marrying his daughter to Amir Jan (9' 02"), conducting me down Dubgari Road (11' 19"), and playing *tabla* in Master Ali Haidar's *deyrah* (13' 30"). In the film Master Ali Haidar is wrongly subtitled as Mushtar Ali Haidar.

Figure 3.2   Sattar Khan, Peshawar 2000

from a barber-musician background. And Sattar acquired a strong ally who was outgoing, outspoken, a good communicator and savvy in business dealings.

Getting to know Sattar better I found that he was very well informed about Hindustani (North Indian classical) music. He had studied with several *ustâd*s in Lahore, and was currently learning from Lal Khan, a music teacher with a large circle of students in northern Pakistan, who he would visit on his frequent peripatetic tours. Right from the start of my visit Sattar wanted to share his knowledge with me. In this way he taught me a number of unusual compositions. For example: a composition in *Râg Marwa* in *Jaitâl*, a metric cycle of 12 *matra*s; a composition in *Râg Marwa* in *Uri Dhamar*, 14 *matra*s; a composition in *Râg Kirwâni*, in *Kultâl*, 9 *matra*s; a composition in *Râg Bhimpalasi* in *Japtâl*, 10 *matra*s; a composition in *Râg Funkar*, also in *Japtâl*; a composition in *Râg Jait* in *Panj o Nim Tâl*, 5½ *matra*s. For these unusual *tâl*s such as *Jaitâl*, *Uri Dhamar*, *Kultâl* and *Panj o Nim* he gave me the *tabla* mnemonics (*bol*s). He also showed me the scales and characteristic melodic phrases for the rarely heard *Râg Bhatiyar* and *Râg Anand Beiru*. Sattar was something of a collector of rare compositions.

To demonstrate these pieces he would play them on the *'armonia* and have somebody accompany him on *tabla*, while I would record the compositions and at the same time try to play *rubâb* along with him. I am not sure why he was so generous with this material. Many musicians make the most of the material they know, spinning it out over a number of lessons.[5] Sattar did not seek payment for the things he showed me, nor was it that these were old pieces that should not be forgotten; on the contrary, I think these were mainly recent compositions of Pakistani musicians like Lal Khan who delight in creating new pieces in obscure *râg*s and *tâl*s. Perhaps he simply wanted to be helpful, but I think also that he wanted me to know that he had a good knowledge of classical music, both as a singer and as a *tabla* player. He was a far more advanced musician than Amir Jan in that respect. I also realized that he was not much appreciated as a singer, not in demand, not usually asked to perform at a gathering. I think this was due to his not having a very distinctive voice. He sang in tune and in time, but there was nothing special about his sound and he lacked the charisma of the successful musician. Some musicians are good performers, and some are good teachers, and he was more the latter.

An incident that illustrated his knowledge arose from a Thursday evening *samâ'* (spiritual concert) at the Sufi shrine of Sattar Shah Badshah, not far from Dubgari Road. It was a special night, the anniversary of Prophet Mohammad's *mirâj* (visit to heaven) and an occasion for special celebration. In the *samâ'* it is usual for several singers to take turns to perform (*mojrei dâdan*). Sattar and I had gone along together (Amir Jan was called away to play elsewhere). Sattar had been expecting to take his turn and sing, and had prepared his programme. But in the event another younger singer and his *tabla* accompanist had appropriated the whole evening for themselves, which meant that they carried off the admittedly modest monetary donations offered by the audience. Sattar was annoyed. The next day I asked him what he *would* have sung if he had been given the opportunity. His account was impressive.

He would have *offered* (his choice of words is significant) a sequence of *ghazal*s associated with the Chishti Sufi Order, in Persian, Pashto and Urdu, in praise of Khwaja Sahib (Khwaja Mohinnuddin Chishti), whose burial place is in Ajmer, Rajasthan. He would have started with *Ai sarwar sardar Khwâja Ajmeri* (*You are my King, my Ruler*) Then a famous *ghazal* by Amir Khusrau, *Namidânam chi manzel bud*, about a vision beyond time and space.

> I do not know what place it was, where I was last night
> On all sides there was dancing in ecstasy, where I was last night
>
> There was one fairy-faced beauty, tall as a cypress, tulip-cheeked
> From top to toe a heart ravisher, where I was last night
>
> Rivals, listening to the song, were flirting, but I was fearful
> And could not speak, where I was last night

---

[5]   Amir Jan Khushnawaz once remarked that he was teaching me a complete multi-part composition in one session, whereas other musicians would teach each part in a separate lesson.

God Himself presided over the sublime assembly, Khusrau,
And Mohammad was the light of the gathering, where I was last night.[6]

He would have sung these *ghazals* in different *rāgs*. And he would have offered something classical, in *Rāg Megh* for Khwaja Sahib, in *Rāg Nat Beiru* for Nizamuddin (whose burial place is in Delhi). If Amir Jan had been there, he said, he would have been more in the mood to play, but he was not, and the *'armonia* was out of tune; he did not feel like performing. 'I'm a poor person, it would not have been seemly to put myself forward, in front of everybody else.' These were hardly the words of a man full of pride and self-confidence.

Influx of Musicians from Kabul Fleeing the Internecine Fighting

We have already seen in Chapter 2 that musicians in Kabul enjoyed rather good conditions during the communist period (1978–92). Some singers were ready, perhaps eager, to sing in praise of the regime. Others remained neutral. Some took risks and performed songs that could be interpreted as critical of the regime. Some left the country, perhaps because they had been requested to sing for the regime and refused, or just for more general reasons, to avoid being involved in the conflict. It seems that those who were close to the regime received special perks. They were allocated apartments in the modern blocks of Microrayan, they were given official cars and they received priority health care. All that came to an end with the fall of Kabul to the *mujahideen* in 1992. I heard graphic descriptions in Sattar's workshop about what happened when the *mujahideen* took Kabul, five months earlier.

The musicians in Kabul, especially those connected with RTA, soon felt the brunt of the anti-music policies of the new government. Singers who had sung in support of the regime were particularly vulnerable to punishment. Musicians at RTA were abused and mistreated. Some had their heads shaved to shame them, some that were dressed in western suits and ties were stripped to their underwear in public. The era of the mandatory beard and the compulsory wearing of traditional *piran o tâmbân* (long shirt and baggy trousers) had started. Apartments and motorcars that had been given to top musicians by the communist governments were confiscated. Lots of goods were tipped into the Kabul River, including bottles of alcohol, videos, photos and films. The cinemas and nightclubs were closed. The club where the famous wife and husband team of Naghma and Mangal sometimes played, with drinking and dancing, was destroyed. The polluted rubble was removed and a mosque was being built on the site, I was told.

All that was bad enough. Although there was some clandestine music making at weddings, work was becoming hard to find. Before long there were outbreaks of fighting between the various *mujahideen* parties (as described above). The Kucheh Kharabat area was hit by a number of rockets. Many of Kabul's musicians now

---

[6] Translated by Bruce Wannell.

left with their families, some for Mazar-e Sharif in the north, which was under the control of General Dustam's mainly Uzbek *Jumbish* forces, some for Peshawar, some for Quetta, some to other destinations. Naghma and Mangal had gone to Dubai. Some musicians avoided stopping in Peshawar, which was the base of the *mujahideen* and dangerous for those in any way associated with the PDPA. Ustad Rahim Bakhsh had passed through Peshawar with a large number of his extended family, and gone on to Lahore. Haji Hamahang had likewise come with a large party of dependants, and continued on to Quetta, where he had relatives. Quetta was less dominated by Pashto speakers than Peshawar. It had a large community of Hazaras in exile, and lots of music loving Kandaharis. In Peshawar you had to sing in Pashto, not Dari.

Recently arrived musicians I met in Peshawar included Ghulam Hussain (*rubâb*) and his brother Olfat Bashir (vocal and *'armonia*), Qassem Bakhsh (vocal and *'armonia*), Sharif Ghazal (vocal and *'armonia*), Ghulam Farid (clarinet) and Fazal Ahmad (*tabla*). Some of them I knew personally, others just by reputation. This was rather different from the wave of Afghan musicians I had encountered in 1985, who were mainly 'Pashtun' musicians from the Jalalabad area. Now there was an influx of musicians from the Kharabat itself, escaping the fighting in Kabul. I met a number of them in Sattar's workshop and had the opportunity to record some of their stories about what had happened in Kabul when the *mujahideen* arrived, the fighting that had ensued between the various parties, the rockets falling on the Kharabat, and the musicians' flight to Pakistan.

One of the most memorable of the newly arrived exiles was the singer Qassem Bakhsh, a student of Ustad Rahim Bakhsh (though not a blood relation), and one of the luminaries of the Kharabat. He told me how he and his family left Kabul because of the fighting; a number of rockets hit the Kucheh Kharabat and many people were killed and wounded. He came to Peshawar with his extended family of about 30 people. They left everything behind; clothes, carpets, everything was left there. They were currently living in a rented house that had no furniture, nothing. They had decided to go back to Kabul soon, even if it was still being rocketed. 'We don't have any relatives in Peshawar to help us. When we came we had nowhere to go. Where can you go when you don't have any relatives, when you don't know anyone? Fortunately we had friends like Amir Jan and Sattar, who were here to help us.'

Amir described how he had come home one night, opened the door of the house and fell over lots of baggage.

> I thought they were cleaning the house, but I was told we had guests from Kabul, 30 or 40 people. I didn't go any further because there were women in there, so I went to Sattar Khan's father's house to sleep there. There were about 20 or 30 friends from Kucheh Kharabat. The men went to stay the night at Mena's house. The next day we found a house for them, with six rooms but the landlord wanted a lot of money in advance and they didn't have any money. I was not in a good way myself; I didn't have much money myself. They had so many children,

there was not much water, the bazaar was a long way off. There's another place where there are many Afghans. It's called Boot, 2 or 3 kilometres from the town. They went there. All the shops there belong to Afghans, and houses are cheaper there. There are some refugee camps nearby, like Nasserbagh. There are lots of houses they rent out to the refugees.

Qassem expressed his gratitude to Amir:

They looked after us a lot and we are thankful to them. As far as I can see if you don't know somebody, nobody will help. People might help in their own country but in Pakistan we don't know the language. These people, Amir and the others, they helped us a lot. They took a lot of trouble. We spent the night in their home and they looked after us. When we left Afghanistan this poem came to my mind.

O God, why is there war in our land?
O God, my heart is tired of this venture

O God, the devastating war
Brought cities and villages to ruins

Thousands of citizens became homeless and
Separated from their families, friends and tribes

Peoples' land and orchards were destroyed and
Thousands of lives fell to the ground

Hundreds of youth lost limbs
Mothers and fathers became grief stricken

Young brides wear the black dress
To mourn the death of their bridegrooms

O God, bring peace to this country
Whose people are tired of war

He recited this poem, then at my request sang it to his own *'armonia* accompaniment.

I was impressed with the way the recent wave of refugee musicians had been received and helped by those already in Peshawar, even though they represented competition for the limited amount of work available. Moreover, there were other factors at play. Amongst the Afghan musicians in Peshawar there was a hierarchy of praiseworthiness based on when you had left Afghanistan. Musicians like Amir Jan had been in Peshawar for years and could take pride in the fact that they had not compromised themselves. They were well embedded in the local community and had good business contacts. The recent influx included people who had worked under the regime, even worked for the regime, and could be singled out for criticism. Yet I did not detect too much bad feeling on this account. The refugees from Kabul spent a lot of time socializing with each other in Sattar Khan's workshop, or in the rooms of other established musicians, and this entailed a good deal of playing music to entertain each other.

I returned to Islamabad with Amir. Bruce Wannell had arranged a gig at the German Embassy for Amir and Ustad Arif. We took with us Ghulam Farid, a clarinetist and saxophone player, who was a grandson of Ustad Sarahang (through Sarahang's daughter's marriage to the Kabuli clarinet player Ahmad Bakhsh). This was a memorable evening, with the musicians playing in various combinations. Martin Barber was a guest and I was able to plan my future visit to Herat.

Herat 1994

> Admire the wine-drinking libertines of this ruinous tavern
> For in this obscure school you will find learning, not fame
>
> (Bedil)

In 1994, with the help of Martin Barber and Brigitte Neubacher of UNOCHA, I was able to visit Herat, after a hiatus of 17 years. In this period Veronica and I had received very little information about the whereabouts of our Herati friends, though I knew that Rahim's father had died. Veronica paved the way to Herat, making a visit in March 1994, and I followed six months later. We were able to travel on the UN flights between Islamabad and Herat, and stay at the United Nations Development Programme (UNDP) guesthouse in Herat.[7] I went to Herat well equipped for research, most importantly with a S-VHS camcorder, a Sony Walkman Professional audiocassette recorder, a radio-cassette machine, copies of some of my field recordings, copies of my Herat films and many photos from the 1970s research to give out to those photographed or to their relatives. My principal objectives were to document the current situation of music and musicians in Herat, and to explore the city in its post-war state.[8]

The Governor of Herat was Ismail Khan, a commander within Rabbani's *Jam'iat Islâmi* (Islamic Association) and a highly successful *mujahideen* leader during the *jihâd*. He was also known for his commitment to education, for girls as well as boys, in areas of western Afghanistan under his control. Much can be learned about Ismail Khan from Radek Sikorski's book *Dust of the Saints*, which recounts his clandestine journey through Afghanistan in 1987 to report on the situation

---

[7]   After a few nights I moved to the small Minarets Hotel, just a large house with a garden, but I often went to UNDP in the evenings to eat and socialize with ex-pats.

[8]   I had two subsidiary areas of inquiry, on the practice of Sufi *zikr* in the Qadiri *khânaqâh* at Kawarzan, some miles from the city, and on Afghan perceptions of birdsong, see Baily (1997a) for the latter. There is no space to discuss these further.

in Herat, to get first hand testimony about life there under communist control and to gather information about the uprising in 1979. In terms of the physical state of the city, it was clear that there had been a lot of destruction on the western side, the area facing the *mujahideen* forces, but it was hardly the 'Hiroshima' of Afghan *jihâdi* propaganda. I visited the mass grave hidden behind a low hill near to Gazer Gah. This grave was mentioned by Ezat Jan Mujadidi in *Amir* when describing the uprising in Herat in 1979.[9] Here I was, standing on that great mound of earth, now turned into a memorial for those who perished. A number of shafts had been dug into the ground, each covered with a glass-topped viewing point so one could gaze down at the corpses below, many with a bullet hole to the head.

The situation in Herat was quite different from that in Kabul. In 1994 the city was at peace, with none of the internecine fighting that was destroying the capital. The reconstruction of Herat was underway, to make it the most developed city in Afghanistan. I was well received by officialdom in Herat; Ghani Niksear, an old friend from the 1970s, was still in the local office of the Ministry of Information and Culture, and was very helpful. Abdul Ali Ahrary, a Herati journalist and author who enjoyed good relations with the local regime, also helped a lot, and through him I was able to get a permit to use the video camera in public places other than military installations. I always wore local dress and filmed without restriction in the streets of Herat. Altogether I shot 27 hours of video, and many years later edited some of this footage into the film *Ustad Rahim: Herat's Rubab Maestro* (Baily 2008b). This is not included on the DVD accompanying this volume.

Profile: Ustad Mohammad Rahim Khushnawaz (Rubâb Player)

The day after my arrival I went to find Rahim Khushnawaz, the *rubâb* player mentioned several times in Chapter 1. He had moved from the family's old house and I had some trouble locating his new residence near the Grand Mosque from the description Veronica gave me. Eventually a neighbour led me to the house, and knocked loudly on the door. No response. He knocked again. There was a faint shout from inside; I shouted back, *'Mehmân-e shoma âmad ast'* ('Your guest has arrived'). Rahim appeared. He did not recognize me immediately, but then it was all hugs and kisses. 'Gada's here,' he said as we went upstairs to a small room overlooking the *serâi* and I could hear the gentle strains of a *rubâb* being plucked. There sat Gada Mohammad, my erstwhile *dutâr* teacher. He did not recognize me immediately either – kisses and a tear or two on both sides, but not the extreme emotions I had feared might accompany these re-encounters after such a long separation.

Mohammad Rahim Khushnawaz, then commonly known as Ustad Rahim, came from a family of hereditary musicians in the city of Herat. His paternal grandfather Mohammad Hassan was active as a semi-professional *tabla* player in the 1920s, at a time when the urban music of Herat was closely connected with

---

[9]   *Amir* – 35' 03" (Baily 1985a).

the art music of Iran. This connection with Iranian music was a hallmark of what became the family's musical style. Mohammad Hassan had three sons who became professional musicians: Chacha Ghulam, who played *tabla*, my erstwhile teacher Amir Jan, a singer who also played *'armonia, rubâb* and other instruments, and Mohammad Karim, *tabla*. In the 1930s the two older sons received training in the newly established art music of Kabul from the singer Ustad Nabi Gol, who visited Herat several times and resided in the city for three extended periods (see Chapter 1). Amir Jan and his older brother Chacha Ghulam became his *shâgerd*s (students) for singing *ghazal* and *klâsik*, and playing *rubâb* and *tabla*. On his first two visits Ustad Nabi Gol brought musicians with him from Kabul, but on his last visit he came alone because by then he had these Herati students who were competent to serve as his accompanists. In this way knowledge of the art music of Kabul was transmitted to Herat (Baily 1988a: 28–9).

From this time until the late 1960s Rahim's father Amir Jan Khushnawaz was the pre-eminent professional singer in Herat, performing mainly *ghazal*s and a little *klâsik*, in the form of *khyâl* and *tarâna*. Chacha Ghulam died young and Mohammad Karim took his place as *tabla* player. Amir Jan had four sons: Rahim, *rubâb*; Naim, *tabla*; Salim, motor mechanic and semi-professional *tabla* player; and Mahmud, vocal and *'armonia*. Once his sons were skilled enough to play professionally in public (aged 12–14) Amir Jan was able to form a family band, which concentrated income into the family. It was at this time he took on the family name of Khushnawaz, meaning 'Happy Player'. Amir Jan's status as Herat's top singer and bandleader was undermined in the early 1970s by the residence of a celebrated Kabuli singer in the city, Amir Mohammad. Rahim and *dutâr* player Gada Mohammad became the interloper's accompanists, and remained in this capacity for many years. In the mid-1970s young Mahmud became the Khushnawaz band's singer, and Amir Jan took over as the *rubâb* player in the family band. He died in 1982.

I first met Rahim on 20 October 1973. Amir Mohammad and his band were playing in the Badghisi Hotel in Herat, where they had a contract to play every night during the month of *Ramazân*. Knowing that I was keen to listen to the *rubâb* as played by Rahim (I had already heard domestic cassettes of his playing), a young Herati friend took Veronica and me to hear him with Amir Mohammad's band. Late on in the evening Amir Mohammad took a rest from singing and Rahim played two pieces with *tabla* accompaniment, a *râg* and a Herati *chahârbeiti*.

In my first year of fieldwork in Herat (1973–74) I saw and heard a good deal of Rahim with Amir Mohammad's band playing at wedding parties and *Ramazân* concerts (Baily 2011a). Early in 1974 I conducted three recording sessions with Rahim. For the first he came alone and recorded a number of Herati pieces, for the second he came with his brother Naim to play *tabla* for Herati and classical pieces, and for the third, in addition to their instruments, they brought two canaries in cages from the family home, knowing they would be stimulated by the sound of the instruments to sing. Birdsong added to the sound of music was for many Heratis the acme of musical enjoyment. I had already started learning the *rubâb* at

Figure 3.3   Ustad Rahim Khushnawaz, Herat 1994. © Veronica Doubleday

this stage, from Ustad Mohammad Omar, and while I had no lessons from Rahim I learned a lot from these recordings, some of which were published on the CD *AFGHANISTAN Le rubâb de Hérat / The rubâb of Herat* (Baily 1993).

Rahim was acknowledged as the outstanding *rubâb* player in Herat (Figure 3.3). He was a brilliant accompanist, especially for the *ghazal* singing of Amir Mohammad, and master of the technique known as *parandkâri*, which uses the shortest sympathetic string as a high drone in complex rhythmic patterns. This is employed extensively in accompanying *ghazal* in the regularly recurring fast instrumental sections known in Herat as *duni* (and in Kabul as *tâduni*). In addition to *ghazal*, Amir Mohammad's band played popular songs from Kabul and Iran, dance music and ritual wedding songs. And there was Rahim the solo *rubâb* player, with *tabla* accompaniment. There were two sides to his art as a soloist, the classical music of Kabul, and the local (*mahali*) music of Herat. His classical repertoire embraced two principal genres, both with Indian connections. One was the *lâriya*, a type of multi-part composition often played as a group instrumental at the start of a concert of music, intended to warm up the instruments, the musicians and the audience.[10] Rahim had learned many of these pieces from playing them with his father, who in turn had got them from Ustad Nabi Gol in the 1930s.

---

[10]   The origin and correct name for this type of composition is controversial (Sarmast 2007). The old name was *lâriya*. Amir Jan Khushnawaz, who dictated to me many such compositions called the genre *naghma-ye kashâl* (extended instrumental piece) while Ustad Mohammad Omar used the term *naghma-ye chahârtuk* (four part instrumental piece).

Rahim had also had some lessons from the great *rubâb* player of Kabul, Ustad Mohammad Omar. The other type of classical pieces seemed very reminiscent of the *âlâp* and *rezakhâni gat* of North India, with simple melodic improvisations. In Afghanistan this type of piece is usually called *naghma-ye klâsik* (classical instrumental piece). More idiosyncratically, Rahim also played Kabuli *ghazal*s as instrumental pieces, a most unusual practice that reveals a brilliant transfer of vocal into instrumental music.

In terms of Kabuli art music there were other *rubâb* players equal to Rahim in Kabul, but in the field of the local *mahali* music of Herat he was unrivalled. The music of Herat has strong connections with that of Iran; most obviously in the use of neutral seconds in some of the melodic modes of Herati music, notably in that mode called *Shur* in Iran, and *Bairami* in Herat, a corruption of the Indian term *Bhairavi*. These neutral seconds, intermediate in size between a minor second and a whole-tone, cannot be played in the fretted range of the *rubâb*, which gives a chromatic scale of 12 semitones to the octave. To overcome this limitation Rahim's father Amir Jan Khushnawaz had added an extra fret to the *rubâb*, and Rahim had added a second extra fret, allowing one to play the neutral seconds of Herati songs. Armed with this innovation, Rahim had made a specialty of playing the melodies of Herati local song as instrumental pieces on the *rubâb*.

An important form in the vernacular poetry of Afghanistan is the quatrain known as *chahârbeiti*, with its AABA rhyme scheme.[11] The term *chahârbeiti* also refers to a set of melodies for the singing of such poetry, often unaccompanied and in free rhythm. In Herat the best known of these is *Chahârbeiti Siâhmu wa Jalâli*, which celebrates the true story of the unrequited love of the shepherd Jalali for the rich man's daughter Siahmu. Abdul Wahab Madadi encountered it in Badghis, when he was a child, and it became widely known through radio broadcasting from Kabul. Madadi was the first to sing it on radio. Being in free rhythm, the *chahârbeiti* has an obvious connection with the *âvâz* of classical Persian music. Rahim had turned *Siâhmu wa Jalâli* into a substantial work by interposing other song and instrumental melodies. Many other musicians in Herat copied this innovation, especially *dutâr* players such as Gada Mohammad, and it has become part of the standard repertoire of 'traditional' Afghan music.

I did not see much of Rahim during my second year of fieldwork in Herat (1976–77). For reasons I never fully understood, he had fallen out with his father, though he continued to live in the family home in the old city. His mother had died the year before and his father had taken a new wife, a widow, but this had not been a success, and they separated soon after. Probably Rahim's close association with Amir Mohammad had something to do with the rift, for this change of allegiance had effectively broken up the family band. Amir Mohammad had prematurely ended Amir Jan's career as a singer, and Amir Jan had then taken over

---

[11] Since a *beit* is a couplet (two lines of verse) the proper name for the quatrain form is *dubeiti*, 'two couplets', but for some reason the quatrain is usually known as *chahârbeiti*, 'four couplets'.

as *rubâb* player in the reconfigured family ensemble. Moreover, I had become closely attached to Amir Jan as my *rubâb* teacher, and the father was sometimes dismissive of his son's abilities, saying that he had 'a good hand' but did not know much about music theory. From Amir Jan I notated a valuable collection of old compositions of the *lâriya* type (published in Baily 1997b). He taught me by the dictation of note names in the *sargam* system, a method of teaching that was very revealing about his musical cognition (Baily 2001b: 91–3).

When I met Rahim again in 1994 everything changed. During the 52 days of my visit to Herat I spent time with Rahim during 36 of them. He was incredibly kind, hospitable and helpful. He and his relatives treated me as a family member and I was now free to socialize with his wife and sisters and sisters-in-law. Much of the time we spent together was in his house, either in the small room upstairs where he kept his instruments and taught his students, or downstairs in the family living room. Rahim insisted I sleep there one night. He took me to visit other musicians, and helped me with my video work in the city, especially with interviewing various craftsmen, as I was interested in possible connections between the manual skills of musicians and those of other crafts, such as weaving. But most of our time together was spent 'doing' music.

Up to this point I had learned a lot from the recordings I had made of Rahim but we had never sat down together in a teaching situation, with the intention of conveying knowledge from him to me. Now all that changed and we spent a lot of time playing two *rubâb*s together. Sometimes I would pause every now and then to write down what it was I was learning, using the Indian *sargam* note name system. Sometimes I just recorded on tape what we were doing. I made many recordings of him playing alone, to put particular items of his repertoire 'on record' so to speak. He was particularly keen to pass on to me certain old compositions that had to a large extent been forgotten, just as his father had been keen to preserve pieces he had learned in the 1930s from Ustad Nabi Gol. Sometimes we composed together new *palta*s (variations) or *seh*s (rhythmic cadences). I also showed him things I had learned from recordings of other *rubâb* players to get his opinion, and I had fun with a *gat* in *Râg Todi* that Narendra Bataju, my *sitâr*-playing friend in Paris had composed for me to play on the *rubâb*. This particular composition has some tricky cross-rhythms, very different to the usual Afghan *rubâb* compositions and I was interested to see how difficult it was for him to learn it. Altogether we worked on 20 *râg*s during this period: *Talang, Des, Beiru, Bhimpalasi, Pilu, Pâri, Sindi Bhairavi, Kesturi, Madhubanti, Shivaranjâni, Durga, Todi, Gujeri Todi, Chandrakauns, Âhir Beiru, Yeman, Âsâ, Bhupâli, Lagankauns* and *Kaushi Dhani*.

Sometimes I videoed him playing the *rubâb*. Particularly important for me were the occasions when he allowed me to video the movements of his right hand in the high drone *parand* technique, where he would play variation after variation, sometimes commenting verbally on their rhythmic characteristics. I had already analysed his right hand technique from listening to audio recordings, and had formulated a motor grammar underlying these patterns (Baily 1987, 1989b), but now I could clearly see the movements. While he came up with certain patterns

I had not encountered before, the set of grammatical rules I had formulated seemed to be correct.

Altogether working with Rahim was a wonderful experience and greatly enhanced my *rubâb* playing. But why did he help me so much? There are perhaps several answers to that question. He had been given a copy of *Music of Afghanistan: Professional musicians in the city of Herat* (Baily 1988a) by Veronica, where he could see the photograph of his father in the frontispiece and other photos of himself, and could realize that I was a serious scholar who was putting his family on record. He was happy with the CD of his playing I had published the previous year, and there was the possibility of being invited for a concert in Paris, a matter which I had come to help organize. Veronica had made some very good recordings of his *rubâb* playing during her visit, and got him to teach her some new songs, and this paved the way for my own work with him.

The Situation of Music under Ismail Khan

Herat under Ismail Khan was a city in a condition of deep austerity. With the return of wealthy businessmen who had been in exile in Iran the economy was recovering. Many new buildings were going up, some at the expense of fine old buildings that were being demolished to make way for Iranian style markets. For many years Herati labourers had been employed in the construction industry in Iran, and in the rebuilding of Herat they brought modern ferro-concrete construction skills to bear.

Senior religious figures had an important say in how the city was run, and an Office for the Propagation of Virtue and the Prevention of Vice had been established in order to monitor and control public behaviour. Various edicts affecting the day-to-day lives of ordinary people were issued. For example, Heratis were keen pigeon fanciers, and many men (including Rahim) kept pigeon lofts on the roofs of their houses in the old city, and would fly their flocks of birds as a hobby, bringing them back to their lofts with large nets fastened to the ends of long poles. This activity was banned on the grounds that it could lead to men spying into the courtyards of their neighbours' houses, observing their womenfolk unveiled. Rahim told me that when the ban was announced on local television the point was emphasized by several pigeons being killed in front of the camera. Likewise, there was a ban on flying kites from the rooftops, in case young men were on the lookout for girls to spy upon.

The cinema and the theatre were closed, although the actors from the theatre (*Herât Nanderi*) were still employed by the Ministry of Information and Culture, and gave occasional performances on Herat TV. There was heavy control over music, but a certain amount of musical activity was allowed. Professional musicians had to apply for a licence, which stated that they could perform only songs in praise of the *mujahideen* and songs with texts drawn from the mystical Sufi poetry of the region. This cut out a large amount of other music, such as love songs and music for dancing. The licences also stipulated that musicians must play without amplification.[12]

Male musicians could play at private parties indoors, but Herat's women professional musicians were forbidden to perform, and several were briefly imprisoned for having transgressed this ordinance. Technically, male musicians were permitted to perform at wedding parties, but experience had shown that often in such cases officials from the Office for the Propagation of Virtue and the Prevention of Vice, religious police, had arrived to break up the party. They would confiscate the instruments, which were usually returned to the musicians some days later when a fine or bribe had been paid. Veronica reported just such an incident earlier in the year, when a band of musicians was playing at a *Now Ruz* country fair held in the grounds of a Sufi shrine. The performance was stopped; the instruments were confiscated, and recovered the next day. Rahim had a broken *rubâb* in his house which he told me had belonged to one of his students and that it had been smashed when the religious police had broken up a music party (Figure 3.4).

There was very little music on local radio or television. Due to technical problems and shortages of fuel to power the generator, broadcasting time was severely restricted to about one hour in the morning and an hour in the evening. But occasionally a musical item would be transmitted. If a song was broadcast on television one did not see the performers on screen, but a vase of flowers was shown instead, a practice adopted from Iran. Names of performers were not announced on radio or television. But I was pleased one morning to hear on Herat radio a *ghazal* sung by Amir Jan Khushnawaz that I had recorded in 1974, a copy of which I had presented to the radio station a few days earlier. Herat television showed parts of my film *The Annual Cycle of Music in Herat* and I also recorded in the studio some pieces on *rubâb* to be broadcast. It is clear that the religious lobby was exercising tight control over music, but not in anything like as severe a form as the Taliban were to display when they took Herat a year later.

The *dutâr* maker Paindeh Mohammad had re-opened his business in one of the main streets, and resumed the making and repair of musical instruments, though keeping an eye open for the religious police. A *rubâb* maker was also active. The audiocassette business continued, with a number of shops in the bazaars of Herat selling music cassettes and videos, some of Herati musicians. Professional musicians like Rahim could hardly make a living from playing music. They depended on the generosity of their long-standing patrons, often from the wealthy business class, who would pay them to play at house parties, or simply give them financial aid.

---

[12]   We have met this issue of amplification before, in Peshawar in 1985, when the mullahs tried to stop Shah Wali playing at an Afghan wedding. I was amused to note that in 1994 the Grand Mosque of Herat had installed an extremely powerful amplification system that could awaken the whole city with the early morning *âzân* (call to prayer).

Figure 3.4   Rahim with broken *rubâb*, Herat 1994

During the seven weeks I spent in Herat in November–December 1994 I attended a number of musical events, all but one held in the daytime. A curfew operated at night, and musicians in particular would not want to be apprehended after dark. And in the months of November and December it was much warmer in the daytime, the weather being generally sunny. I describe here four such events that together reveal a wide range of musical activity (amongst men).

Rahim took me to a wedding party in the extended Golpasand musician family, deep in the complex of alleyways where they lived. Compared to the luxurious wedding parties I had attended in Herat in the 1970s this one seemed fairly low-key. There was no bandstand, no PA system, no *takht-e dâmâd* (bridegroom's throne) ritual, and minimal decoration of the courtyard. Amir Mohammad's son Aziz Amiri, who sounds just like his father, was singing when we arrived, followed by two other singers, Sadiq Shaek and Naimatullah. When the music came to a stop a meal was served in the courtyard, and there was a little music after lunch. A party for the women was held in an adjacent *serâi*, I could hear a *dâira* being played at some point, probably when the bride was being paraded.

A much bigger event was held in the function room of the Alemyar family, built in the communist era to accommodate large wedding parties. Our host was Seid Ahmad Alemyar, one of several brothers who ran a prosperous carpet business, including a shop in Zurich. As well as Rahim, many of Herat's musicians were invited: Karim Dutari, Gada Mohammad, Hamed Alemyar, Quduz, Naim Khushnawaz, Azim Hassanpur, singers Ghulam Salwar, Qassem, Sorud, Mahmud Khushnawaz, and the singer/comedian Naimatullah. All of these musicians took their turn to perform, singing or playing *rubâb* or *dutâr* instrumentals. Also invited was Herat's veteran playwright, actor and comedian, Ustad Olfat Herawi, who entertained the company with two of his famous comic sketches. At the end of the party all the musicians and singers gathered together on the large bandstand and performed the Herati wedding song *Olang Olang*, that in some ways serves as Herat's 'national anthem'. It was a moment of affirmation of solidarity amongst the musician community, having survived the war and now faced with the pressures against music coming from the mullahs. I had never encountered such a performance before. With a number of singers singing together as a chorus it was a profoundly moving experience.

Mohammad Karim Herawi (Karim Dutari), inventor of the 14-stringed *dutâr* invited me to a *mehmâni* for young men at his house, and told me I should stay the night, which I did. Early in the evening Karim played *dutâr*, accompanied by his son Arif on *tabla*. The young guests were mainly Arif's friends, and later on we were treated to an extended performance of 'new music', provided by a young singer who accompanied himself on a small Casio keyboard with a microphone jammed up against it, connected to a ghetto-blaster for amplification. Arif himself had improvised a drum kit consisting of two large plastic jerry cans laid on their sides, and a cymbal made from an *aftau lâgan*, the hand washing set consisting of a metal water jug with a spout, and a large metal bowl. When guests are entertained, a junior member of the host family goes from guest to guest, pouring a thin stream of water into the bowl while they wash their hands. Arif used the upturned bowl as a cymbal, balanced on top of the water pot. He played his kit, which he termed his *jâz*, with two metal spoons. They played mainly dance music, with two young men taking it in turn to do solo dancing. This performance was significant in the way that it reproduced at the local level the new keyboard-based Afghan popular music that had developed in Kabul and the diaspora.

The most interesting and significant music event I attended during this visit to Herat was a *gormâni* ritual. Clearly modelled on the *ganda-bandhan* as practised in the Indian Subcontinent, this takes place when a senior musician formally accepts an advanced student at a gathering of musicians. The central part of the ritual is the tying by the teacher of a chord of seven differently coloured threads around the right-hand wrist of the student, the feeding of the student with a spoonful of *halwâ* (sweet food) and the distribution of sugared almonds amongst the assembly. At such a ritual the musicians present take it in turn to sing and play after the string-tying part of the ritual. The *gormâni* is a central element of musical life in the Kharabat, and treated with great respect, the string being thought to represent an unbreakable chain between teacher and student. The institution was presumably introduced into Herat along with Kabuli art music in the 1930s, when Amir Jan became the student of Ustad Nabi Gol; in Herat it is incorrectly called *gorbandi*. I had only seen this ritual once before in Herat (Baily 1988a: 121–3).

For this enactment of the ritual the *ustâd* was Rahim, and the *shâgerd* one Nazir, a young builder and *rubâb* enthusiast who was already receiving musical instruction from Rahim. This was a big party, there must have been a hundred of us, with many of Herat's musicians and Nazir's friends present. The conduct of the ritual was led by Ali Ahmad Delahang, the senior member of the Golpasand family of musicians. Having asked whether everybody was present Ali Ahmad asked Nazir, 'Why we are all here?' Nazir described his passion for the *rubâb* and how he wanted to become the *shâgerd* of a *rubâb* master. Ali Ahmad named various *rubâb* players in Herat, which of them did he want? Nazir replied that he wanted to be the *shâgerd* of Ustad Rahim, explaining that he felt a special connection with him. Ali Ahmad asked Rahim if he was willing to take Nazir on, to which Rahim replied:

> I know nothing about *lay*, nothing about *gor*, nothing about *sor*, nothing about *thât*, nothing about *ârui* and *amrui*, but if my students are satisfied with what little I know, I am at their service. It's his choice. This is how much I know. I don't come up to the shoes of the great masters. (Baily 2008b, 36′ 37″)

Karim Dutari recited a brief prayer in Arabic, Rahim prepared and tied the string round his student's wrist, and there was a round of applause from the assembled gathering. Rahim touched his own face, then Nazir's face, and fed him a sugared almond and a spoonful of *halwâ*. Nazir leant forward, grasped Rahim's hand, into which he placed an envelope of money. Rahim said he should not do that, offered the money to Karim Dutari, who refused it, offered it to Ali Ahmad, and then to the company at large, and was refused by all, after which he tacitly accepted the gift himself. Somebody picked up the tray of *noqol* and started handing them out to the guests. Karim Dutari recited a long prayer in Arabic, then Rahim suggested they pray for the doyen of *rubâb* players, Ustad Mohammad Omar. Rahim offered his money again, then took up his *rubâb*, and the music started.

There was a long succession of singers: Joma Gol, Nasrullah, Ghulam Sadiq, Ghulam Nebi Azizyar, Naimatullah, Aziz the son of Amir Mohammad, then after a break for the meal, Mahmud Khushnawaz and Ali Ahmad. Ali Ahmad introduced each artist and asked from whom he had learned his art. Aziz's introduction was of particular interest. He said, 'I ask everybody's permission to play. Since today we have remembered Ustad Mohammad Omar, there's a song that Ustad Mohammad Omar used to sing before he had to quit because of health problems and took up the *rubâb*. At that time when he was a singer my father was his student. This song I'm going to sing was taught to my father by Ustad Mohammad Omar.' He then sang a *ghazal* by Bedil from the Kharabat tradition, subtitled in the film *Ustad Rahim* as follows.

> The morning breeze seeks the laments of the lover in the land of the beloved
> If you see the mirror's truth, you will seek God's perfection
>
> Admire the wine-drinking libertines of this ruinous tavern
> For in this obscure school you will find learning, not fame
>
> Bedil's night will surely turn to day
> When you, the sun rise over our land
>
> Like the luminosity slowly arising from the East
> The morning breeze seeks the laments of the lover in the land of the beloved
>
> At this crossroads of disappointment a poor man's heart is crushed
> If we endure and offer a hand, it will stir a revolution at the school of
>   the beloved
>
> May his soul rest in peace, my late father used to tell my teacher
> 'Teach my child nothing but love'
>
> If we endure and offer a hand, it will stir a revolution at the school of
>   the beloved
> The morning breeze seeks the laments of the lover in the land of the beloved

After finishing Aziz said, 'My apologies if I have been disrespectful in this gathering of *ustâds*. This is not a place where I should be singing', to which Rahim replied, 'This party belongs to you.'[13]

Once the singers had had their turn, Ali Ahmad introduced the second part of the programme. This gave a chance for the *rubâb* and *dutâr* players to perform: Rahim's student Abdul Karim the *rubâb* maker, Abdullah, Gada Mohammad, Rahim's son Nasim, myself, Nasim again, Rahim's new student Nazir, then Rahim himself. Finally, Joma Gol's seven year old son played a short *tabla* solo, with Azim, his teacher, looking on benignly.

This *gormâni* ritual was an opportunity for musicians in Herat to affirm their allegiance to the protocols of the Kharabat, observing the rules of behaviour for

---

[13]   The ritual is shown in Baily 2008b, Chapters 9 and 10.

formal occasions. For example, before singing or playing it is important for the musician to ask for permission from those gathered together. Rahim's humility, somewhat undermined by his naming all the technical terms that he claimed to know nothing about, and his offering of his payment to others, are good examples, as were Aziz's apologies at the end of his fine performance. And at this *gormâni* Karim Dutari's ability to recite lengthy prayers in Arabic, with apparently very good pronunciation, was also noteworthy.[14]

The Trip to Paris

I went to Herat in 1994 with a plan for Rahim and Gada Mohammad to go to Paris for a concert in the *Théâtre de la Ville*, a very prestigious venue in the heart of the city. This idea came from Jean During, who wanted Rahim, Gada Mohammad and a *tabla* player to play a concert and make a CD for the Ocora label of Radio France. I discussed the matter with Rahim and Gada from time to time and they were naturally keen to go. While I was in Herat the official invitation arrived by fax. It was now necessary to go about obtaining approval from the administration of Ismail Khan, and for the musicians to be issued with passports. Abdul Ali Ahrary, the aforementioned Herati journalist and author, facilitated this process. In the event, Ahrary was sent to Paris with the three musicians to act as interpreter and minder. Rahim and Gada spent some time practising for Paris, continuing their long-term partnership. The concert was going to be purely instrumental, and they worked out a number of 'question and answer' (*soal-jawâb*) routines, or divided a tune between them, passing the melody from one to the other.It seemed paradoxical that musicians could be sent abroad as cultural ambassadors, while their voices at home in Herat were stifled. But it was not unprecedented. On several recent occasions Herat's musicians had been requested to play for visiting delegations from Iran, with little or no payment. It suggests that the tight control over music in Herat at that time was not initiated by the administration itself, that is, Ismail Khan, but came from powerful figures in the religious hierarchy who expected to be rewarded for their role in the prosecution of the *jihâd*. It is the same rhetoric I heard in Peshawar in 1985 when the mullahs tried to stop Shah Wali performing at a wedding.

The three musicians, accompanied by Abdul Ali Ahrary as translator, went to Paris in the early summer of 1995. Their concert was a great success, and they recorded a CD in the studios of Radio France, released as *Afghanistan. Rubâb et/ and Dutâr*. Veronica and I sat on the floor with the musicians in the vast studio, capable of accommodating an entire symphony orchestra, reminding the musicians of the agreed play list and making sure that at the end of each piece they kept absolutely still until the sound had died completely before talking, coughing, or noisily putting their instruments down. Veronica accompanied them to Switzerland

---

[14]   Karim's *qirâ'at* was judged to be fully correct by Arabic speakers such as A.W. Saljuqi in the USA and Maulana Rizvi in the UK.

for two more concerts, and then brought them to the UK. Rahim, Gada and Azim stayed with us in our home in Brighton for a few days, then Azim went to London to stay with Ustad Asif Mahmoud, who was going to accept him as a *shâgerd* through the string-tying ceremony. We attended a very small *gormâni* in Asif's apartment, when Azim became Asif's official student. Unexpectedly, Rahim then tied a string around my wrist, too, and I became his 'official student'. At the end of the week Ahrary accompanied them back to Herat. I next saw Rahim three years later, in Mashhad, Iran, where he and other musicians from Herat had taken refuge from the new order under the Taliban.

Chapter 4
Taliban Times

Yonder Come the Taliban

In 1994 a new troupe of actors arrived on the Afghan stage – the Taliban. Much has been written about the origins of this new Islamist movement and it is unnecessary to go into details here (see, for example, Griffin, 2001; Maley, 1998; Marsden, 1998; Misdaq, 2006; Rashid, 2000).

Prompted by the state of complete anarchy and lawlessness in Kandahar, the Taliban took control of that city in October 1994. At that time Kandahar Province was controlled by a patchwork of local militias in conflict with each other, with many roadblocks impeding the movement of goods and people, and tolls to be paid at every transit point. Abuses were rife. There were reports of two local commanders engaged in a tank battle over the favours of a dancing boy. The trigger for the release of the new movement was the rape of two women by a local commander. A group of militant Islamists, calling themselves Taliban, went to apprehend the commander, who was hanged from the slowly raised gun barrel of one of his own tanks.

In September 1995 the Taliban conquered Herat, and in September 1996 they overwhelmed the forces of the Rabbani Coalition and took control of Kabul. However, they never managed to conquer the whole country. Ahmad Shah Massoud, the 'Lion of the Panshir', held out in the remote mountains of northeastern Afghanistan. It is generally supposed that the Taliban received direct support from Pakistan in terms of armaments and military manpower, channeled through the ISI networks that had previously aided the *mujahideen* during the *jihâd*.

At first, for many Afghans, the Taliban represented some measure of security, law and order after the chaos of the preceding regimes, despite the harshness of the conditions they imposed. The Taliban initially enjoyed the benefit of the doubt in the West, which was interested in the pacification of Afghanistan, and the development of trade and the exploitation of rich oil fields in Central Asia, with proposals for trans-Afghanistan pipelines for oil and gas. The Taliban had a certain allure as a kind of student movement reminiscent of protest movements in Europe in 1968, for the *tâlib* is a theological student, and many of the Taliban emerged from the *madressa*s in Pakistan where so many young Afghan males were cared for and educated. But the Taliban leaders were not students, and many, like the movement's leader Mullah Mohammad Omar, were former *mujahideen* who fought against the Soviet forces. The great majority of the Taliban were Pashtuns, who upheld the traditional code of honour known as *Pashtunwâli*, even though this had little to do with Islamic precepts as such. Pashto, rather than Dari, was the language of the Taliban, and there was a clear ethnic dimension in resistance to the Taliban in many parts of the country, perhaps most notably amongst the Hazaras, who had for long felt themselves oppressed by Pashtuns (Mousavi 1998).

It was not until the Taliban took over Kabul that the darker side of their ideology became apparent to the outside world. Whereas Najibullah had remained safe in the UN compound in Kabul after the Coalition takeover in 1992, the Taliban had no hesitation in seizing him and his brother, executing them with extreme brutality and displaying their mutilated bodies in Pashtunistan Square, in the centre of Kabul. Public executions were to become a hallmark of their system of justice. The Taliban soon fell from favour in the West once the full range of their policies became clear, most notably the very severe restrictions they imposed on women, particularly concerning dress, work and education:

> The imposition of many restrictions stemmed from the Taliban's interpretation of urban and secular society as essentially corrupt, Godless and immoral. ... Thus, in many newly 'liberated' urban areas, Kabul included, the perceived anti-Islamic influences brought by indigenous modernizers and foreign occupants, such as western styles of clothing and hair styles, television, music and the emancipation of women, represented focal points for the activities of the Taliban's religious police force ... . (Skuse 2002: 273–4)

Kabul, having been much more westernized than other cities, seems to have been singled out for special retribution. Only three countries recognized the Taliban as the legitimate government of Afghanistan: Pakistan, Saudi Arabia and The United Arab Emirates.

Taliban and Music

When the Taliban took control of Kabul in 1996, they imposed an extreme form of music censorship, including banning the making, owning and playing of all types of musical instrument other than, perhaps, the frame drum (Doubleday, forthcoming). In Afghan culture the concept of 'music' is closely connected with musical instruments and the sounds they make, and a ban on music meant a ban on musical instruments. Unaccompanied singing does not, according to this definition, constitute music, a convenient fiction that allowed the Taliban themselves to enjoy their own very musical renditions of Taliban songs. As explained by Andrew Skuse:

> Under the Taliban's interpretation of Muslim *Shari'at* law, music was perceived as a distraction from the remembrance and worship of God, the logic behind this injunction being that it arouses the passions, lust and causes deviation from piety, modesty and honour. Similarly, restrictions on the broadcasting of female voices, which has no legal grounds in Islam, were imposed so as to keep radio from becoming seductive, arousing or inspiring carnal desires such as adultery. (ibid., p. 273)

The Taliban issued a number of decrees, including the following concerning music (the English is the Taliban's, the added punctuation mine):

2. To prevent music ... In shops, hotels, vehicles and rickshaws cassettes and music are prohibited ... If any music cassette found in a shop, the shopkeeper should be imprisoned and the shop locked. If five people guarantee[,] the shop should be opened[,] the criminal released later. If cassette found in the vehicle, the vehicle and the driver will be imprisoned. If five people guarantee[,] the vehicle will be released and the criminal released later. ...

12. To prevent music and dances in wedding parties. In the case of violation the head of the family will be arrested and punished.

13. To prevent the playing of music drum. The prohibition of this should be announced. If anybody does this then the religious elders can decide about it. (Rashid 2000: 218–19)

The meaning of the term 'music drum' is unclear. So far as I have been able to determine it refers to the frame drum (*dâira*), predominantly the preserve of girls and women, for playing at home to accompany their singing and to play dance rhythms (Doubleday 1982). The use of the drum is sanctioned by *hadith* (Robson 1938: 78–9). Nevertheless, women were very careful about their domestic music sessions. According to one young lady, 'Kabul and the whole country was like a prison for women. It was not a happy place. Every family knew the Taliban were watching. We would only risk playing if we were 100 per cent sure it was safe. Look-outs were posted to watch for Taliban coming. Then we'd silence our music and hide our tambourines [*dâira*s]' (Broughton 2002, 31′ 46″). But the term 'music drum' might also refer to the *dohol*, a double-headed barrel drum much used in traditional Pashtun music (rather than the *tabla* or *zirbaghali*). This instrument has an important role in performance of the *attan*, the national dance of Afghanistan that is strongly associated with the Pashtuns. There is clear evidence that the dance continued to be performed in Taliban times, even by the Taliban themselves, to the rhythms of hand-clapping, vocalization, or the *dohol* (BBC staff member Painda Sargand, Kabul, 25 April 2006).

The disemboweled audiocassette, nailed to a tree or post, tape waving in the breeze, became the icon of Taliban rule. Musical instruments were destroyed and hung from trees in mock executions or burned in public in sports stadiums. In a sense the Taliban simply exacerbated the anti-music sentiments already present in the preceding Rabbani period. In Herat in 1994 the Coalition was against public performance, but tolerant of private performance, while the Taliban condemned both public and private performance, and at same time created a new musical genre, the Taliban *tarâna*. A new segment of the cassette recording industry arose to record this novel kind of 'music without instruments'. Shops that previously sold music cassettes now sold the Taliban *tarânas*, while other types of 'real music' were provided secretly, 'under the counter'.

For a variety of reasons it was difficult to collect first-hand statements about the censorship of music in Afghanistan during the period of Taliban rule. One reliable source, a man I have known for many years who visited his aged mother in Herat in 1999, provided the following account a year later when I met him in the USA. I asked him about music in Herat during his recent visit (I have only slightly changed his English):

> Music is not allowed. If somebody tells Taliban that in this house is wedding and they put stereo cassette, audio cassette, and there is a little dancing the Taliban come to the house and they say, 'Who is the owner of this wedding?' They say, 'I am the owner.' They take him to office of *Amr Bil Marof Wa Nahi Anil Munkar* [Office for the Propagation of Virtue and the Prevention of Vice, the religious police]. The owner of this wedding, the leader of this wedding is carried to the office, they say, 'Oh man, you know that this is not the time of music. This is not the time for dancing. We know that you had music and we heard your VCR or your stereo. We'll let you free but after this no music in the wedding for a certain time. Maybe one day you will have music [again], not now.' And give him a paper to sign that I don't do anything any more, and let him to go. (Baily 2001a: 38)

But if the host of the celebration refused to sign the paper or started to argue, saying, for example, 'Music is good, without music we cannot have a good wedding,' then he was likely to be imprisoned, for the Office for the Propagation of Virtue and the Prevention of Vice was allowed to incarcerate people for a few days without trial. I asked my contact whether he had seen musical instruments being destroyed. He replied that he had, and told me:

> The *Jahrchi* [like a town crier], the man in a Taliban car, [came round] announcing: 'Oh people, tomorrow at ten thirty in the morning you come to the stadium. We want to burn some music instruments and some hashish plants, and some stereo cassette[s] and audio cassette[s] and some toys.' Okay, I heard this. When I heard this I said to myself I have to go. The next day I called somebody who has taxi, I go to stadium. At ten o'clock I went. There were about five or six hundred people, most of them came by force … 'Come on, come on!' the Talib said. They were sitting on the terraces, you know the stadium has terraces. They came all together, making a circle. First they put the *dutâr*, *rubâb*, *'armonia*, and put gasoline on them and set fire to them. And then the stereo cassettes, audio cassettes, a lot of boxes of audio cassettes and video cassettes, they were burnt. All the music instruments [equipment] like VCR and TV were burnt, and at the last time one hundred and fifty hashish plants was burnt too. Then the plastic toys, they were burnt. And [then they] said '*Allah O Akbar*, [God is Great] *Allah O Akbar*, *Allah O Akbar*' … I saw this burning, the plants, the toys, the music instruments, I saw with my [own] eyes. (ibid., pp. 38–9).

The accuracy of his account was confirmed by an article in the local Herati newspaper *Itafâq-e Islâm* for 10 December 1998 which announced that Herat's Office for the Propagation of Virtue and Prevention of Vice had seized a number of unlawful instruments and goods, which were set on fire and destroyed in Herat's stadium. The newspaper cited the following *hadith* to justify this action, 'Those who listen to music and songs in this world, will on the Day of Judgment have molten lead poured in their ears.'

Faced with these difficulties it is not surprising that many musicians remaining in Afghanistan left if they could. Of course, many could not, for family or other reasons. And there was a good deal of clandestine musical performance for individual enjoyment or to entertain others. Music acquired a new significance as a protest against the regime:

> Many NGOs and other organisations providing humanitarian assistance in Afghanistan consider that high ranking Taliban officials may be relatively moderate but are limited in the policies they can put into effect by the fanaticism of the younger Talibs, who are the people in the front line of a war that still continues against Ahmad Shah Masud and the remnants of the Rabbani coalition. As a distinguished anthropologist and tireless champion of Afghan welfare put it: 'If they get too moderate, the Taliban leaders lose the loyalty of these young boys who are their cannon fodder' (*The Observer* 12/7.98). Thus it is the radical students themselves who set these social agendas. (Baily 2001a: 41)

The foreign press delighted in stories of how people evaded the Taliban ban on music, as illustrated by the following account from Pakistan:

> One ploy is to keep the few tolerated cassettes in the vehicle along with those containing the forbidden, instrument-based music. So tapes with recitations from the Holy Quran, Na'ats praising the Holy Prophet Mohammad (pbuh) or Taliban political chants are kept handy to be played at checkpoints. Once out of sight, it is back to popular Pashto and Persian singers like Nashenas, Ahmad Zahir, Qamar Gulla [sic], Farhad Darya, Farzana, Shah Wali, Abdullah Moquray, Naghma and Mangal. (*The News*, 3 April 2000)

During the period of Taliban ascendancy I made three fieldtrips to work with Afghan musicians, visiting Mashhad, in Iran, Peshawar in Pakistan (for the third time), and Fremont, in California. The visits to Peshawar and Fremont in 2000 resulted in 'fieldwork movies', *Across the Border: Afghan musicians exiled in Peshawar*, and *Tablas and Drum Machines: Afghan Music in California*. I was also invited by the Danish human rights organization Freemuse to write a report on the censorship of music in Afghanistan. For some time I declined to help them, fearing that such a report would close my door to Afghanistan permanently, but a visit to Switzerland in the autumn of 2000 caused me to change my mind.

Elizabeth Rubi, a teacher of cello in Berne, someone with a deep knowledge of Sufism and its musical manifestations in Afghanistan and Pakistan, and in whose house in Peshawar I had stayed in 2000, organized a visit to Switzerland by some Afghan musicians. The band consisted of the classical singer Sharif Ghazal, his brother Ghulam Farid, clarinet – I had met them both in Peshawar in 1992 – Amir Jan Herati, *rubâb*, and Ustad Arif Mahmoud, *tabla*. Bruce Wannell and I went over to Switzerland to help. I found myself introducing the musicians in their concerts with the statement: 'This is the music you cannot hear today in Afghanistan', followed by a description of the current political situation. At a concert in Zurich an old acquaintance came to tell me how he had recently heard from his brothers in Herat that my friends and teachers Gada Mohammad and Karim Dutari had been apprehended by Taliban while playing at a party out in a village far from the city. They had been treated harshly and had their instruments destroyed. I was very upset and I felt an urgent need to write the report, which was published by Freemuse as *'Can you stop the birds singing?' The censorship of music in Afghanistan* (Baily 2001a). I supplied an accompanying CD of Afghan music that included two examples of Taliban *tarâna*s, arguing that these were in fact Pashtun folk melodies with new texts. The report was published in the spring of 2001, just a few months before the al-Qaida attacks of 11 September 2001.

Tehran and Mashhad 1998

The sight and love of Herat will bring youth to my heart,
O, I will go, I will go
                              (composer unidentified)

After the Taliban took Herat in 1995 I heard that many of its musicians had moved to Mashhad, one of the holiest cities in the Shia Muslim world, the burial place of Imam Reza (765–818), the Eighth Imam of Islam. His tomb lies at the centre of what has become one of the largest mosques in the world, greatly expanded after the Iranian Revolution of 1979. Mashhad is an important site of pilgrimage, which has brought great prosperity to the city. For Shias from Afghanistan, including many people from Herat, it was a good place to be, at least emotionally; the signs and symbols of their faith were everywhere.

By then I had new ways of being in contact with the musicians from Herat. The most useful channel of communication was my correspondence with Nasruddin Saljuqi, from an illustrious family of Herati scholars and theologians, who was then resident in Mashhad. He had graduated from Kabul University in 1985 with a degree in Persian literature and had worked in the Ministry of Telecommunications in Kabul, where he became Director of Planning. He left Kabul in 1992 and after a complicated series of journeys shuttling between Iran and Pakistan had settled in Mashhad, where he was working as a teacher in a school for Afghan children. He also served on a voluntary basis in the Afghan Consulate, helping refugees sort out their problems with documentation, identity papers, visas and permits of many kinds, a position that gave him status and a reliable postal address. He wrote to me about an association of refugee actors and musicians he had set up in April 1998 to help those in exile in Mashhad. The same letter gave me the tragic news that Rahim Khushnawaz's young son Tamim had drowned in a swimming accident in a lake near Mashhad. Then I started to receive e-mail messages from Rahim himself, via an Iranian computer programmer called Mazyar, one of a group of young amateur Iranian musicians with whom he was in contact. This was the first time I had received e-mail from an Afghan friend. A visit to Iran seemed to be required.

After the Islamic Revolution of 1979 there had been severe pressure against music in Iran. In a speech to radio and television employees in Tehran, Ayatollah Khomeini was reported to have denounced music as 'the opium of youth'. However, it does not appear that this statement had the status of a *fatwâ*. Nonetheless, following the spirit of his speech, music departments in the universities stopped teaching, though the faculty members seem to have continued to receive their salaries. There was also very little music on radio or television apart from 'revolutionary songs' (*tarânahâ-ye enqalâb*) performed in a strongly martial style. The ban on music lasted until the end of the war between Iran and Iraq (1982–88), and was justified in terms of respect to those who had lost their young men in the fighting. It was not a time for merriment.

After 1988, when Ayatollah Khatami was Minister for Culture, official attitudes to music gradually became more relaxed, and when he was elected President in 1997 the ban on popular music was finally lifted (Nooshin 2009: Chapter 10). It was becoming possible for visiting academics to get into the country and the British Institute for Persian Studies (BIPS) started to put its large modern building in north Tehran back into commission. I was able to get financial support from BIPS to make contact with musicologists in Iran and to investigate the teaching of music in the higher education sector; to conduct research on the Khorasani *dotâr* of Torbat-e Jam, a type of long-necked lute found in eastern Iran which is closely related to the Herati *dutâr* of Afghanistan (the object of my original research in Herat 1973–74); and to contact Afghan refugee musicians from Herat known to be in exile in Mashhad. I also wanted to meet Abdul Wahab Madadi to get his help in preparing biographies of six Afghan musicians for the second edition of *The New Grove Dictionary of Music and Musicians*.

On 2 November 1998 I arrived with some trepidation at Tehran Airport in the middle of the night, not knowing what to expect. Following instructions from BIPS, I took a taxi to the Institute in Golhaq, an exclusive part of North Tehran, and rang the Institute's bell. Eventually the caretaker came to let me in. After years of neglect only a small part of the Institute was habitable, there were few guests and I had the run of the place to myself for most of the time. After a few hours' sleep I made phone calls to several contacts in Tehran, Hooman Asadi, a graduate student in Tehran University, Catherine Squire of the International Consortium for Refugees in Iran (ICRI) and Abdul Wahab Madadi, former Head of Music at RTA. On receiving my call Madadi immediately came to collect me and took me to his apartment in central Tehran.

Profile: Abdul Wahab Madadi (Radio Singer and RTA Music Director)

Abdul Wahab Madadi is one of the most remarkable and talented Afghans it has been my privilege to meet. He was famous as a singer on Radio Afghanistan and as a composer, setting the poetry and lyrics of others to music. He was a radio personality, a journalist, and the author of an important book about music and musicians in Afghanistan published in Iran (*Sar-guzasht Musiqi Mu'âsir Afghânistân* (*The Story of Contemporary Music in Afghanistan*) (Madadi 1996). He spent most of his career at RTA, working in various capacities, as producer, presenter, archivist, and was formerly Assistant Head and later Head of Music at RTA. He has a prodigious memory for facts and figures, and is a man of great courage and integrity.

He comes from a land-owning family in Herat Province. He was born in 1938, in the village of Torkan-e Payan, a predominantly Taimuri village near the city of Herat. His father died in a cholera epidemic when Wahab was a baby and he was brought up by his father's brother Abdul Ra'uf, who was head teacher in one of the city's secondary schools. As a boy Wahab was very interested in music and often heard Amir Jan Khushnawaz and his band playing at wedding parties in Herat, performing both *ghazal*s in the Kabuli style and local Herati songs. His family had some interest in music and Abdul Ra'uf kept a *dutâr* in the house, which the young Wahab liked to play on when his uncle was out. One day he caught the young Wahab playing with his *dutâr* (Figure 4.1) and was so angry that he smashed the instrument, worried that the neighbours might get to hear that Wahab was playing music, and so bring dishonour to the family. He was sent to school in Kabul in 1955 for eighth and ninth grades and was then enrolled as a student in the Afghan Institute of Technology for tenth to twelfth grades. This institution taught in English.

As a schoolboy in Kabul he went for an audition at the radio station and sang over the air under the name of Abdul Wahab Herati. When the maths teacher at his school found out his pupil had sung on the radio he gave him a severe thrashing to discourage his musical proclivity. A year later the boy dared to sing again on the radio and this time was threatened with failure in his exams if he did not stop. Once enrolled in the Institute of Technology, he sang once more on the radio, now under the pseudonym Ranjur, 'Sufferer'. When the Director of the Institute found out he was sent for and roundly abused, with remarks such as 'Death to you', and 'I'll cut your tongue out if you do it again!' Furthermore, his mother sent him a letter saying that she disowned him for his singing, but a year later she wrote to him again, saying how she missed him and longed to hear his voice once more on the radio. By this time a new Director of the Institute of Technology had been appointed who was a music lover and he encouraged Wahab to sing. Wahab reappeared on the airwaves, with the pseudonym of Madadi, 'Helper', which in due course became his official surname and the name by which he is generally known.

Figure 4.1   Abdul Wahab Madadi with 2-stringed *dutâr*, Tehran 1998

He graduated from the Institute in 1960 and started working for the Afghan Air Authority as a Morse code operator in the weather forecasting section. Morse code was a skill that he learned at the Afghan Institute of Technology. He worked for the Air Authority for a little over four years. At the same time, he was a regular performer on Radio Kabul, singing mainly Herati folk songs. These were usually broadcast live; although the radio station now had tape recorders, these were restricted in use to recording newly composed songs. In 1962 he was invited to join a delegation of radio artists to visit India, and after prolonged negotiations between Radio Kabul and the Air Authority he was given leave to go to India for a month. He travelled along with three other singers, Ustad Sarahang, Khyal and Zaland, with instrumentalists Ustad Mohamad Omar, *rubâb*, Ustad Hashem, *tabla*, Ustad Salim Sarmast, mandolin, and Salim Qandahari, *delrubâ*.

A year later he was invited to join another delegation, this time to Iran. The Air Authority made a fuss about granting him a second leave of absence but the Minister of Information and Culture, Sayed Qassem Reshtia, stepped in and offered him a job as a staff member at Radio Kabul, which would also allow him the opportunity to sing over the airwaves. Furthermore, he was promised the opportunity to go to Germany for two years to study radio journalism at Westdeutscher Rundfunk (WDR) in Cologne. This he did, and at the same time attended courses in western art music appreciation. The knowledge he acquired enabled him to produce and present regular programmes about western art music in later years. He returned to Kabul in 1967 and became Deputy Director of the Music Department in the new Radio Afghanistan in Ansari Wat. One of the first things he did was to catalogue the burgeoning number of tapes in the radio archive, a very important step; from that time on new recordings were well catalogued in card-index format, and individual items could be quickly retrieved.

The next few years were difficult. Madadi became highly critical about certain practices at Radio Afghanistan, and in 1972 he wrote a controversial article for *Pashtun Jakh*, a magazine published by the Ministry of Information and Culture (Madadi 1972). The article was entitled '*Uruj wa nuzul-e musiqi dar Afghânistân*' ('The rise and fall of music in Afghanistan'). It criticized arrangements for pensions for musicians, the lack of sick pay for musicians, and inequalities in the payments of singers and musicians from Kabul as distinct from those who came a long distance from remote areas at a time when road transport was extremely slow and difficult. Madadi was threatened by the President of Radio Afghanistan, Dr Latif Jalali, with imprisonment and prosecution. He immediately left for Germany, leaving his wife and infant son in Kabul. After several months working in a factory in Cologne, he was given a position in WDR. Two years later he returned to Afghanistan. Zahir Shah had been deposed by Daud Khan and Madadi's enemies at the radio station had been replaced. He resumed his work as Director of the Music Department of Radio Afghanistan.

Perhaps because of Madadi's prominent position in Radio Afghanistan, Herat was very well represented in the archive. When I visited Radio Afghanistan in March 1977 I found there were recordings by 44 singers and instrumentalists from Herat. Most had just a few recordings in the archive but Madadi himself had no less than 121 songs. Herat was much better represented than other provincial cities: Kandahar had eight singers, Ghazni five, Mazar-e Sharif five, Jalalabad 20, Pakhtia 15, and Logar 20. Madadi's own recordings show a very interesting progression. His first recording, made in 1960, was *Siâhmu wa Jalâli*, a song he made famous. As a boy he used to stay with relatives in Badghis, in western Afghanistan, where this song about the unrequited love of the shepherd Jalali for the local khan's daughter Siahmu was popular with local singers.[1] The song became very well known through his performance of it on radio, and Rahim Khushnawaz developed it into an elaborate instrumental piece, as described in Chapter 3.

During his early years at Radio Kabul Madadi was taken under the wing of the court singer Ustad Ghulam Hussain, who was employed as a staff member, with the official position of *montazem*, 'arranger'. He coached Madadi's singing and composed songs for him to perform. Madadi's was the 'Voice of Herat' on the radio at that time; he set the agenda and created the Herati canon of local *mahali* songs. He was like a recording star, but his recordings were in the radio archive, not available in the bazaar. Many of his early recordings of Herati songs with a small ensemble show all the features of the radio popular music of the time, with accelerations of tempo, pronounced rhythmic cadences, and pre-composed instrumental sections with geometrical melodic structures. But later he

---

[1]   This vernacular folk poetry was supposedly composed by Jalali. The quatrains were collected by Mayel Herawi and published in Kabul (Herawi 1968).

developed a more western style of orchestration and the recordings he made with the *Arkestar-e Bozorg* (see Chapter 1) are very different in style.

Madadi stayed on at what then became RTA throughout the communist era, but he was never a member of the PDPA. In 1980, after Babrak Kamal became president, he recorded the song *Watan* (*Homeland*), which might be interpreted as being supportive of the new regime. The melody of this song was borrowed from a recording by Mikis Theodorakis, with new words by Nasser Tahuri:

> My country, my love for you is my honour
> My country, I'm ready to sacrifice myself for you
> My country, to me your clean dust is heaven
> My country, even your bathhouse furnace is like a garden
>
> My country, I'm in love with your glory
> Your mountain rocks are better than pearls
> Wherever I may be
> You are everything to me, my country.
>
> My country, you are my heart and everything I have
> All my veins are full of your blood
> Being with you, my heart opens like a flower
> Whether it be autumn or spring[2]

This song was apparently the very first piece of music broadcast by RTA after the fall of the Taliban in 2001. In 1982 he recorded for television a song about the martyrs of Afghanistan, once again using the melody borrowed from Thedorakis, but set to a very slow tempo, with poetry by Latif Nazimi. This was a dangerous song to perform, for although both sides in the conflict could claim its martyrs, it was clearly intended to commemorate the death of those who were fighting for the *mujahideen*.

> O martyred fighter of my homeland
> You, whose name is recorded in blood
> You, who were killed by villainous demons
> The garden of our country is red with your blood
> With your blood you have written an epic
> You made a sacrifice of pure love for your country
>
> You left, but it was a bitter journey
> Look at your mother waiting for you
> You left, and look at the flood of tears
> Flowing down your wife's cheeks

---

[2]   Translated by Veronica Doubleday.

You raised the flag of martyrdom
And put the nation into mourning

O martyr, O unknown brother
I swear on the tears of your children
You, who are eternally on this journey of love
I swear on your precious soul
Your personal sacrifice is the story of our tomorrows
Your epic is the story of our generation[3]

Madadi made video and audio copies of the recording and sent them to Germany. The song was broadcast only once in Afghanistan. The next day Madadi was brought before the Minister for Information and Culture, the Deputy Minister for Foreign Affairs, and a member of the Central Committee of the PDPA. 'Why did you sing that song? We love you so much, we helped you so much', they asked. Madadi told me that he could have been killed, but they needed him at RTA. After that he did not broadcast any new songs. He left Kabul in 1992 when the *mujahideen* started fighting amongst themselves for control of the city. He and his family stayed three months in Herat, and then went to Tehran.

Madadi was well respected by the Iranian authorities, notably by *Hauz-e Honari*, the 'Arts Centre', which was answerable to The Supreme Leader (Ayatollah Khomanaei) rather than to President Khatemi. *Hauz-e Honari* helped Madadi with his residence visa, and published his book *The Story of Contemporary Music in Afghanistan*, the hand-written manuscript of which he had been able to rescue from his apartment in Kabul. The Iranian ethnomusicologist and composer Mohammad Reza Darvishi was particularly helpful; he read the manuscript and recommended it for publication. The book is largely a compendium of the biographies of a large number of Afghan singers and musicians. It sold out in a few months, and was reprinted in 2011, with added photos. Some time later *Hauz-e Honari* invited Madadi to record a cassette of his singing, the production of music cassettes being another part of their work. He was accompanied by Herati musicians exiled in Mashhad, who were brought to Tehran for the recording. The recordings were later released on CD in the US, by Watan Music in Virginia.

I visited Madadi a number of times during my visit to Tehran in 1998. We worked together on biographies of Ustad Qassem, Ustad Mohammad Omar, Mahwash, Khyal, Ahmad Zahir, and Sarahang for the second edition of *The New Grove Dictionary of Music and Musicians*, and we became good friends. In 1999 he made his way to Germany, with the help of his sons and a daughter who were already there, and in due course he was given political asylum and a visa that allowed him to travel freely in Europe. For a while he was in demand for concerts accompanied by the Herati *rubâb* player Ghulam Mohammad Atay.

---

[3]   Translated by Veronica Doubleday.

We invited him to Goldsmiths for a seminar and a concert with Ensemble Bakhtar in 2004, and later that same year he sang in the Semley Festival with Veronica and myself playing *dutâr*. Recordings from this concert were released on the CD *Sweet Nomad Girl*. Since then I have had various meetings with Madadi, and the opportunity to gather much of the information given here. He is highly regarded in the diaspora, especially amongst Heratis, who are extremely proud of him as a representative of the Herati cultural tradition.

Music in Mashhad

After four days in Tehran I flew to Mashhad. I was met at the airport by a small reception committee: Rahim Khushnawaz (Figure 4.2), Nasruddin Saljuqi and Ahmadi, a young Herati businessman and amateur singer who also owned a car – which proved to be a very useful asset. They took me to the Jahan Hotel, where I was booked to stay. Having unloaded my bags we proceeded to Rahim's house to hold a small *fâta* (memorial) for his son Tamim. Rahim recounted how he had been playing at a big outdoor celebration a few miles from Mashhad and had taken his sons with him. Tamim had gone to bathe with some other boys in a nearby lake. He had enjoyed himself so much he had returned alone, got out of his depth, and drowned. Rahim was able to give me the date, which Saljuqi calculated to be 30 August 1998, around 2.00 pm. About 20 people attended the *fâta*, where Rahim displayed a photo of the banner they had prepared at the time of the burial.

Figure 4.2   Rahim Khushnawaz and his brother Mahmud, Mashhad 1998

In the evening we went to Nasruddin Saljuqi's house and he explained something about the situation of Afghans in Iran. There were, he told me, about half a million refugees from Afghanistan in Iranian Khorasan, in Mashhad, Torbat-e Jam, and many other places in the province. They seemed to be much more restricted than Afghan refugees in Pakistan. There were all sorts of problems to do with identity papers, passports, visas and freedom of movement. Afghan children were not given access to Iranian schools or universities. Refugee camps in Iran were more like places of detention. Saljuqi described his experience of camp life in Torbat-e Jam; once he had been woken up in the middle of the night to go and clean the latrines. There were thousands of refugees living in Mashhad, but they were not allowed to rent houses for more than six months at a time and people were constantly having to move from one place to another. All this no doubt was to discourage permanent settlement. On the other hand, Afghans were a vital part of the Iranian work force, especially as labourers in the construction industry.

Nasruddin told me about the three family bands from Herat then resident in Mashhad. There was the Khushnawaz band, with Mahmud, vocal and *'armonia*, Rahim, *rubâb*, Rahim's older son Nasim, *rubâb*, and Rahim's brother Naim, *tabla*. There was the Delahang (Golpasand) band, with Jalil Ahmad, vocal, his son Wahid, *rubâb*, and his nephew Sami, *tabla*. And there was the Hassanpur band, an offshoot from the Khushnawaz group, led by Karim Hassanpur, the younger brother of Amir Jan Khushnawaz (Rahim's father), and his sons Hakim, vocal and *'armonia*, and Azim, *tabla*. Karim had in the past been Herat's leading *tabla* player, but in later years he took to playing *rubâb* in the family band. The Hassanpurs had in fact been living in Mashhad for many years, having left Herat during the communist era. For much of the time they had not been able to follow their traditional occupation of musician due to the pressures against music. Hakim had supported the family working as a shoemaker. In addition to the hereditary musicians, there were several Herati *dutâr* players who worked with these groups, and a number of amateur singers such as Ahmadi, the man with the useful car. Two of Herat's leading musicians, Gada Mohammad and Karim Dutari, had stayed in Herat, as noted above.

I spent a little over a week in Mashhad, and my hotel was just outside the *Haram*, the mosque complex. The shrine of Imam Reza is notable for having a *naqqârakâna* (kettledrum house), an ancient type of ensemble of shawms, long trumpets and kettle-drums that played at dawn and at sunset. I used to sneak in to listen to the dawn chorus; non-Muslims were not permitted to enter the inner parts of the *Haram* where the *naqqârakhâna* was located.[4]

---

[4] On another visit to Mashhad in 2004 Rahim Khushnawaz insisted on taking me to the inner sanctum, to the gilded enclosure surrounding the tomb of Imam Reza, where we had to fight our way through the dense crowd to grasp a bar of the enclosure in supplication. Rahim was very pleased that I had succeeded and felt a personal achievement in having got me there.

It was a hectically busy time, described later by Nasruddin Saljuqi as 'The Week of Music': an exceptional week of hospitality (*mehmân nawâzi*), seemingly inspired by my visit. Every day there was a lunchtime *mehmâni*, parties with a substantial meal and live music, and several in the evenings, too. I noted new styles of eating, using individual plates and cutlery, rather than shared dishes and hands, though we still sat on the floor. After eating there would be music, when different singers and instrumentalists took turns to perform, rather like a *gormâni*. I was usually requested to play the *rubâb*, not just out of politeness, in that the guest should be asked to take his turn as a social obligation; my Herati friends wanted to hear how I was getting on, to assess the *khareji* (foreigner) who had learned to play their music quite well, and become in some ways one of them.[5] The music making was invariably videoed, usually with wobbly hand-held cameras, sometimes with an elaborate set-up to allow the audience to see the performers and themselves on a television set as the performance was being recorded. This could have its embarrassing moments for a guest caught unawares.

The music was largely familiar, with many *ghazal*s in the Kabuli style, and some new songs too, such as the very popular *Kâbul Jân*, which struck a new note of optimism about a return to Afghanistan.

Beloved Kabul, tomorrow I am going to you,
O, I will go, I will go

I go to Afghanistan with a hopeful heart,
O, I will go, I will go

The air and sight of my land will bring life to my heart,
O, I will go, I will go

They say, Kabul is but a ruin, no matter, to the ruined land I go,
O, I will go, I will go

The sight and love of Herat will bring youth to my heart,
O, I will go, I will go

They say, Mazar is a ruined land, no matter, to the ruined land I go,
O, I will go, I will go

I go with a heart full of hope and good wishes
O, I will go, I will go
(composer not identified)

---

[5]   In this respect I, and Veronica, have joined the ranks of ethnomusicologists who have become accepted as legitimate performers by the communities with whom they have worked.

Local Iranian musicians were invited to several of these *mehmâni*s and there were interesting interactions between the Afghan and Iranian musicians, finding a shared repertoire and learning new pieces from each other. For the Heratis this was a renewal of the contact with the art music of Iran that had dominated the urban music scene in Herat during the 1920s (see Chapter 1). It was also good for them to make contact with local musicians, who might be supportive in the future. Both Afghan and Iranian musicians knew what it was like to be under pressure from the religious authorities. And there was a genuine enthusiasm for playing together and exploring musical similarities.

Listening to an audio recording I made of Rahim and the Iranian violinist Motabasam playing together it is striking how 'at home' Rahim seemed to be and it shows the very strong element of Persian influence in his style, especially the use of the extra frets tied to the *rubâb* and the novel tunings he devised for its long drone strings. Rahim had a number of Iranian students learning Afghan music on the *rubâb*, including some girls, and he also taught his own two daughters. In 2011 Nasruddin showed me a video of Rahim with two of his Iranian students in Tehran, young women, in a very luxurious apartment. I realized that there had been many more opportunities for him as a teacher in Iran than in Herat.

As well as working part-time at the Afghan Consulate in Mashhad, Nasruddin was much concerned with helping the actors and musicians from Herat. At their request he had in April 1998 established the *Etedâdi-ye Honarmandân-e Musiqi wa Teâtreh Mohâjerin-e Afgâni dar Mashhad*, the 'Association of Afghan Refugee Musicians and Actors in Mashhad'. The Association had three Artistic Directors: Ghulam Mohammad Farhat, Ali Jewadi and Hussain Ebrahimy, all three formerly well-known actors and playwrights in the Herat Theatre. The Music Director was Rahim Khushnawaz. One night Nasruddin and I produced a document on Mazyar's computer, in English, to spell out the objectives, current situation, future prospects and special needs of the members of the Association. This was intended to be submitted to organizations like UNHCR and ICRI in Iran:

1. To maintain the traditional music and theatre arts of Afghanistan at a time when no music or drama is allowed in Afghanistan.

2. To support and protect Afghan musicians and actors who are refugees in the Mashhad area.

3. To bring traditional music and theatre to the Afghan refugee communities, to enable Afghans to celebrate their weddings and other festivities according to custom, and to bring comfort to the refugees through the proven beneficial effects of music and theatre.

4. To foster good relations between the Afghan communities and their Iranian hosts, through a shared interest in traditional music and theatre and to promote a more positive image of Afghan refugees in Iran.

Members of the Association had already participated in a number of cultural activities in Mashhad, sometimes at the invitation of Iranians. Thus, they had performed at the Mashhad Engineering University, at the Iran Tourism Fair, for celebrations at the tomb of the poet Ferdowsi and in the Golestaneh Cinema. The Association also provided occasional music for the Dari Service of Radio Khorasan, which was broadcasting for two hours a day from Mashhad, targeted at Afghanistan and Afghan refugees in Iran. During my visit the musicians were rehearsing for a radio broadcast to celebrate Prophet Mohammad's birthday.

Soon after my visit the Association presented a comedy entitled *Shekam Salâr*, which approximately translates as *The Man Who Worshipped his Stomach*. This was tremendously successful, with a two week run in a cinema in Mashhad, with three shows per day. Every show was sold out to a paying audience of about 300 people, and this generated quite a lot of money for the actors and musicians, who insisted that Nasruddin take an equal share of the profits. The audiences were mainly Afghan, plus invited Iranian guests. Saljuqi later sent me a video of the show, which ran for nearly three hours. Most of the performance was in the form of a concert, with a number of singers taking their turn to play: Jalil Delahang, Hakim Hassanpur, Mahmud Khushnawaz, Naimatullah Hussainzadeh, and several others. Rahim Khushnawaz and his son Nasim played *rubâb* solos, and Azim played a *tabla* solo. The music was traditional in terms of instruments, with *'armonia*, *rubâb*, *dutâr* and *tabla*. There was no electronic keyboard or other modern western instruments. Even at the time when pop music was banned, the Iranian authorities had promoted the performance of local traditional music from different parts of the country, and perhaps unwittingly had encouraged a notion of 'authenticity' that spilled over into the practices of the Afghan musicians in exile.

The theatrical component of the show consisted of two lengthy comedy sketches, featuring Naimatullah, who was equally well known for his comic theatrical roles as for his very Herati style of singing. The first sketch was one I had seen live in Herat in 1994, called *Bil-e Me* (*My Spade*). This was about a farm labourer's search for his spade, which has been stolen when he took a nap while at work. The sketch leads to a song about his search for his spade, naming the different parts of Herat city he visits. In the second sketch, *Shekam Salâr* (*The Man Who Worshipped his Stomach*), Naimatullah played someone afflicted by a disorder which meant he could not stop eating. The efforts of a modern doctor were ineffectual in curing him but in the end it was a *hakim*, a traditional healer following the Greek system, who effected a cure.

Rahim's Visit to Tehran and Subsequent Events

Before I flew to Mashhad there had been discussion with Iranian musicologist Mohammad Reza Darvishi about bringing Rahim to Tehran to give a concert organized by the *Hauz-e Honari*, which was part of the Islamic Propaganda Organisation (IPO). But there were problems. In order to travel far from their place of registration, Afghans in exile were required to have a travel pass, but there was no time to organize this. Such a permit would be essential for travel by air. In the event, Rahim, accompanied by Nasruddin, made the journey by overnight bus, hoping they would not be apprehended. On arrival they were taken to stay at the IPO guesthouse. The concert took place in a former Bahai mausoleum that had been appropriated by the Iranian authorities after the revolution of 1979 and turned into a concert hall.[6]

The programme was in three parts: first, Darvishi gave a slide lecture about the *rubâb* in Iranian Baluchistan. Then I gave a lecture on the *dutâr* of Herat and its relationship to the *dotâr* of Khorasan, and played several pieces on a large *dotâr* I had bought in Mashhad. Finally, Rahim played a solo *rubâb* programme, with no percussion accompaniment, concentrating very much on his Herati repertoire. In appreciation for our participation Rahim and I were given a fine 'illuminated address' apiece and I received a set of 32 audiocassettes published by *Hauz-e Honari* of the *Regional Music of Iran*, recorded by Mohammad Reza Darvishi. Madadi attended the programme and the next day the four of us were invited to his apartment for a lavish Afghan luncheon.

There were a series of developments after my departure from Iran. As part of our campaign to give Afghan musicians in exile special protection, Saljuqi had given details of the Khushnawaz and Delahang families to the local authorities in Mashhad. Back in the UK I received an e-mail from Rahim's Iranian friend Arash saying that members of the families had been arrested as unregistered immigrants and that they were in the process of being deported back to Afghanistan. For musicians to be surrendered to the Taliban in this way could have had fatal consequences. However, Saljuqi and I were able to contact ICRI in Tehran and UNHCR in Mashhad, the deportation orders were rescinded and the Herati musicians and their families allowed to return to Mashhad.

Rahim and his family were later offered resettlement in Denmark, but declined this generous opportunity. Rahim remained in Mashhad for several more years. We visited him in 2004 and made a trip with him and Hooman Asadi to Torbat-e Jam for further research on the Khorasani *dotâr*, staying in the house of a prominent singer and *dotâr* player named Pur-Atay. Nasruddin and his family were offered resettlement in Ireland and, at the end of 2000 moved to Dublin, where I visited them at the beginning of 2001. As noted above, Abdul Wahab Madadi, his wife and younger daughter were able to make their way to Germany. Hooman Asadi completed his PhD at the University of Tehran, and Mohammadreza Darvishi was awarded the Society for Ethnomusicology's Klaus Wachsman prize for an outstanding publication in the field of organology for his compendium of chordophones in Iran.

---

[6]   The Bahais were regarded as apostates by the Iranian Shia clergy and subject to periodic persecution.

Peshawar 2000

The music from my instrument is the intoxication of melody
We would be ashamed to get ecstatic in any other way
(Ashghari)

After my visit to Mashhad I realized the need to devote more of my academic time to the music of Afghanistan. Following publication of a short paper on music and refugee lives in *Forced Migration Review* (Baily 1999) I was becoming increasingly interested in issues of music and migration. My Pro-Warden for Research at Goldsmiths, Professor Chris Jenks, granted me 0.5 status for two years to give me more time for research and in early 2000 I made visits to Peshawar and to Fremont, to make a comparison between near and far sites of Afghan settlement outside Afghanistan.[7] I acquired one of the new digital camcorders to use as a research tool. In due course this led to making a series of four 'fieldwork movies' about Afghan music, three of them to be found on the DVD that accompanies this book.

I had heard that many of the musicians from Kabul's Kucheh Kharabat were now living in exile in Peshawar. Ustad Asif Mahmoud in London put me in contact with members of his wife's family, who were the children and grandchildren of the late Ustad Sheyda. They were living in Peshawar, and Asif asked me to visit them and bring back some videoed messages.

In addition, I was concerned about the status of the *rubâb*, and whether the instrument was still being made and played. 'Bring Back the Rubab' was the title of a short piece I published in *Afghanistan – Reflections* (Baily 2000a). Brigitte Neubacher was still with the United Nations Office for the Coordination of Humanitarian Affairs (UNOCHA) in Islamabad, and once again was a great help. She arranged for me to stay in the house of our Swiss friend Elizabeth Rubi in Peshawar, and persuaded her erstwhile driver and helper, Ezat Mir, from the Panjshir, to accompany me. At that time Ezat was working as a self-employed taxi driver, and I hired him and his taxi for two weeks. Brigitte also arranged for me to make a quick visit to Herat on the ICRC aeroplane, but for this I needed an Afghan visa. My application was unsuccessful. In retrospect I attribute this to my photo on the visa application form, unbearded, wearing a very loud sports jacket, and looking overly cheerful, not an image likely to appeal to a Taliban immigration official. Phoning the Afghan Consulate in Islamabad a few days later to ascertain the progress of my application I was put on hold for a few minutes, and was delighted to hear Scott Joplin's piano rag *The Entertainer* (as used in the Oscar-winning film *The Sting*) playing away as hold music while I waited to be connected to the relevant office. This seemed very odd, given Taliban attitudes to music.

---

[7]   Sometimes referred to as the near diaspora and the wider diaspora (Van Hear 2003).

Khalil House

We drove to Peshawar in Ezat Mir's yellow taxi and with a great deal of trouble found Elizabeth Rubi's house, at No. 2C Rahman Baba Road. The problem was that No. 2C was a good half-mile from Nos 2, 2A and 2B. Elizabeth was away in Switzerland and two young servants looked after her rented home. The day after my arrival in Peshawar Ezat Mir and I discovered Khalil House, a modern four-storey apartment block on University Road, one of the main thoroughfares in Peshawar. When the Taliban took over Kabul in 1996 most of the musicians from the Kucheh Kharabat who had remained in or returned to the capital were forced to leave for economic and political reasons. They could no longer make a living from music, and were in danger of severe punishment if exposed as former musicians. Many of them moved to Peshawar and set up new business premises in Khalil House. Between 25 and 30 bands were located in this and an adjacent building. The singer Faiz-e Karezi (not in fact a denizen of the Kharabat) was the first to hire a room, in about 1996, when it was still a residential building. Other musicians moved in, and the Pakistani former residents moved out, presumably not wanting to be embedded in a nest of musicians.

As was the case in the other music business areas of Peshawar, Dubgari Road and Qesakhani Bazaar, the musicians did not live in Khalil House: each apartment, essentially a single large room, sometimes with en suite facilities, became the *daftar* (office) of a group of musicians. Some offices were modern in style, with sofas, armchairs and telephones. Others were more traditional, with people sitting on *toshaks* (thin mattresses) on the carpeted floor. Potential patrons would come to hire musicians for their wedding parties or other musical events, going from one music office to another, to see what was on offer, and to negotiate payment with the group of their choice. Discerning patrons might even compile their own ensemble for the night, with a favourite singer from one band, a *rubâb* player from another, a *tabla* player from a third group. On the outside of Khalil House, facing the main road, were large billboards advertising some of the famous musicians with rooms in the building, such as Rafi Hanif, Daud Hanif, Sultan Hamahang and Shabeer Hamahang. There was nothing secret about Khalil House (Figure 4.3), and it would have been only too easy for Taliban sympathizers to detonate a car bomb outside and put the whole place out of operation. But that never happened – it is possible that protection money was being paid.

Khalil House was essentially the Kucheh Kharabat in exile, where Dari was the main language. In this respect it differed from the music offices in Dubgari Road and Qesakhani Bazaar, which were more for Pashto speaking musicians from southeastern Afghanistan. Amir Jan Herati, though a frequent visitor, had no professional link with this community of Kabuli musicians. Khalil House, as a sort of artists' colony, was a hotbed of musical activity. There was a lot of teaching and practising going on, and informal music sessions where musicians competed in turn to show off their virtuosity and technical skills were common. Some of the musicians in Khalil House ran private 'music schools' in their music offices.

Figure 4.3   Khalil House, Peshawar 2000

Ghulam Hussain, a *shâgerd* of Ustad Mohamad Omar, had a large chart of the wall in his *daftar* charting the lineage of what he called the 'Ustad Mohammad Omar school of *rubâb* playing', with small ID photos of all his teacher's *shâgerd*s.

Younger musicians were in charge of the various rooms for much of the day. The senior musicians would come along in the late afternoon when patrons would be arriving to hire musicians and that was the time for the informal music sessions, which of course also impressed the punters looking for bands. Life in Khalil House encouraged the musicians to maintain the social organization and social hierarchy of the Kucheh Kharabat. The protocols of the Kharabat were strictly observed: respect for elders, asking for permission to play, expressing humility, and recognition of the importance of the *ustâd-shâgerd* system as embodied in the *gormâni* string-tying ritual for taking on a new student.[8]

Overall, the instrumentarium had not changed much from how it had been in Kabul. *'Armonia, rubâb* and *tabla* remained the principal instruments, used to accompany singing, and players of *dutâr, tanbur, sarinda, delrubâ, doholak* and

---

[8]   *Across the Border* – 11' 41" (Baily 2007c).

clarinet could also be found.[9] The hereditary musicians were, of course, expert in the performance of Afghan art music, vocal and instrumental, and conversant with North Indian music theory and terminology. They also played popular music and dance music when they went to work at wedding parties.

There were also some modern Afghan bands based in Khalil House, such as the Daud Hanif group, made up of five brothers, grandsons of the Kabuli singer Ustad Nabi Gol. Daud Hanif sang and played keyboard, and his brothers played electric guitar (Rafi), electric bass (Ahmad Shakib), saxophone (Sharif), congas, drum kit, and drum pads (Shafi). I had never seen this sort of lineup before in Afghanistan and it may well have developed in the communist era. But overall, the general picture of Afghan music in Peshawar was one of 'minimal change'.

Profile: Homayun Sakhi (Rubâb Player)

One of the outstanding younger musicians in Khalil House was Homayun Sakhi (Figure 4.4). His father, Ghulam Sakhi, was from the Kharabat, a *rubâb* player and a *shâgerd* of Ustad Mohammad Omar. Ghulam Sakhi became Mohammad Omar's brother-in-law when the Ustad took his sister as his third wife and this no doubt gave him privileged access to Ustad's teaching. I had met Ghulam Sakhi in 1976, in company with the *rubâb* player Ghulam Jailani, one of the five musician sons of Ustad Nabi Gol (see Chapter 1). Ghulam Jailani had been an outstanding *rubâb* player, with an individual and very fluid style, close to Indian music, with long improvised melodic passages. He was sometimes criticized for playing the *rubâb* as though it was the *sarod* (Baily 1988a: 78).[10] One night I had found him and Ghulam Sakhi playing together as a *rubâb-tabla* duo in a tourist hotel in Kabul, taking it in turns to swap the two instruments around, and they seemed to be good friends. I mention this because Ghulam Sakhi's son Homayun also plays in this *sarod*-like style.

Homayun was born in Kabul in 1976.[11] He moved with the rest of the family to Peshawar in 1992, but I do not seem to have heard of him when I visited the city that year (see Chapter 3). Eight years later he was the toast of Khalil House, acclaimed by other musicians, young and old, for his brilliant *rubâb* playing. He had visited the USA two years earlier, sponsored by an enterprising Afghan businessman, to give concerts in San Diego, Los Angeles, Fremont and New York. He also had two CDs released that were recorded in Pakistan, one of Pashtun music, another of song tunes associated with Ahmad Zahir, but at that stage he had not yet made any commercial recordings of classical music.

Homayun had his own music office in Khalil House. Above the door a painted sign read (in Dari): MUSIC COURSE FOR *RUBÂB* AND OTHER MUSICAL

---

[9]   I was delighted to discover Masjidi, player of the very large *dohol* sometimes used in Kabul. He had been a *shâgerd* of Ustad Hashem and incorporated a number of *tabla* compositions in his playing, see *Across the Border* – 22' 04" (ibid.).

[10]   Two examples of Jailani's playing can be found on http://www.oart.eu.

[11]   According to the booklet that accompanies his Smithsonian CD.

Figure 4.4   Homayun Sakhi, Peshawar 2000

INSTRUMENTS. HOMAYUN SAKHI. I visited this room a number of times. It was very simply furnished, with *toshak*s and cushions on the carpeted floor, and lots of photos of Ustad Mohammad Omar on the walls. Homayun was not usually present, but his father would be there in charge of things. Ghulam Sakhi no longer played the *rubâb*, having suffered an injury to his right hand, which meant that he could not grip the plectrum easily. His role had become that of teacher. In the *daftar* he often played *lehra* on the *'armonia* to accompany *tabla* solos. I spent many hours in his company, listening, videoing performances, and sometimes playing *rubâb* myself.

I met Homayun on my second visit to Khalil House. Amir Jan Herati took me to his *daftar*, where I found Ghulam Sakhi. He greeted me warmly, remembering me as a *shâgerd* of Mohammad Omar. He sent for Homayun, then in his mid-20s, good looking with a fine head of black hair, smartly dressed, very affable, evidently star quality. One of his *shâgerds* played a *naghma* in *Yeman* that I videoed, with some *palta*s that were new to me. Homayun prompted him at certain points. I, Amir Jan and some others in the *daftar* were then invited to the Sakhi family home, an apartment next door to Khalil House. Homayun tuned up a very large *rubâb* and started to play the well-known *naghma-ye chahârtuk* in *Râg Pilu*, accompanied by the *tabla* player Nasim Jan Bahi.

I was transfixed. I had never heard or seen anything like it; the sheer strength, stamina and speed of the man were incredible. He seemed to have full command of the difficult unfretted upper range of the instrument on all three melody strings, with very *sarod*-like extended melodic improvisations. In this respect his playing was reminiscent of Jailani. He played complex *parandkâri* patterns, with lots of cross-rhythms. Homayun Sakhi had carried this approach to new levels of complexity, going far beyond the variations of Ustad Mohammad Omar. He also cultivated use of the upstroke in fast down-up-down-up patterns, another *sarod*-like aspect of his playing. He denied having studied with any *sarod* players, only his father and what he had innovated himself, but this does not eliminate the Jailani influence, transmitted via his father. Another innovation was his rendition of *shakl* (the unmetered introduction to an instrumental piece, like *âlâp* in Indian music). For this he made use of the sympathetic strings, plucking them as though he was playing the *santur*.[12] The performance lasted 27 minutes, long by *rubâb* standards. The audience responded with great enthusiasm.

He then played something completely different but equally (or perhaps even more) innovative, now accompanied by the young Sanam Gol on *tabla*. This sounded like a very free improvisation that had little to do with Afghanistan, with lots of chords, and even using the left hand on top of the frets like the tapping technique employed by some jazz guitarists. It transpired that he could also play the guitar, though I never heard him. The three melody strings of the *rubâb* are tuned in fourths, like the bottom three strings of the guitar, and triadic chords are easy to play. 'This man is evidently destined for the world music circuit', I said to myself, imagining him playing with Yusuf Mahmoud on *tabla*, a dream that was realized when Homayun came to London in 2011 to play a concert in The British Museum during the *Afghanistan: Crossroads of the Ancient World* exhibition.

It was stimulating to be in contact with musicians who were so close to the practice of Kabuli art music and in particular to the Ustad Mohammad Omar school of *rubâb* playing. I was able to refresh and update my knowledge, clarify certain issues that puzzled me and correct some mistakes. What I had learned in Herat about this art music was very important, but Kabul was where the music had been created, in the time of the music loving Amirs (Chapter 1), and Kabul was the fountainhead of the tradition. Here I mention a few of the matters I discussed in conversations with Homayun and his father.

I gave Homayun and his father a copy of my paper 'The *naghma-ye kashâl* of Afghanistan' (Baily 1997b). This is a collection of two pieces I learned from Ustad Mohammad Omar in 1973, when I started playing the *rubâb*, and the 12 pieces I had collected from Amir Jan Khushnawaz in Herat in 1976–77, notated in both *sargam* and western staff notation. They looked at the notations carefully and wanted to know where they came from. I said the ones I learned in Herat ultimately derived from Ustad Nabi Gol, and they were satisfied with their pedigree. They confirmed that these compositions had been made up by the prominent *ustâd*s

---

[12]   This technique is also used for playing the Kashmir *rubâb* and the Dulan *rewap*.

of the past, before the time of Ustad Mohammad Omar. They described how the members of a band would sit together and make up new sections for a *naghma*, almost as a game, and would then play it when it was time to perform.

They were impressed and at the same time unimpressed by my work: Ghulam Sakhi was keen to make the point that one cannot learn music properly from books and notations, it needs to be *siha be sina*, 'chest to chest', that is, through direct interaction between a teacher and a student. They also criticized the term *kashâl*, which literally means 'long', 'extended', 'stretched out', and has slightly negative connotations as something overly lengthy and boring. I received this same criticism from Ahmad Sarmast, Ghulam Hussain the Kabuli *rubâb* player, and from Madadi. They told me the correct name for this type of piece was *naghma-ye chahârtuk*, a 'four part instrumental piece', or the older term *lâriya*, which in India simply means an instrumental composition. I had heard these terms, too, but *kashâl* was the term Amir Jan had used for these compositions, and I had followed his usage in my publication. Amir Jan had held these compositions in high regard and certainly did not think them to be boring. In performance such pieces, played at the beginning of a wedding party or a concert to warm up the instruments, the musicians and the audience alike, are sometimes very long. In 1976 I made a recording of Ustad Rahim Bakhsh and his band at a *Ramazân* concert in Herat where the introductory *naghma*, in *Râg Yeman*, lasted 20 minutes, very long for a group instrumental in Afghanistan.

Of particular importance for me was the matter of right hand technique. In *rubâb* playing the down stroke is the main stroke, and the up stroke is weak by comparison, which allows for a variety of rhythmic patterns according to the sequence of down and up strokes. Of special interest is the use of the high drone in the *parandkâri* technique. I had made a detailed study of these patterns and formulated a set of rules (a simple grammar) underlying their structure. Amir Jan Khushnawaz had once revealed to me a 'trade secret' about these patterns. Referring to the triplet pattern VΛᵛ VΛᵛ VΛᵛ VΛᵛ he showed me that one could start the pattern with the upstroke – Λᵛ V Λᵛ V Λᵛ V Λᵛ V – or with the high drone – ᵛVΛ ᵛVΛ ᵛVΛ ᵛVΛ.[13]

Starting with the upstroke he called this *chapa*, which variously means 'upside down', 'inside out' or 'back to front'. In my grammar I had extended this principle to a longer asymmetrical eight stroke pattern, ᵛVΛᵛ VΛVΛ ᵛVΛᵛ VΛVΛ, often used by *rubâb* players, where exactly the same sequence of strokes generates eight slightly different-sounding patterns, depending on which point in the stroke cycle you start. I called this principle 're-phasing the stroke pattern'.

On the first evening at the Sakhi house, after thrilling us all with his playing I was asked to play. This was something of a challenge, but they wanted to see what this student of Ustad Mohammad Omar could actually do. I played a *naghma-ye klâsik* in *Râg Yeman*, using lots of *parandkâri*, and playing the three *chapa* triplet patterns, which can be quite challenging for a *tabla* player. I was well

---

[13] V = down stroke, Λ = up stroke, ᵛ = down stroke on the high drone string.

satisfied with the reception and felt I had acquitted myself well, especially having to follow Homayun. The next time we met, Homayun told me he knew what I was doing with *shahbâz chapa dâdra* (an 'upside down plectrum pattern in a six beat cycle'). Several days later I videoed him playing to an enthusiastic group of fellow musicians in his *daftar* and he went through an extended series of right hand variations, including some *chapa* patterns which he most obviously directed towards me sitting behind the camera, as if to demonstrate that he knew that I knew what he knew.[14]

Homayun was invited for a concert tour in the USA soon after I met him in Peshawar, and he quickly became a super-star of *rubâb* in the USA, settling in Fremont, California. His successful career as a musician owes a lot to patronage by the Aga Khan Music Initiative. This organization has sought to develop him as a composer, with some success, as his recordings with the Kronos Quartet demonstrate.

The Life of Afghan Music in Peshawar

My fears about the possible demise of the *rubâb* proved groundless. There was a plentiful supply of new instruments, from the workshops of two instrument makers. One was a local Peshawari, Wilayat Khan, a grandson of the highly regarded *rubâb* maker Wasel; he had a workshop off Dubgari Road. The other was Essa Qaderi, a son of the famous Bacha Qader, who before the war had had a workshop near the Kucheh Kharabat. Essa was in exile, with a workshop near to Khalil House, while his aged father remained in Kabul and periodically sent down blocks of mulberry wood for his son to carve into instruments. The Kabuli *rubâb* is a little different in shape to the Peshawari model, with a rather deeper body and fuller chest. It has four frets, whereas the Peshawari type has three. The Peshawari *rubâb* does not usually have the shortest sympathetic string raised by a protuberance on the bridge, for the *parandkâri* technique is not usually used by *rubâb* players on the Pakistani side of the border.

One day in Essa's workshop I was excited to find that a small instrument he had opened to replace the velum (the skin belly) had the shells of three chicken eggs glued inside. He explained that these have an effect on the quality of the sound, boosting the resonance, though how this works I have been unable to discover. Only certain, small, *rubâb*s are said to benefit from the addition of internal eggshells.[15]

Nearby Khalil House were shops selling everything needed for a wedding, such as wedding dresses and accessories, videographers' businesses to record the events, and banqueting rooms where large wedding receptions could be held, with separate parties for men and women. Afghan musicians in Peshawar earned their living in part by playing for weddings. Not only did good music confer prestige, a programme of music was important for structuring the wedding party as an event,

---

[14]   *Across the Border* – 13' 37" (Baily 2007c).
[15]   *Across the Border* – 37' 59" (ibid.).

and certain ritual songs had to be performed. At women's wedding parties the music would be supplied by recordings or by bands of pre-pubescent boys from the musician families. The only wedding I attended was organized in the Hazara community in a banqueting hall near Khalil House. The music was provided by the aforementioned Daud Hanif band, vocal with keyboard, electric guitar, bass guitar, saxophone, keyboard, congas and drum pads. Despite its westernized instrumentation, the repertoire was mostly familiar Afghan songs, with an occasional Bollywood hit, but there was nothing new about Afghan musicians performing *filmi* songs. After all, Nashenas had told me he was the Afghan Saigal.

In Daud Hanif's *daftar* in Khalil House I met with the blind singer Joma Gol Khushkhui, aged about 55. He spoke very good English, having been educated at a school operated by the Noor Eye Clinic in Kabul. He told me that he had been to Kabul recently to record some unaccompanied *na'ts*, songs in praise of Prophet Mohammad, for Voice of Shari'at Radio, as Radio Afghanistan was now called (the television part of RTA had been closed). As far as he knew, he said, the music archive of Radio Afghanistan remained intact apart from some songs in praise of the communists that had been erased. The musical instruments in the studios had not been destroyed, either. Since he was blind I could not be sure about the veracity of his statements, but he said that he himself had used the grand piano in the studio to check his *karj* (tonic) before recording. This was interesting stuff indeed. He told me the Taliban are not against music as such, but against lascivious music. And with so many dead in the war it is not the time for music anyway, he said.

It is appropriate here to say something about the Taliban *tarâna* as a form of musical expression. While banning musical instruments and the songs they accompanied, the Taliban had their own sonic art. The western press usually referred to these as 'Taliban chants'. More accurately they are called Taliban *tarânas*, 'Taliban songs', or *tarâna bidun-e sâz*, 'song without instruments'. They may be sung solo, by two singers together, or by a group. They may be in free rhythm, or they may be strongly rhythmic. The texts (usually, but not always, in Pashto) are of a religious nature, with frequent mention of the Taliban themselves, and of their *shahid*s (martyrs) killed in fighting with anti-Taliban forces.[16] The Taliban are mostly Pashtuns, and music is an important part of Pashtun culture. Taliban singing in Pashto uses the melodic modes of Pashtun regional music, is nicely in tune, strongly rhythmic, and many items have the two-part song structure that is typical of the region (Baily 2001a: 52). Without musical instruments it is not, from the Afghan viewpoint, to be classified as 'music'.

Recordings of Taliban *tarâna*s often feature prominent use of electronic devices such as delay and reverberation, much favoured in secular music of the region. More recent recordings that have come into my hands 10 years later are notable for their use of what is technically called 'pitch-correction', or 'auto-tune', which gives a 'robotic' quality to the voice. It is an effect frequently heard in western popular music in recent years. The Taliban certainly value good voices, like that of

---

[16]   Johnson and Waheed (2011), Said (2012).

Joma Gol Khushkhui. The BBC film *Breaking the Silence* (Broughton 2002) has interviews with two singers from RTA with very good voices, Aziz Ghaznawi and Nairaz, who remained in Kabul and were obliged to sing Taliban *tarânas* over the air. It is not that the Taliban have no music: they have their own version of music, which is structurally like secular music but without instruments, and with very specific song texts. In other words, they have their own music aesthetic.

In London, Ustad Asif had asked me to visit his wife's relatives in Peshawar. I had met his brother-in-law Ahmad Shah, a tabla player, in Khalil House several times, though he was not connected to a particular *daftar*. He invited me round for a meal one evening and treated me as a member of the family, allowing me to mix with the women. Ahmad Shah is a son of Ustad Sheyda, one of the great *ustâds* of the Kharabat who sometimes performed for King Zahir Shah. Sheyda, his son Mia Sheydai, and six other musicians were all killed in a car crash on their way to perform in the Shomali area sometime in the 1960s.

Before eating I videoed the family, who sent their greetings and gave their news, one by one, to Asif's wife and the rest of their relatives in London. After eating it was time for music. Songs were sung, one to offer congratulations to Asif's son Yusuf in London, who had recently become engaged to a daughter of Ustad Sarahang. Ahmad Shah played a *tabla* solo, which he addressed to Asif in a spoken introduction:

> With the permission of Uncle Asif, the Great Ustad. You are my teacher, but I'm out of practice because there are many problems in life here and I cannot continue to improve my playing. I have five young children, and I have to deal with too many problems. They have needs and I'm not able to practice much. But still God is kind. And here I present one of the pieces you gave me, which I'm very honoured to have. I also seek Yusuf Jan's permission, whom I have heard so much about.[17]

An important aspect of life in the Kucheh Kharabat had been the connection with Chishti Sufism, a form of mystical Islam which is especially strong in India and Pakistan, and which uses 'real music' in its ritual. *Qawwâli*, as this genre is called, became well known on the world music concert circuit in the West, with super-stars such as Nusrat Fateh Ali Khan. In Kabul there was a Chishti *khânaqâh* (place for holding Sufi spiritual concerts) near to the Kucheh Kharabat. Many musicians not otherwise engaged would go there on Thursday evenings for all-night music sessions in which they would take turns to perform. I had attended such a session there in 1976.

In Peshawar I visited an Afghan *khânaqâh* that had been established by the son of Abdul Hamid Asir Qandi Agha, an acknowledged expert on the poetry of Bedil. Qandi Agha was known as the poetry teacher of Ustad Sarahang, who had set many of Bedil's *ghazals* to music. The son was known as Bacha (Son of) Qandi Agha, and he also was an expert on Bedil's poetry. This *khânaqâh* was unlike others I

---

[17]   *Across the Border* – 34′ 19″ (Baily 2007c). The speech is a good example of Kharabati protocol, asking permission to perform across time and space.

have encountered, such as Sattar Shah Badshah (Chapter 3), because it was not located at the tomb of a Sufi saint but in the courtyard of a private house (probably that of Bacha Qadi Agha himself). Its regular gatherings were held on Thursday afternoons, and began with two hours of discussion about the deeper meanings of the poems of Bedil and other Persian language poets. This was followed by the *samâ'*, the 'spiritual concert', when the musicians from Khalil House, and others, would perform Sufi poetry. This *khânaqâh* had something of the air of a gentleman's club; many who attended were former professional men – engineers, doctors, lawyers, judges, bureaucrats – now struggling to survive in exile. The music was predominantly the performance of mystical poetry in the *ghazal* style of Kabul, with an occasional vocal *râg* or instrumental piece. The instruments were those associated with the Kharabat: *'armonia*, *rubâb* and *tabla*, with the addition of stone clappers (*qairaq*) and jingling tongs (*chimta*).

I attended two such sessions. At one, the Kharabat singer Alem-e Shauqi sang the following *ghazal* by the contemporary Afghan poet Ashghari. This is of particular interest because it references music and musical instruments.[18]

> The lip of the wine glass is a lip that does not smile
> Like a vein, the string of an instrument pierces the heart
> The music from my instrument is the intoxication of melody
> We would be ashamed to get ecstatic in any other way
>
> I have a pale and yellow complexion
> And my heart bears scars of many colours
> On judgment day, when I arise, I will shamefully say
> O Lord, I'm scarred by separation from you – don't scar me more with firebrands
> And my heart bears scars of many colours
> The music from my instrument is the intoxication of melody
>
> Of all the instruments, I love –
> O God, we are but the strings of instruments – what to do?
> Bring *tabla* and *sârang* to play at my funeral
> Of all the instruments, I love
> The *tabla*, *delrubâ* and *sârang*
> The music from my instrument is the intoxication of melody
>
> See Laili through the eyes of Majnoon
> Whose poor soul did not seek such heartache
> Do not tell someone their beloved is ugly
> They have criticized me for being shameless
> No one sees flaws in others unless they are shameless themselves
> The music from my instrument is the intoxication of melody

---

[18]   *Across the Border* – 44' 27" (ibid.).

Out in the desert the poet Ashghari was saying
My dear, just look at Ashghari
Never mind if he sits on a rush mat
Out in the desert Ashghari was saying
To my eyes this world seems so small
The music from my instrument is the intoxication of melody
We would be ashamed to get ecstatic in any other way

(Ashghari)

Fremont 2000

O girl, don't believe my words
Your ring is still in my pocket

My research in Fremont, California, focused more on issues of migration than my work hitherto, perhaps because I was in receipt of a grant from the British Academy and had to write a proposal that addressed more general issues. I spent six weeks in Fremont, much longer than some of my field trips. Also, this was my first research on music in the wider diaspora, far away in terms of geographical and cultural distance. For the first three weeks of my stay I was the guest of Kabulis Tareq Mehdavi and his family, who welcomed me into their home and treated me as a family member, and helped me in many ways with my research. Through them I was instantly embedded in the Afghan community. Tareq's older son, a student at a community college, acted as my driver and also became my student for *rubâb*. I carried with me an instrument sent as a gift to the Mehdavi family by Ghulam Hussain. After three weeks I moved to a studio flat, much against the wishes of my host, but I was beginning to feel the need for privacy and to have a place where Afghans could visit and talk about matters they would not necessarily want to discuss in a more public space.

At that time there were about 15,000 to 20,000 Afghans living in the area of Fremont, Union City, Hayward and Newark, in the San Francisco Bay Area of California. I use the term 'Fremont' to include all four areas. There had been very few Afghans living in Fremont before the communist takeover of Kabul in 1978. The first Afghan exiles arrived in the early 1980s. I do not know how and why they gravitated to California, but certainly rents were low and the climate was attractive. The Afghan exiles in Fremont were predominantly educated people from the principal cities of Afghanistan, but especially Kabul, and were mostly Pashto and/ or Dari speakers. Oeppen (2009) refers to them as members of 'the Afghan elite'. Many who were granted political asylum in the USA had formerly worked for western diplomatic, educational, cultural or aid agencies. This was a very different section of the population to that which had settled in exile in Pakistan or Iran.

Many Afghan businesses were established in an area around the railway station known as Centerville. There were a number of so-called 'Afghan markets', which typically stocked all the necessary ingredients for Afghan cuisine, herbs and spices, dried fruits and nuts, pulses, dried milk products, *halal* meat and freshly baked Afghan bread. Such groceries usually also carried CDs and DVDs of Afghan music, and many audio and video recordings of Indian film music, which was and remains very popular with Afghan audiences. In addition to the Afghan markets there were Afghan travel agents, insurance agents, restaurants, chiropractors, shops for photocopying, electronics, even, in Newark, a music shop selling instruments, mainly keyboards, electric guitars, electric basses and guitar amps. All in all, the Afghans in Fremont seemed to constitute a highly successful business community. It is tempting to connect this with the very long history of Afghanistan as a centre of commerce and business activity, where a culture of entrepreneurialism prevailed. The Afghans in Fremont had requested that Centerville should be re-designated as 'Little Kabul', but this proposal did not find favour with the City of Fremont authorities.[19]

Despite their success as a business community, Afghans had found it hard to adapt to life in the USA. They were in a completely new alien milieu, which promoted a fear of transgressing unheard-of and unimagined US laws. They often found themselves dealing with officious social service agencies, especially those concerned with the welfare of children. One of the main areas of difficulty for Afghan society in the USA concerned inter-generational differences. Age is deeply respected in Afghan culture, and being described as a 'white beard' or as 'white haired' is a mark of respect. The older generation aged 50–70+ were people who were brought up in pre-war Afghanistan and left from 1980 onwards. They embodied the older values of Afghan culture. As refugees they had lost much of their dignity. They were impoverished, lived on welfare or had to take on poorly paid and low status jobs. They suffered a loss of self-esteem and self-identity. This can only be equated with a crisis of experiencing oneself as a valuable human being. A medical survey by Lipson and Omidian (1993) revealed a community with a lot of stress, depression and other mental problems, and a high mortality rate, the result of traumatic experiences in the past, separation from home, the challenge of a new culture, and possibly physical differences in altitude, climate and diet. I stepped into this environment in the company of Ustad Asif Mahmoud, the Kabuli *tabla* player.

Profile: Ustad Asif Mahmoud Chishti (Tabla Player)

Ustad Mohammad Asif Mahmoud Chishti (Figure 4.5), to give him his full chosen name (which connects him with the Chishti Sufi order) is from one of the most prominent and highly respected families of the Kharabat. His ancestor Gamuddin Khan, a *tabla* player, was from Kasur, near Lahore. Gamuddin was part of that influx of musicians, singers and dancers who had originally come to Kabul from India in the time of Amir Sher Ali Khan. Asif's father, Ustad Mahmoud, a famous *tabla* player, in the Panjab *gharânâ*, 'stylistic school', had three talented sons:

---

[19]   See http://www.littlekabul-centerville.blogspot.com for details of this controversy.

Figure 4.5   Ustad Asif Mahmoud Chishti, San Diego 2000

Hashem, Asif and Arif. I had had some contact with them in Kabul 1976–77. Ustad Hashem, who not only played *tabla* but also sang *ghazal* and *rág*, played *sitâr*, *sarod*, *rubâb* and various other instruments, and was something of a composer. In Kabul I noticed that he had cultivated friendships with a number of young westerners (Peace Corps Volunteers amongst them) who were interested in the Chishti way. In 1977 the three brothers went to the USA to give concerts arranged by their American Sufi friends. I made several visits to Hashem's soirees in his apartment in Microrayon. In the *jihâd* era Ustad Hashem made his way to Germany, where he was later killed by a deranged *shâgerd*.

In 1988 Asif and his family left Kabul and moved to Delhi, where other musicians from Kabul had migrated, such as Ustad Sarahang's son Eltaf Hussain. Asif knew Delhi well from the two years he spent there as a young man getting advanced instruction for *tabla*. He arrived in London in 1990 and was granted political asylum. He came at the same time as I took up my Senior Lectureship in Ethnomusicology at Goldsmiths. He was in very difficult circumstances at that time, both economic and psychological, living in cramped communal accommodation with other asylum seekers, far away from his wife and children. We at Goldsmiths were able to employ him as a visiting instrumental tutor for two hours per week, to teach Indian *tabla*, which was certainly good for his self-esteem. He had a systematic approach to teaching, and despite limited English was able to train several of our students to a high level of proficiency for their practical examination in the MMus in Ethnomusicology.

In London it had been a great asset for me to have such a musician on hand, direct from the Kharabat. I could regularly practice *rubâb* with his *tabla* accompaniment, and I was also able to do some research with him, getting his comments on recorded performances of others, notably the 1970s field recordings of Ustad Amir Mohammad (Baily 2011a). He was also able to help me by identifying musicians in old photographs. In the early 1990s we took part in many concerts and workshops. With Veronica and the Herati *dutâr* player Aziz Herawi, who came over from California, we played in Discovering Afghanistan – London's First Festival of Afghan Arts and Culture in 1992, and at the Falun Festival in Sweden in 1995. There were other concerts in Acton Town Hall, with the female singers Hangoma and Fereshta, over from Germany, and with Farida Mahwash, who came from California. Asif and I played a number of *rubâb* and *tabla* programmes, with strong emphasis on his *tabla* playing, so that our performances were more like duets rather than solo instrumental with percussion accompaniment.

Early in 1999 Asif spent some months in Fremont, to start what he termed a 'school of music'. In practice it would more accurately be described as a *tabla* course, mostly for young Afghans. While I was at Ohio State University to give some lectures, I made a brief visit to Asif in Fremont. We played a concert, sharing the bill with Farida Mahwash at the Radisson Hotel. We also broadcast a two hours' programme of playing and talking for a small Afghan independent radio station in Fremont, Radio 24 Hours, run by Farida Awary, who had previously worked as a presenter for Radio Afghanistan. This round of frenetic activity showed the possibilities of more detailed research in Fremont. In 2000 Asif went again to Fremont to reactivate his music school, to give his students further training and to recruit more students. His young friend Zaki Ahmadi, who ran an insurance business in the city, sponsored this visit, which involved a lot of legal paperwork. Here we see the continuation of a well-established pattern of peripatetic teaching, like Ustad Nabi Gol's visits to Herat in the 1930s.

I arrived in Fremont a few days before Asif and moved in with Tareq's family. I was able to observe the whole process of Asif setting up the school, which is depicted in detail in the film *Tablas and Drum Machines: Afghan Music in California* (Baily 2005). Asif rented an office in a small two-story office block shared with other Afghan businesses, including Zaki Ahmadi's insurance premises. The office had a small washroom attached, with a toilet and washbasin, and no cooking facilities apart from a kettle. Asif's bed was hidden behind a curtain. To take a shower required a visit to the local sports centre. Friends and students brought in meals, or one could eat in one of the several Afghan restaurants nearby. It was all very 'Afghan', in the sense of making do with limited facilities.

During the next few weeks I helped Asif with editing documents in English, photocopying and giving some *rubâb* lessons in the school. I soon became aware of the respect Ustad Asif commanded amongst the Fremont Afghans. He was regarded as a national treasure, someone keeping Afghan music alive through his teaching, addressed in terms such as 'You are our nightingale'. He was treated almost as a Sufi *pir* (spiritual leader), with people wanting to help him all the time, feeding him, running errands and ferrying him about as required. As well as being busy with the music school we played a number of concerts together, in the Museum of Art at Brigham Young University in Salt Lake City, the Soufi Restaurant in San Diego, Paradise Mission in Fremont, and various *mehmânis*. With so much time to practise and perform I was probably at my peak as a *rubâb* player during this period. Sponsored by my American friend the blues singer and guitarist John Harrelson, we drove down to Los Angeles to make a *rubâb* and *tabla* CD, with John Harrelson playing *tânpurâ* with us. I released the CD under the title of *John Baily & Ustad Asif Mahmoud: From Cabool to California* (Baily 2000b).[20]

Ustad Asif returned to Kabul in 2003 under the Returned Professionals Scheme to work at Radio Afghanistan, and he started teaching at the Aga Khan Music School in Kabul (and later in its school in Herat). He rebuilt a house in the Kharabat and divides his time between Kabul and London, where five of his children live. His son Yusuf Mahmoud is also a virtuoso *tabla* player, and his son-in-law Timor Sheydai a fine *ghazal* singer.

The Life of Afghan Music in Fremont

Compared with Mashhad and Peshawar, Fremont presented a more liberal face of Afghan culture. One rarely saw Afghan women with any kind of veiling, and at big open-air public events like the *Now Ruz* celebrations described below, it was striking how many young women were dressed in tight jeans and T-shirts. The liberal attitude was also manifest in certain other ways. Dr Farid Younos, with a PhD in anthropology and education, described himself as 'reformist'. For seven years he had a regular programme on Afghan community TV in Fremont in which he discussed Islam in the modern world. He told me:

> According to time things change, there are some rules and regulations, without touching the Quran or the *sunna* of The Prophet we could make some modifications in our interpretations according to time ... I have written more than 30 articles about research on Islamic values. For example, time management. Does anything exist about time management within Islam? Because now they are teaching time management in the universities. I brought some verses from the Quran and then interpreted them according to time management. (Interview 29 March 2000)[21]

---

[20]   The CD was pirated in Pakistan and as a result became used in the soundtrack for the Australian feature film *Son of a Lion*, directed by Benjamin Gilmour (Gilmour 2008).

[21]   In retrospect I see that Farid's focus on time management was rather significant; Afghans are notoriously unpunctual, and often make jokes about it.

Farid Younos had lots to say about the various issues facing the Afghans in Fremont, such as reconciling traditional Afghan attitudes with American ideas regarding the equality of the sexes, the benefits of freedom of speech, the absence of fundamentalist attitudes and intergenerational tensions. On the subject of the lawfulness of music, he told me:

> Music is not forbidden ... There were incidents in the time of Prophet Mohammad Peace Be Upon Him that there were musicians and they played and he watched them, he helped his wife Aisha to watch them ... Avicenna, one of the Muslim scholars, he was the one who has written, before Mozart, Beethoven and Tchaikovsky, he has written musical notes, and Iranian notes of traditional music of Iran, it's based on those notes. And Farabi was another one who was very music oriented and there are some of the top notch Muslim scholars that someone could bring as a proof that music is not *harâm*, or forbidden. (Ibid.)

Farid Younos's liberal attitude towards music was echoed in other quarters. The *Qeri* (reciter of the Quran) in the Hazrat Abubakr Sadiq Mosque, a Pashtun in his mid-30s, brought from exile in Pakistan to fulfil this role in Fremont, enjoyed listening to music and also liked to watch the dancing in Bollywood movies. The film *Tablas and Drum Machines* has a sequence of him enjoying a ride on the roundabout on the San Francisco waterfront with Tareq Mahdavi's young son.[22] But while there seemed to be no overt oppression of music, and an acceptance of music as a part of normal everyday life in the USA, there were surely some families that disapproved of it.

California was the domain of amateur and amateur-turned-professional Afghan musicians. There was an older generation of exiled singers who were well established in Afghanistan before 1978, such as Zaland, Haidar Salim and his sister Salma, Mahwash and Aziz Herawi the *dutâr* player. There was also a younger generation of musicians who had grown up in Afghanistan and developed their musical skills in that environment. In Fremont that included singers such as Khaled Omar, Khalil Ragheb, Rahim Jahani Sulaiman Hamsada and Abdullah Qassemi. And there was an even younger generation of musicians who had grown up and been educated in the USA, and been frequently exposed to contemporary US popular music: these included Qader Eshpari, Habib Qaderi and Ehsan Aman. In 2000 Ustad Asif was the only hereditary musician in Fremont to represent the pre-eminence of the Kharabat in matters musical. In the long-standing competition and dispute between *kesbi*s and *shauqi*s, between professionals and amateurs (see Chapter 1), it was the *shauqi*s who had control of the music business in California.

Young musicians in Fremont were much concerned with performing a new kind of Afghan music, vocal with keyboard accompaniment, fast, loud and basically intended for dancing, not for listening. The origins of the 'new music' are a somewhat confused matter. As discussed in Chapter 2, there were significant

---

[22] *Tablas and Drum Machines* – 10′ 04″ (Baily 2005).

developments in popular music in Kabul during the communist era, with the use of electric guitars, bass guitars, keyboards and drum kits. At the same time, parallel developments were taking place in Fremont. Whether these were stimulated by what was happening in Kabul, or occurred independently, taking advantage of the latest technology available in the USA, is not clear. A key player in the creation of new Afghan music in Fremont was Qader Eshpari, who told me, 'There's been a revolution in our music.' In 2000 he had just opened a music store, where he sold mostly western instruments such as electric guitars, guitar amplifiers, PA systems, keyboards and other electronic equipment. At the back of the shop he had a small recording studio, and behind the shop counter he had a mixing desk and computer which allowed him to carry out much of the work necessary in producing his own and other people's CDs when business in the store was slack.

Qader Eshpari told me (in English) that in 1986:

> I came up with this keyboard made by Yamaha. The keyboard was capable of programming your own rhythm, your own bass line and chords. You could do a show with one keyboard, a one-man-band thing. I programmed that keyboard rhythm section in Afghani, like 7/8, 3/4, 4/4, *Mogholi, Dadra, Kerawa.*[23] I programmed all those rhythms ... From there I added the bass line that goes with the rhythm and also the chords that go with the rhythm. That created the whole arrangement. You could perform at a big wedding, a big concert, just you; you didn't need a drummer, a bass player, anything. That was my first step.[24]

Eshpari kept up with technical developments and new models, moving progressively through the expanding range of keyboards, from the Technics 1000, the 2000, then to the 5000. 'Recently I switched from Technics to Korg because the sounds are a little more professional, you can do more with it,' he said. He played me bits of a new song he was working on. He had commissioned the lyrics, which were posted on the wall above the keyboard, and was composing the music around the lyrics. When I asked him what was *Afghan* about the music he created, he said:

> I try to keep the originality, a touch, of Afghan music. I don't want to lose that originality, the flavour of our music, but ... I'm using different tools, different instruments, electronic instruments to produce the sounds of instruments we don't have ... [As well as composing new songs] I try to find sometimes older songs, good ones that our people has good memory from those songs and I try to re-do the whole song, with new instruments and new way of playing the instrument. I try to make it more modern.

---

[23] These are the principal metric cycles (*tâls*) of Afghan folk and popular music. *Kerâwâ* is more commonly called *Geda* in Afghanistan.

[24] *Tablas and Drum Machines* – 15′ 28″ (Baily 2005).

He seems to have been generous in helping other musicians, giving out copies of the software he created for the various Afghan rhythms. 'Our music compared with [that of] other countries, we are a little behind in that way ... I want to help.' He handed out advice to customers who wanted to know how he achieved his sounds, and could sell them the necessary electronic modules to produce them.

From Eshpari's account it seems clear that utilizing the possibilities of the new technology was an exciting and creative activity. In the new format the central figure remained the solo singer, now playing keyboard rather than *'armonia*. The drum machine built into the keyboard provided rhythmic accompaniment. Despite the emphasis on the one-man-band concept, in live performance at a big event a *tabla* player would often be added, which potentially gave more rhythmic interest, and a symbolic contact with the Kabuli music of the past. The musical style had undergone some degree of westernization, with the introduction of simple harmonic principles borrowed from western music. For Eshpari, the harmonization of Afghan music came from the chord generator built into the keyboard he used. But some other young Afghan musicians came to understand something about chords and harmony by taking piano lessons, or showing Afghan songs to the music teacher at school to get help. They discovered that three or four chords were usually enough for the 'average' Afghan song.

Inevitably, young Afghans in Fremont received a lot of exposure to western poplar music. I met Eshpari's sister Maryam in the store and she told me that she was practising being a DJ. Asked what kind of music she liked she replied:

> My main interest is trance. I love trance music. A lot of people don't like it, either you like it or you hate it, 'cause if you like it you're in it forever, and if you hate it, it's because it's the kind of music that makes you want to let yourself go. A lot of people are afraid of that, to let themselves go, be in touch with your both sides music ... You can listen to trance music anywhere, it could be in the middle of 100 people or 200 people, and if you're listening to something it's just you and the music in your mind. It separates you from everybody and everything. It's a personal thing.[25]

A perceptive critique of the new music came from Dr Farid Younos:

> The music that's allowed in Islam, that should be nourishing the mind, not disturbing the mind. Within the Afghan community in Fremont there are some of the older generation who like Ustad Qassem, Ustad Natu, Sarahang and all that, because they grew up with that concept of music. And for the younger generation, of course, those singers are very boring. Why? First of all they don't know the language. Second, they don't have that poetic sense anymore ... . It's a cultural gap. It's the same thing with music, they just don't understand it.

---

[25] *Tablas and Drum Machines* – 14' 19" (Baily 2005). This interest in trance is possibly connected with a Sufi view of music.

So the music which is aligned with the western music, with a lot of high-pitched rhythm and dancing attitude and all that, they like that. So when we go to these weddings, it's a hidden atmosphere [there is an underlying tension], young people want to stand and dance and all that, and the older generation always complain that it's too loud ... because they grew up with the idea that music should nourish the mind, and they should not sit and talk but there should be some music to listen to. That's the problem between the young and the older generation ... . I prefer *tabla*, *rubâb*, that's our traditional music. If you want to preserve our cultural identity, all these keyboards and instruments, I'm not against them but it's not *ours* ... . [Regarding the songs of Faiz-e Karezi] They want to perform his songs with a modern instrument. It's not the same thing, it's not ... I don't know how to express it, but it's just not the same thing, it doesn't have the same rhythm, it doesn't have the same taste, doesn't have the same nourishing of my mind. Everything is lost because of the different instrument, because this instrument [*rubâb*] by its own components and structure, it's not just a piece of wood and some strings, there are some values in each of these strings. And those values are not transmitted with any other instrument than that one [the *rubâb*] ... that box with those strings ... the sound of it transmits a culture. (Interview 29 March 2000)

At a large *shirinikhori* (engagement party) I attended in Fremont, for something like 400 guests, the music was provided by Ramesh (vocal and keyboard) and Mustafa, a young *tabla* player. The *shinikhori* followed the usual sequence of events for such an occasion but I was very surprised by the dancing that occurred once the bride and groom, attended by several bridesmaids, had slowly processed into the large hall and taken their places on the bridegroom's throne (a massive sofa), surrounded by close family members. In front of them was a large dance space in which a great number of women and men, young and old, danced together. The men wore dark suits, the women their best evening dresses, while the younger women wore what looked like graduation gowns. Men and women danced together, but not holding each other, in small groups of two, three or four. The dancing was comparatively free in style, with lots of raised arm movements. A *shirinikhori* is considered to be primarily a women's party, and as such it was perfectly in order for women to dance, but for women and men to dance together in this way was for me quite unexpected. I had never seen anything like this in Herat, where such parties were strictly segregated. But in cosmopolitan Kabul it seems that mixed dancing at wedding celebrations was more common, at least amongst the middle and upper classes. As they danced, the singer Ramesh sang:

O girl, don't believe my words
Your ring is still in my pocket
I am very upset, come to me
Your lips are like sweeties
O God, you have to look at the face of the lover

Tell her about my sadness
(composer not known)[26]

I was also struck by a performance of the *attan*, the national dance, by a group of women at this *shirinikhori*. The dance was led by several older women, probably members of the bridegroom's family, followed by a number of young women, and finally a line of young girls who had yet to learn the intricacies of the dance. Their performance overall was sedate and uncomplicated, lacking the many pirouettes to the left and to the right characteristic of the dance when performed by men.[27]

A very different music and dance event took place at Pleasanton, an open-air showground some miles from Fremont, where the Afghans celebrated *Now Ruz* (Afghan New Year) on the occasion of the spring equinox. There was live music, with both traditional instruments (*rubâb*, *tabla* and *'armonia*) and keyboards playing together, and the sound was heavily amplified. A succession of singers took turns to perform. There were also a number of quizzes and games on stage, and a long series of jokes and stories from the comedian and actor Haji Kamran, whom we last met in Kabul leading the applause for President Taraki (Chapter 2).

The event was attended by a large number of family groups, mostly sitting on carpets or mats on the grass, with some older Afghans in deck chairs. Particularly striking were the many children dancing in front of the bandstand. The majority were girls dressed in brightly coloured traditional Afghan (Pashtun) dresses, pantaloons and headscarves, while the boys were in casual clothing. The children were dancing in a very free manner, but not just playing about to music. It was evident that some groups of girl friends had worked out dance routines together.[28] Their casual dress notwithstanding, mature girls and women did not dance at all; to do so would have been unseemly. The only adult dance was an *attan* performed by a group of men, two of them wearing traditional dress, with turbans, the others in casual clothing. As usual in performances of the *attan*, the dancers exhibited very different ways of doing the dance, expressing perhaps the Afghans' love of individuality in community.[29]

Naghma and Mangal Controversy

When I visited Fremont briefly in 1999 I had met Sher Ahmad, founder and head of International Immigrants Services. It was he who had originally sponsored Ustad Asif, and housed him in a room in his office block, where Asif ran his *tabla* course. Sher Ahmad was a great lover of music, and a believer in its power to bring people together. In a conversation with me, in English, he made the following statement, which I have quoted in several publications.

[26] *Tablas and Drum Machines* – 22' 31" (ibid.).
[27] *Tablas and Drum Machines* – 23' 58" (ibid.).
[28] *Tablas and Drum Machines* – 37' 27" (ibid.).
[29] *Tablas and Drum Machines* – 41' 30" (ibid.).

Music brings unity to the people, old and young together, and helps us not to lose our identity. We Afghans have some differences, but the concerts are the only times when we forget about everything, all people from different parts [of the country], different sects, different parts, we come and buy our tickets and go to the concerts. (Baily 1999: 12)

In 2000 Sher Ahmad sponsored a visit to Fremont by the well-known wife and husband duo Naghma and Mangal, along with their three accompanists, Mahmud Logari on *rubâb*, Toryali, *tabla* and his brother Morai, *tabla* and *doholak*. The visit was highly controversial, and for several reasons. First, Naghma and Mangal were mainly singers of Pashto songs, and this did not suit the Dari speaking section of the Afghan community in Fremont. Second, Naghma and Mangal had remained in Kabul for much of the communist era and were rumoured to have been PDPA members. They were said to have sung in support of the regime and to have been members of the Kabul police force, if only as members of the police band. Their imminent arrival in March 2000 divided the community and their concert at the Holiday House banqueting hall 'stirred up some of the rivalries and historic ethnic schisms that many Bay Area Afghans hoped to leave behind', as a local American-run newspaper put it.

A few days before the concert they were invited to play at a large house party in Fremont. Starting at 10.00pm they performed for several hours to an enthusiastic crowd of Afghans, who as is usual at such performances with professional musicians, presented *bakhshish* (donations of money) to the band. There was a lot of dancing, and when a donation was made the note was waved over the heads of the dancers, or simply brushed against them, before being placed on the floor before the band. The pile of money grew higher and higher, notes of all denominations, but I noticed quite a few $100 bills amongst them. They must have made several thousand dollars in this way before they came to an end at 2.30am. No doubt Naghma and Mangal took most of the money. The police arrived at one point to try to quieten the loud music, but it seemed to make little difference. Ustad Asif and I were rather put out, as we had also been expecting to play, but it was impossible to break off while the pile of money beckoned enthusiastic punters to continue with their generosity. The situation became acutely embarrassing for Asif, but after Naghma and Mangal had finished I persuaded him to play for half-an-hour. However, not much money was laid before us!

At the concert in the Holiday House banqueting hall (tickets $25 in advance, $30 on the door) the scene was much the same as at the party, with lots of dancing and lots of *bakhshish* for the band. It was attended by an enthusiastic Pashto speaking audience, while Dari speakers boycotted the event. In this case the attempt to bring together the community was thwarted because of differences between Pashtuns and Tajiks. As Farid Younos remarked, when we had discussed the topic of music and unity some time before the arrival of Naghma and Mangal, 'Music brings unity … if it's the right music.' Naghma and Mangal's was evidently not the right kind of music.

Chapter 5
Kabul after the Taliban

Two Towers and the Fall of the Taliban

Following their capture of Kabul in 1996 the Taliban were unable to consolidate their success by taking control of the whole of Afghanistan, despite the covert military assistance they 'allegedly' received from the ISI in Pakistan in terms of fighting men and munitions. The complicated narrative of advances and defeats, of shifting alliances and allegiances is far beyond the scope of my narrative; Michael Griffin's *Reaping the Whirlwind* (2001) has all the details and takes the story up to 2000, before the fall of the World Trade Center.

Three areas of the country proved particularly difficult for the Taliban to conquer. One was the city of Mazar-e Sharif, in the north, controlled by the Uzbek warlord General Dustam and his *Jowzjâni* militia, also known as the *gilemjam* (rug-stealers) 'because they looted everything that came to hand, including *gilems*, rugs' (Misdaq 2006: 162). In the 1980s the *Jowzjâni* had served as a communist militia, and after the fall of Najibullah became involved in the internecine battle for Kabul, during which they changed sides several times. The Taliban succeeded in taking Mazar on 24 May 1997, but were defeated several days later, with the loss of 2,500 of their men, plus as many civilian casualties again in an anti-Pashtun pogrom carried out by Hazaras (Griffin 2001: 174). Taliban forces returned a year later, capturing Mazar on 8 August 1998, and in revenge for their earlier losses launched a massacre of the Hazaras living in Mazar.[1]

A second area of difficulty for the Taliban was the Hazarajat Mountains of central Afghanistan, the homeland of the Hazaras. Of special importance here is the fact that the Hazaras are mostly Shia, while the Taliban are Sunni Pashtuns. There has been a long history of repression of the Hazaras from the time of Amir Abdur Rahman (late nineteenth century). Many Pashtuns had been relocated in the Hazarajat to exercise control, and there was long-standing enmity between the Hazaras and the Pashtun incomers. As in Mazar, the Taliban were eventually able to subdue the Hazarajat, again with great loss of life on both sides. The third area of conflict was the Panjshir and other regions in northeastern Afghanistan controlled by Ahmad Shah Massoud, whose forces were able to make repeated incursions into the very fertile Shomali area near Kabul.

---

[1]   In Chapter 18 of *The Rugmaker of Mazar-e-Sharif* (Mazari and Hillman 2008) Najaf Ali Mazari gives a graphic description of his own imprisonment by the Taliban, of being beaten day after day with whips fashioned from electric cables to confess to being involved in the uprising.

During the last years of President Najibullah's presidency there had been international plans to construct an oil and gas pipeline from newly independent Turkmenistan to the Pakistani coast through Afghanistan as a way of avoiding using Iranian territory for shipment of oil and gas. Planning continued during the Rabbani Coalition period (1992–96), but was held up by the fighting between the various *mujahideen* factions. As explained in Chapter 4, the arrival of the Taliban was initially greeted in the West as a possible end to the conflicts and chaos that marked the Rabbani presidency. The USA was particularly interested in the exploitation of Turkmenistan's gas and oil through pipelines avoiding Iran, and various consortia of oil companies emerged.[2] By 1998 the USA was ready to excuse the Taliban their women's rights policies, which were hardly more severe than those in Saudi Arabia. But before construction of the pipeline there had to be an internationally recognized government of Afghanistan, and that never came to pass.

But then the USA had another problem in the form of Osama bin Laden, the Islamist leader from a large and very wealthy Yemeni family settled in Saudi Arabia that had close links with the Saudi royal family. Bin Laden had studied economics and business administration, and perhaps also civil engineering, at university; his family's wealth came from the construction industry. He had become involved with supporting the Afghan *mujahideen* and in 1984 set up the Afghan Service Bureau in Peshawar to train Arabs coming from a variety of countries to fight in the *jihâd*. Griffin (ibid., p. 131) estimates there were between 14,000 and 25,000 'Afghan Arabs' involved in the war, strong supporters of the fundamentalist Wahhabi school of Islam. With the end of the last communist government of Najibullah, the Arabs in Afghanistan largely dispersed to fight insurrections in other parts of the world, including Kashmir and Chechnya.

Bin Laden returned to Saudi Arabia after the Soviet withdrawal. He frequently condemned the presence of US troops posted there in the build-up prior to the 1991 Gulf War, and their continued presence afterwards in the sacred land of Islam. His outspoken criticisms of the Saudis on this matter led to his banishment and in 1992 he moved on to Sudan. He was stripped of his Saudi citizenship in 1994 and returned to Afghanistan in 1996 on a private plane, at the end of the Rabbani period, to Jalalabad, not yet in Taliban hands. It is worth noting that the Afghans did *not* invite him to Afghanistan, though he was soon able to pick up links with his former *mujahideen* allies; he was an uninvited guest. With the gathering success of the Taliban he was able to develop his plans to establish the training camps that were going to be necessary to take on the West and its allies, including Saudi Arabia. On 23 February 1998 a CNN team visited bin Laden to televise an interview, in which he announced the formation of the World Islamic Front, or al-Qaida, and called on Muslims to 'kill the Americans and their allies – civilian and military' (ibid., p. 186). This could be construed as a declaration of war on the USA. His presence in Afghanistan was already becoming something of an

[2]   The Union Oil Company of California (UNOCAL) was one of the principal contenders for a contract.

embarrassment to the new Taliban government and they moved him to Kandahar in the hope of keeping a tighter rein on his activities.

On 7 August 1998 the US embassies in Nairobi and Dar-es-Salam suffered devastating suicide bomb attacks attributed to al-Qaida, with the death of 212 Kenyans, 11 Tanzanians and 12 Americans. The USA retaliated with ineffectual missile attacks on bin Laden's training camps in Afghanistan, and on a pharmaceutical factory in Sudan that the USA claimed, wrongly, was used for making chemical weapons. The USA demanded the removal of bin Laden from Afghanistan, demands that were rejected by the Taliban on the grounds that he was a guest and according to the custom of *melmastia* in the Pashtun code known as *pashtunwâli* it was their duty to protect him.[3] In deference to US demands the Taliban put him on trial accused of organizing the embassy bombings, and found him 'not guilty'. The suicide bombing of the US warship *USS Cole* on 12 October 2000 (ibid. p. 251) was the next stage in bin Laden's campaign against the Americans. The surrender of Osama bin Laden became the pre-condition for international recognition of the Taliban as the legitimate government of Afghanistan, which would have allowed them to take over Afghanistan's seat at the UN (still occupied by former President Rabbani), and to recover their various embassies around the world. For example, Ahmad Shah Massoud's brother Wali Massoud was still the ambassador in London.

Amidst all the gloom there was one glimmer of light relief. In November 2000, Kate Clark, the BBC's correspondent in Kabul, reported that although cinema, television and video were all banned in Afghanistan, the film *Titanic* was undergoing an extraordinary surge of popularity. Everybody in Kabul seemed, somehow, to have seen it, in some cases many times. Even the Taliban knew all about it. According to a joke current at the time, a mullah giving his Friday sermon to a crowded audience warned listeners that they were committing many sins. He told them, 'I know you are listening to music, you're hiring video players, you're watching films. You should be careful. You're all going to be damned and drown just like the people in the *Titanic* film!' Leonardo DiCaprio's haircut in the film, a form of Eton Crop known in Afghanistan as the 'Titanic haircut', became popular in Kabul and many barbers were punished for styling it. Clothes, rice, motor oil, handbags and other goods were sold with the Titanic logo. Expensive wedding cakes were baked in the shape of the Titanic, and the most extravagant added the iceberg as a supplement. The bazaar that had recently arisen on the bed of the dried up Kabul River in the centre of the city was dubbed the 'Titanic Bazaar'.

Various reasons could be suggested for the popularity of the film but it is surely relevant that the love story is in the classic Leyla and Majnun or Yusuf and Zulaikha mould. Perhaps at a deeper level, the ship was a symbol of an Afghanistan

---

[3]   In retrospect it seems a little contradictory for the Taliban, so keen to respect the principles of Wahhabism, to have mixed these up with tribal customs that had nothing to do with religion as such. But as an overwhelmingly Pashtun organization it was not possible for them to renounce their long-standing tribal values.

foundering on the iceberg of civil war; or perhaps the Afghans saw *Titanic* as a symbol of the Taliban, seemingly impregnable, but in the event unsound. VHS copies of *Titanic* were probably imported from Pakistan or Iran, dubbed in Urdu or Farsi. There is no suggestion that the film was favoured simply because it was made in the West. The Irish music in one scene of the film's soundtrack may well have been attractive to Afghan ears. Talking about the film allowed people to communicate their resistance to the Taliban state. *Titanic* was everywhere and symbolized dissent. But that window into sentiment was suggestive of current feelings, with no idea of the sooner than to be expected demise of the Taliban.

Two years after the final conquest of the Bamian Valley the two famous giant Buddhas carved into the cliff face were destroyed over a period of days in March 2001, by shellfire and, finally, implanted explosive charges. Mullah Mohammad Omar had given assurances some months earlier that the Buddhas and other parts of the Afghan pre-Islamic heritage would be preserved and protected, but something had led to a change of mind. Mullah Omar issued the following statement on 26 February 2001:

> [A]ll statues and non-Islamic shrines located in different parts of the Islamic Emirate of Afghanistan must be destroyed. These statues have been and remain shrines of unbelievers and these unbelievers continue to worship and respect them. ... all the statues must be destroyed so that no one can worship or respect them in the future. (quoted in Morgan 2012:15)

Morgan (ibid., pp. 20–26) assesses various theories about the motivation for this provocative act of desecration and concurs with the conclusion reached by others that it was due to pressure from al-Qaida. After the embassy bombings and the *USS Cole* attack, with increasing demands from the USA for the expulsion of bin Laden, or even his surrender to the USA, the relationship between the Taliban and Osama bin Laden became ever closer. The destruction of the Buddhas showed the extent to which the Taliban had fallen under the spell of Arab Wahhabism, a gradual trend that had been evident during the *jihâd* period, as noted by Robert Darr amongst others (Chapter 2). It is ironic that the Afghans, for all their pride in having repelled British and Soviet invasions since 1747, found that they had been taken over 'from within', by Arabs.

Having now gained control of Mazar and the Bamian Valley the Taliban were gradually closing in on Massoud, to the point where he held only 5 per cent of the territory of Afghanistan, in the Panjshir and Badakhshan. On 9 September 2001 Massoud was assassinated by suicide bombers posing as a television crew who had journeyed far and waited many days to be granted an interview with the redoubtable commander. The bomb was hidden either in the camera or in a battery belt worn by one of the crew. Massoud died a few hours later in the helicopter taking him for medical treatment. It is widely believed that the assassination was the opening move in the terrorist attacks in New York and Washington two days later, commemorated in the well-worn phrase 'Nine Eleven'. It seems likely that al-Qaida calculated that if the attacks in the USA were successful American retaliation would be inevitable and that Massoud would have a new role to play in fighting the Taliban–al-Qaida alliance with American military support.

Now the Americans had the justification they had been waiting for, to eliminate the Taliban and the terrorist training camps they harboured. The USA demanded the surrender of bin Laden; a demand rejected. The first bomb fell on Kabul on 7 October 2001. A Northern Alliance of anti-Taliban forces, drawn from the remnants of Massoud's army, now under the command of his former deputy, Mohammad Fahim, allied with Dostam and Hazara militias, approached from the north and entered Kabul five weeks later, on 13 November 2001, with BBC journalist John Simpson in the vanguard. The Taliban evacuated Kandahar a few days later, but they never formally surrendered.

Late in November the UN convened a conference in Bonn to establish a transitional government to replace the Taliban, with a *Loya Jirga*[4] to be held six months later to elect an interim President: a full-scale parliamentary election was planned for 2004. Thirty two Afghan delegates were present, with 11 seats for the Northern Alliance (Tajiks and Uzbeks, including several former *mujahideen* commanders), 11 seats for the Rome Group (representing the former King), five seats for the Cyprus Group (with links to Iran) and five seats for Pir Gailani and his followers (Steele 2011: 256). It was a mistake to exclude former PDPA ministers, and professional people who had either stayed in Afghanistan, or were in the diaspora, and no moderate Taliban were invited either. The Americans had already decided that Hamid Karzai was the man to take over as interim leader. He was not present at the conference, because he was involved with US Special Forces fighting the Taliban in Uruzgan Province, but he addressed the conference by satellite telephone.

Hamid Karzai is a Pashtun from a wealthy Kandahari family. He lived in exile in Pakistan during the *jihâd*, was a fund-raiser for Mujadidi's party but did not serve in a military capacity. During the Coalition period he was Deputy Foreign Minister for a short period. He opposed the Taliban and had good connections with the Northern Alliance and the monarchists, and he was seen as the best hope for creating national unity. There was considerable nervousness amongst the western allies about the consequences of the Northern Alliance taking Kabul, remembering the fate of the city when the *mujahideen* took control in 1992. On 20 December the UN Security Council authorized the creation of an International Security Assistance Force (ISAF), confined to Kabul. All Afghan forces were supposed to be withdrawn from Kabul, but Marshall Fahim did not conform to this requirement.

Steele (2011) gives a first-hand account of the *Loya Jirga* held in Kabul in June 2002. There were 1,050 delegates, including 210 women. A number of former *mujahideen* commanders took part, including warlords Ismail Khan and Rashid

---

[4]   The *Loya Jirga* was originally a Pashtun decision-making meeting, a large assembly brought together to consider important political matters. In more recent times such assemblies bring together people from different ethnic groups.

Dostam, whose presence was denounced by a number of delegates. At the start of proceedings many Pashtuns refused to stand for the national anthem, which they claimed was a Tajik song from the Panjshir Valley (ibid., p. 273), a good musical indicator of the sectarian issues that would underlie the difficulties of arriving at a consensus in decision taking. Karzai was elected as President, and in the general election of 2004 was re-elected, with an electoral turnout of 75 per cent.

Overall, the euphoria and optimism amongst most Afghans and westerners after the fall of the Taliban did not last long. Within two years it was apparent to Chris Johnson and Jolyon Leslie, both of whom had worked in Afghanistan through much of the Taliban era, that things were going wrong (Johnson and Leslie 2004). Disillusionment had set in. Many factors were responsible for this. President Karzai had very weak control over his cabinet, recruited largely from former commanders, many described as warlords. There was the failure to disarm former *mujahideen* in Kabul, with Defence Minister Fahim maintaining an army of 10,000 troops in the city. There was rampant corruption, no effective planning, and mistakes were made in the practice of combining aid with military presence. The Iraq War diverted the West from its commitment to Afghanistan and soon there were clear indications of Taliban resurgence.

Kabul 2002

> This is our beautiful homeland
> This is our lovely homeland
> This is our garden
> This is Afghanistan
> (Malang Jan)

Soon after the fall of the Taliban I proposed the creation of an Afghanistan Music Unit (AMU) at Goldsmiths, and this was agreed by my ever accommodating Pro-Warden for Research, Professor Jenks. After several years during which music was banned and musicians outlawed, there was an urgent need to see about rebuilding music culture in Afghanistan. The initial goals of AMU were twofold: to conduct research on the re-emergence of music in public life in Afghanistan, and to provide educational support in the rebuilding of Afghan music culture. AMU was officially launched on 8 February 2002 with a concert in Deptford Town Hall of Afghan, Uzbek, Iranian and Greek music by members of the Goldsmiths Ethnomusicology programme.

The first step was for me to go to Kabul to find out what was going on with respect to music, a visit funded by the British Academy's Committee for Central and Inner Asia. William Reeve, a BBC radio journalist who had been reporting from Afghanistan during the war, surviving an American bomb that hit the BBC's building in Kabul, gave invaluable advice about visiting the city. On 5 October 2002 I flew with Emirates to the sumptuous Dubai airport with its rows of fake palm trees and vast duty-free shopping mall. There I bought the mobile telephone that I had been told was an essential piece of kit in the new Afghanistan. After an uncomfortable night on an airport chair I experienced great difficulty in finding the unmarked Transit Desk E that William Reeve had told me I needed to go to. After an hour's wait, standing in line, we were loaded onto a bus to the very modest Terminal 2, on the other side of the airport, where the freight hangars were located. 'Typical Afghan stuff', I thought, 'everything done at the lowest cost possible'. The Ariana flight to Kabul was ramshackle. The aircraft seemed to have been seconded from Spain or Latin America, with all the notices in Spanish. Passengers were smoking and luggage was everywhere, blocking the aisles. But at least a sandwich and cup of tea was served for breakfast. As we came down over Kabul, we could see how the edges of the airfield were littered with wrecked aircraft, remnants of the war.

At the airport two lots of friends were waiting for my arrival: Ezat Mir, who had worked for me in my visit to Peshawar in 2000, now back in Kabul, and Dr Patricia Omidian, the medical anthropologist whose work in Fremont had been so helpful, and whom I had met in Islamabad in 2000. She was now Kabul director of the NGO American Friends Service Committee (AFSC), US Quakers, mainly concerned with children's education in Afghanistan, with a special commitment to setting up schools for girls after a period when they had been denied education. Dr Pat was the only non-Afghan working for the organization in Kabul, and she was a convert to Islam, so Quakerism at AFSC was evident only in spirit. I stayed a few nights at Ezat's house, and then moved into the AFSC building, a two-storey modern house in Kalula Pashta with offices, upstairs guest rooms and a large front garden filled with children's playground furniture awaiting shipment to their schools. Across the road was a cemetery on a steep hill covered with graves. It was a quiet and very agreeable place to stay.

Living in the building was AFSC's administrator, Aziz Yaqubi; his wife and children were still in Pakistan. Dr Pat lived in an apartment in Microrayan with an Afghan family she had adopted when they were in exile in Pakistan. Life at AFSC was austere, with an extremely monotonous diet. I developed quite a dislike for bread and over-cooked okra twice a day, but then AFSC did not employ a cook; food was prepared by Sultan, a charming middle-aged Hazara, who was one of two *chowkidars* (gatekeepers). Aziz was away much of the time, visiting AFSC schools in the south, and I was left alone in the house at night, when Sultan would lock me in. Only occasionally did this cause me some concern, wondering how I would get out in case of an emergency. I felt at liberty to walk the streets by myself and do lots of filming with my camcorder in public places, but usually I was in the company of Ezat Mir, now driving a 4×4 rather than a yellow taxi, and acting as my guide and guardian. He was proud to be from the Panjshir and had a photo of Ahmad Shah Massoud stuck to his windscreen to announce his allegiance to the Northern Alliance. There was a general feeling of optimism about Kabul. The Taliban were defeated and with western support Afghanistan could look forward to a bright future, and to getting back to where it had been in the 1970s, before the start of the long war.

One of the first things to strike the visitor to Kabul at that time, and later, was the heavy traffic on the roads. When I was in Kabul in the 1970s the amount of motor traffic had been small. Unlike Herat, there had been few *gâdi*s (the two-wheeler horse-drawn trap that served as a taxi in many Afghan cities), but the number of motor vehicles was limited. In 2002 Kabul was overrun with private cars, taxis, buses and trucks, with frequent traffic gridlock. There was complete anarchy and lawlessness on the roads. Few drivers held a driving licence, they had received no training, and passed no driving test. There were no operational traffic signals, and the directions given by traffic police at crucial junctions were often ignored. If there was too much traffic in one direction, drivers created a new lane on the other side of the road. The state of traffic was a good metaphor for Afghan society at that time – chaotic.

I took a *rubâb* with me to Kabul, thinking that it might be hard to find an instrument, and guessing that it would be an asset in my research. One of its frets had come loose and two days after my arrival I set out with Ezat in search of a *rubâbsâz* (*rubâb* maker). We were directed to a workshop in Shor Bazaar that turned out to be the business premises of Yusuf Qaderi, one of three instrument-making sons of the master-craftsman Joma Khan Qaderi, also known as Bacha Qader, who had made a *rubâb* for me in 1974. And who should live next door to Yusuf's workshop in a half-ruined house but my old friend Ghulam Hussain. He gave me direct access to the music scene in Kabul.

Profile: Ustad Ghulam Hussain (Rubâb Player)

Ghulam Hussain (Figure 5.1) comes from one of the hereditary musician families of the Kharabat. His father, Ghulam Hassan, and his uncle, Habibullah, were both *rubâb* players. Habibullah was a brilliant musician whom I had encountered several times in Herat in the 1970s, as a member of Ustad Rahim Bakhsh's band. There the *rubâb* was used very much as the main instrument to accompany Rahim Bakhsh's singing and sometimes to lead the ensemble. Ghulam Hussain himself is one of six musician brothers. I first met him in 1973, when I was newly arrived in Kabul, waiting for permission to do my research in Herat on the *dutâr*. I had been given a letter of introduction to Ustad Mohammad Omar written by a Herati journalist, Zia Haidari, whose father – remembered as Haidar Dandan (Haidar the Tooth) – had been a keen amateur *rubâb* player and student of Ustad Mohammad Omar's. For some weeks I had become a member of Ustad Mohammad Omar's *rubâb* class, held twice a week in his house in the Kucheh Kharabat. Ghulam Hussain was one of Ustad Mohammad Omar's 'official' students, in that he had been through the *gormâni* (string tying) ritual and was 'paying' for his apprenticeship by serving his *ustâd*. He likes to remind me that when I came for my *rubâb* lessons he used to bring the tea. This was the basis of our friendship. I was then aged 30 and he must have been about 13.

I met Ghulam Hussain during my visit to Peshawar in 1992 and again in 2000, where he had a music office in Khalil House, which he also ran as a small music

Figure 5.1   Ustad Ghulam Hussain, Kabul 2004

school, mainly for young musicians from the Kharabat then in exile. He was keen to be recognized as a member of the *Maktab-e Ustâd Mohammad Omar*, the 'School of Ustad Mohammad Omar', which he regarded as the only stylistic school of *rubâb* playing worthy of consideration. So now he was back in the Kharabat, after 10 years of exile in Pakistan, along with many other musicians from Kabul. Some of them were already rebuilding their houses. One day he and his friend Alim, an *'armonia* player, gave me a conducted tour of the ruins of the Kharabat, naming the musicians who had lived in each destroyed house, as shown in the film *A Kabul Music Diary* (Baily 2003). In due course we arrived at what remained of Ustad Mohammad Omar's house:

> This was Ustad Mohammad Omar's house. If you remember, this was the teaching room where you came for your lessons. Here's the entrance, there was a window here. There was another room upstairs, another room here. This was Ustad Mohammad Omar's house. There was a tree here in the courtyard. You came here many times for your lessons.[5]

---

[5]   *A Kabul Music Diary* – 3' 40" (Baily 2003).

Visiting the ruins of this once celebrated hub of musical activity was an emotional experience and brought back so many memories about the place where I first learned to play the *rubâb*. The teaching room, off the courtyard, was small but comfortable, with thin mattresses and lots of cushions. Photos on the wall included one of Lorraine Sakata from the University of Washington, who had studied with Mohammad Omar. I remember there were two very large *rubâbs*, which I came to recognize as excellent instruments, as one might expect in the house of such an *ustâd*. Being so large, they were also rather challenging to play. This was where Ustad Mohammad Omar had held his *rubâb* class for amateurs, most of whom were middle-class educated young men, university students, minor government officials, bank clerks, junior army officers. Students from the hereditary musician families of the Kharabat, like Ghulam Hussain, received a different kind of training. They were exposed to music in their homes from infancy and learned a lot from observing the teaching of the amateurs. As we came to the end of our tour of what remained of the Kharabat, standing by the ruins of Mohammad Omar's house, Ghulam Hussain continued:

> Asif Jan [Ustad Asif Mahmoud] knew it [this house] well; he used to come to pay his respect to his elders. We honour Asif Jan now that he's become one of the elders. From that generation only Haji Hamahang is still here in Kabul. We must honour our elders, like Ustad Asif and Ustad Arif, Eltaf Hussain and Olfat Ahang who came originally from here.[6] And now we're getting older, we must be respected and honoured. Look what's happened to this place of the elders.[7]

Ghulam Hussain has helped me in many ways and became my main contact with musicians in Kabul over the next few years. He has shown me many things on the *rubâb*, including one of Ustad Mohammad Omar's most famous compositions, the *naghma-ye klâsik* in *Râg Âhir Beiru*, in *Jap Tâl* (a metrical cycle of 10 *matra*s). As recounted later, he was one of four *ustâd*s appointed to teach in the Aga Khan Music School in 2003, and in 2010 he became the *rubâb* teacher in the Afghanistan National Institute of Music. He has become the most senior *rubâb* player in Kabul and has given a number of concerts abroad, mainly in the UK and Germany. In 2012 he was one of three musicians who played in the Dari translation of Shakespeare's *Comedy of Errors* in the Globe Theatre in London, as part of the Cultural Olympiad Globe to Globe Festival.

Music in Kabul Ten Months after the Fall of the Taliban

My main objectives in Kabul were to conduct research on the re-emergence of music in public life in Afghanistan, and to see how to provide educational support

---

[6]   Eltaf Hussain and Olfat Ahang are classical singrs from the Kharabat now living in Canada.

[7]   *A Kabul Music Diary* – 6′ 14″ (ibid.).

in the rebuilding of Afghan music culture. What struck me immediately was the resurgence of musical life. There was a plethora of new music shops and music offices in areas near where the musicians had formerly been based, in Sang Taroshi and Shor Bazar. Jan Mohammad's music shop in Sang Taroshi, for example, was full of *tabla*s and *'armonia*s recently imported from Pakistan. Many musicians were now too poor to afford to buy their own instruments and had to hire them from a music shop if they were fortunate enough to be booked for an engagement such as a wedding party or *mehmâni*. Three brothers from the Qaderi family ran three separate instrument-making businesses, making and repairing mainly *rubâb*s but also other stringed instruments such as *tanbur*s and *dutâr*s. Khair Khana, a suburb of Kabul, was another area with lots of music businesses, with a long row of small music offices, with large painted shop signs depicting musical instruments, eastern and western.[8] Nearby, there were banqueting halls for holding wedding parties. In addition, there were numerous shops and street vendors selling recordings, in the form of audiocassettes, CDs, VHS cassettes, VCDs and DVDs, mostly imported from Pakistan. Some were recent recordings, some from the past. There were also many pirated copies of CDs and DVDs recorded by Afghans in the diaspora, especially the USA and Germany.

The radio station in Kabul had been renamed the Voice of Shari'at Radio by the Taliban, and the television studios had been closed, though the television equipment had not been destroyed. Perhaps the Taliban thought they could sell it, or believed that television could be used in the future, as long as it did not show living creatures, especially human beings. I found that RTA had been restored, but it was a pale imitation of its former self. Not much music was broadcast, and none by women performers. The radio station occupied two sites, the original buildings of Radio Kabul, near the old city, by the road bridge over the Kabul River, and the 1960s' building in Ansari Wat, in the suburbs. RTA employed about 30 musicians, and they were housed in the old building, under the direction of the singer Aziz Ghaznawi, who had been forced to sing Taliban *tarâna*s on the radio (see Chapter 4). They received a small monthly salary, and were expected to attend each morning to sign on and rehearse, which they did in a vast and draughty studio, with no electric power and no lighting.[9] Most of the music that was broadcast by RTA came from the audio and video archives; there seemed to be very little by way of recording new songs. Not only were there completely inadequate facilities for composing and rehearsing new material, there seemed to be nowhere for it to be performed. The musicians employed by the radio station actually earned their living from playing at weddings and private parties. NGOs and the UN were important patrons at this time, hiring musicians to play at their social functions.

The fate of the RTA music archive under the Taliban had been a matter of much speculation. Had it been destroyed, like the Bamiyan Buddhas? BBC correspondent

---

[8]   *A Kabul Music Diary* – 16′ 55″ (ibid.).
[9]   *A Kabul Music Diary* – 21′ 22″ (ibid.).

William Reeve visited the radio station soon after the withdrawal of Taliban forces and discovered the archive to be intact. There he met Mohammad Sidiq, one of the custodians of the archive, known to his colleagues as Mr Computer on account of his detailed knowledge of the catalogue (that had been set up by Madadi in the 1960s). In a piece he broadcast on *From Our Own Correspondent* (BBC Radio 4, 16 May 2002) William Reeve explained that he asked Mr Computer, 'How on earth did you save all these tapes from the Taliban?' Mohammad Sidiq explained he had removed all the markings from each box, covered the shelves with blankets, and firmly but very discreetly bolted all the doors. When the Taliban arrived in Kabul they had indeed destroyed what they thought was the archive – one unlocked room with shelves of Iranian and Indian popular music. Mohammad Sidiq and his colleagues simply pretended the Afghan music archive did not exist. It was a nice story but surely not the whole truth. It is clear that senior Taliban management at Voice of Shari'at Radio must have known that the music archive was there, and wished to conserve it. It seems very unlikely that a large space in the building should have been presumed not to exist. There was a symbolic destruction of tapes of Iranian popular music and Indian film music, things that could be replaced. This display was as much for the satisfaction of the Taliban foot soldiers as a gesture for the general public.

When I went to Kabul in October 2002 I knew that I had to gain access to the RTA sound archive. At Radio Afghanistan I was taken to meet Engineer Ashmatullah Atta, who knew all about the complicated history of the various radio transmitters operating at various strengths and on several wavebands. He had received some training in the UK and spoke excellent English. He told me that he had been in Kabul throughout the Taliban period. The American bombing had destroyed the transmitters, positioned on top of Kabul's mountain, and RTA was currently operating with some temporary equipment that reached only the Kabul area. He authorized the issue of a permit for me to come and go at my convenience. I found the people in the radio tape archive very helpful, and Mohammad Sidiq showed me the archive itself, a large room for the main radio archive, and a smaller separate room for the music archive.[10] In yet another room was the Taliban archive, with tapes of Taliban speeches, sermons, *na't*s and *tarâna*s. I asked whether they were going to keep this archive. 'Certainly', he replied, 'it is part of our history.'

When I visited Kabul University I found it had reinstated the Music Department within the Faculty of Fine Arts, which taught what it termed *gharbi* 'western' and *sharqi* 'eastern' music. 'Western' music consisted of harmonized Afghan melodies, with the use of western notation. The Music Department had plenty of second-hand western musical instruments, donated by well-wishers in the UK.[11] In 2002 the

---

[10]   *A Kabul Music Diary* – 19' 33" (ibid.).

[11]   I have to mention the contribution of Sue Paterson, who having heard about the need for musical instruments on the BBC World Service collected together a large number of donated instruments and somehow got them shipped to Kabul. *A Kabul Music Diary* – 34' 05" (ibid.).

main instruments of use to the University were a two-manual electric organ with foot pedals, and a Casio keyboard, for these were instruments that Islamuddin, the lecturer in western music, knew how to play. There was an urgent need to find teachers for the other western instruments, many of which had been used in the past in Afghanistan, in radio ensembles and military bands. By 'eastern' music was meant North Indian classical music. Here the situation was quite different. The Department had an excellent teacher of Indian and Afghan music in Ehsan Irfan, who had studied the *sitâr* in Kabul in the 1980s with Ustad Irfan Khan, who spent several years in Kabul with the Indian Cultural Centre. Ehsan taught *sitâr*, *'armonia* and *rubâb*, using the Indian *sargam* system of notation.[12] There was also a *tabla* teacher. The two of them were handicapped by having very few instruments at their disposal, and those they had were old and in need of repair.

I visited the Ministry for Information and Culture and found that it ran its own Directorate for Music Training, which seemed rather more active than RTA, run by the same Ministry. It hosted four music ensembles: a regional group from Logar Province, a Sufi music group, a mixed eastern–western group, and an Afghan pop music group. My stay in Kabul coincided with the Goethe Institute in Germany sending the electro-rock group Ata Tak from Dusseldorf to Kabul for six weeks. They brought with them sophisticated hard drive recording equipment, a less sophisticated four track recorder, new electric and bass guitars, amplifiers and a PA system. They spent their time in Kabul training young Afghans in the use of the recording equipment, and in performance techniques. There was no doubt that there was a tremendous interest on the part of some young Afghans in modern western popular music.

During my visit Ata Tak gave a concert in the Kabul University Auditorium, which seats 500. Two of the members performed live electronics on laptops, the third member, a young woman, played western drum kit. The venue was completely full, with many people standing at the back. They looked bemused by the sight and sound of the Ata Tak programme. The German group was followed by the Afghan pop group attached to the Ministry for Information and Culture's Directorate for Music Training, using some of the western instruments brought to Kabul. This group consisted of singer, electric keyboard, electric bass and drum kit. Their set was much better received than that of Ata Tak. And the best applauded item was the famous song of Awal Mir *Da zemu zibâ watan*, 'This is my lovely country', a song that is the unofficial national anthem of Afghanistan.[13]

This is our beautiful homeland
This is our lovely homeland
This is our garden
This is Afghanistan

---

[12] *A Kabul Music Diary* – 36′ 31″ (ibid.).
[13] This concert is shown in *A Kabul Music Diary* – 44′ 23″ (ibid.).

This country is our body
This country is our faith
Our young children say
'This is our beautiful country'
This is the land of our parents
This is the land of our grandparents
It's very dear to us
This is Afghanistan

This is our beautiful homeland
This is our lovely homeland
This is our garden
This is Afghanistan

The visit of Ata Tak had another interesting outcome in Kabul, as reported in the *Saudi Gazette* (4 August 2003). Three girls working in the Directorate for Music Training wanted to be given a chance to be involved, and were encouraged to rehearse their own song behind locked doors, with vocal, electric bass and drum kit. They called themselves The Burqa Band. Concealed beneath blue *burqa*s, a performance of their song, lyrics in English, was videoed secretly in the Directorate by Ata Tak. With additional shots of three *burqa* clad figures outside (presumably not the three girls themselves) and added sound, Ata Tak created a cleverly crafted video which was placed on YouTube and made the song *Burqa Blue* something of a hit in Germany.[14]

My mother wears a burqa
My father does it too
I have to wear a burqa
The burqa it is blue

The sky over Kabul is also very blue
The blue is from the burqa
Burqa burqa blue

Blue blue burqa blue

My grandma wears a burqa,
My grandpa wears it too
I won't reject [take off] this burqa
But only just for you [For anyone but you]

Blue blue burqa blue

---

[14]   See http://www.youtube.com/watch?v=x_Y-sw89qTY.

We all now wear a burqa
You don't know who is who
If you want to meet your sister
It can be your uncle too

Blue blue burqa blue

You give me all your love
You give me all your kisses
And then you touch my burqa
And do not know who is it

Blue blue burqa blue

My mother wears blue jeans
And I am so surprised
The things are changing faster
I don't know if it's right

Blue blue burqa blue

Not wanting to compromise themselves further, The Burqa Band did not repeat the experiment and their identities were never revealed. In this they followed the example of radio singers adopting aliases, and they escaped the public opprobrium later heaped upon the Herati singer Setara after her slightly risqué performance in the penultimate round of the television show of *Setâra-ye Afghân* (Afghan Star), as discussed below.

Over the next few years several of Afghanistan's super-stars of popular music in the diaspora visited Afghanistan to give large-scale concerts. Amongst the first of these visitors was Farhad Darya, who recorded with local musicians in several parts of the country, leading to the very popular CD and DVD *Salaam Afghanistan*. His concert in Kabul on 14 May 2004 was held in the football stadium to an unprecedented crowd estimated at 45,000. Farhad Darya later described the event to Simon Broughton:

It was like a national day in Kabul. In the stadium I felt like a cloud flying over the sky of the crowd. What was amazing was the presence of women. Men and women were sitting next to each other for a concert right where they had seen their beloved ones executed. Many of them were dancing and crying. It looked like they had forgotten the misery and pain of the past decades. Even the 700 armed security guys started to dance to the music and enjoy the new wave of hope. I wanted a fresh start in Afghanistan with music and we did it! (Broughton 2008)

I had plenty of opportunities to play the *rubâb* during this visit to Kabul, accompanied by Ustad Asif's nephew Daud Salih on *tabla*. We played at RTA, at a charity concert in the art and carpet gallery of Coordination of Humanitarian Assistance and in the Chishti Sufi *khânaqâh* that had been so much the resort of musicians from the Kucheh Kharabat. We also played at various private parties. Polly Toynbee, sent by *The Guardian* to make an extensive report on whether the war on Afghanistan had been 'worth it' wrote: 'Things here are often not what they seem. At a party of Afghan returners [sic] in an old Soviet-era concrete flat one night, a man in full Afghan rig was playing the rebob – a kind of Afghan sitar. Was he a musician returning after the Taliban music ban? No, he was Dr John Baily, reader in ethnomusicology from Goldsmiths College' (Toynbee 2002). Well, she was not so far off the mark; in a way I was a returning musician.

The highlight of my experiences of *rubâb* playing during this visit to Kabul was to entertain the elderly Zahir Shah, the last of the music-loving Amirs, and his family in the royal palace. I had chanced to meet his daughter Princess Maryam in Chicken Street, still well known for its Afghan handicraft shops, several days earlier. She was looking for antique jewellery, discretely accompanied by two security men who I took to be ordinary citizens until she pointed them out when I asked about her security. Maryam Jan lives in London and had returned to Kabul when her father came back from his long sojourn in Italy. I told her I would love to play for her father, the King, and she arranged it. It was a Thursday night, *shab-e joma*, traditionally an evening for music making, the eve of *joma* (Friday), the day for congregational prayer. Ezat Mir drove Daud Salhi and me to the Arg, the royal palace, where Daud Khan (Zahir Shah's first cousin and brother-in-law) and his family were massacred in 1978 by Taraki's supporters in the army and air force.

The Arg is set in spacious grounds, adorned by some ancient and carefully preserved trees. We passed through four checkpoints, the last in the Arg itself, where we were checked by an American soldier, gun in hand. The occasion itself was very informal. We were shown to a large drawing room, with armchairs and sofas. Maryam and her niece came to personally rearrange the seating and set up a *takht* for us to sit on while playing. Daud and I got in tune. Other members of the extended royal family and their guests drifted in, several with camcorders. Zahir Shah arrived and sat in an armchair facing us. We played extensive compositions in *Yeman*, *Bhupali* and, at Zahir Shah's request, *Bihâg*. Daud and I were called to meet Zahir Shah, and were awarded bronze medallions, bearing his portrait on one side and his seal on the reverse.

After playing we went to eat with the royal family and their guests in an adjoining room. This was not a very elaborate meal, served by two waiters. The chilled Coca Cola cans on the dining table added to the sense of informality. After dinner it was the turn of an acclaimed Afghan boy of about 12 singing classical music accompanied by *tabla*, *delrubâ* and a member of the royal family on *rubâb*. I was told that Zahir Shah himself had had *rubâb* lessons from Ustad Mohammad Omar. Daud, Ezat Mir and I had to leave the party at around 11.30pm in order to get home before the nightly curfew. The other musicians presumably stayed overnight, probably sleeping on those comfortable sofas.

The Continuing Censorship of Music

During the war of 2001 that led to the defeat of the Taliban, spontaneous outbursts of music greeted the liberation of the towns and cities. Music in Afghanistan has for long been associated with joyous occasions, such as wedding festivities and the country fairs held over a period of 40 days in the spring. For most people, the end of Taliban control was the occasion for rejoicing and for music making, whether by playing cassettes loudly in the streets or by playing musical instruments. The very sound of music became a symbol, even a signal, of freedom. Once music was heard coming from a local radio station, people knew that the Taliban had lost control over that area. The sound of music heralded a return to (comparative) normality, for the chronic absence of music is symptomatic of a dysfunctional society. Madadi was keen to tell me later that his song *Watan* (see Chapter 3) was the first piece of music to be broadcast in Kabul by the radio station after the fall of the Taliban.

However, heavy censorship of music continued during the post-Taliban period. For a while there was a complete ban on women singing on state-run radio and television, or on the stage or concert platform. Women could announce, read the news, recite poetry and act in plays, but they could not sing and they certainly could not dance. This ban was the subject of intense argument within the radio and television organization, under the control of the Ministry of Information and Culture. The explanation offered for the ban was that to do otherwise would give the government's fundamentalist enemies an easy excuse to stir up trouble. In the case of television, further reasons given were that there were no competent women singers left in Kabul, and that the tapes in the video archive (dating from the communist period) showed women wearing clothes that would now be considered too revealing. This last excuse obviously did not apply to women singing on radio. Another reason – that it would place the women in danger of attack – could not be accepted either, since most of the music broadcast was from the RTA archive. The danger of attack was offered to explain why women were not allowed to sing at a live-broadcast concert in Kabul on 15 December 2002 to celebrate the 70th anniversary of the BBC World Service.

If there was some censorship of music in Kabul, protected and patrolled by the International Security Assistance Force (ISAF), outside the capital much tighter restrictions were imposed by local fundamentalist commanders. The lengthy Human Rights Watch report '"Killing You is a Very Easy Thing For Us": Human Rights Abuses in Southeast Afghanistan', published in July 2003, catalogued a string of abuses, including attacks on musicians in areas close to Kabul. Paghman, located in the foothills of the Hindu Kush and once a royal resort, had a particularly poor record under the governorship of Zabit Musa, a prominent member of the powerful

Ittehâd-e Islâmi party led by Abdur Rasul Sayyaf. In a village near Paghman two musicians were killed when hand grenades were thrown at a wedding party. Whilst it is not certain that this attack was specifically anti-music in motivation, it seems likely. One of the musicians, a well-known and respected *doholak* (drum) player, Abdul Paghmani, might well have been deliberately targeted.

A resident of Paghman described a visit by Zabit Musa and his gunmen to the local bazaar:

> I was there – I saw the whole thing. It was morning ... He had three or four soldiers with him. When he got to the bazaar, he went towards some shopkeepers who were listening to tape recorders, to music, and he grabbed them and pulled them out of their shops. He yelled at them: 'Why do you listen to this music and with the volume so high?' A shopkeeper said, 'Well, it is not the time of the Taliban. It is our right to listen to music!' But the governor got angry and he said, 'Well, the Taliban is not here, but Islam is here. Shariat [Islamic law] is here. We have fought for Islam – this fight was for Islam. We are mujahid. We are Islam. We did jihad to uphold the flags of Islam'. And then he took them out of their shops and started beating them with his own hands. He beat up two people himself, along with his troops, slapping them, kicking them. And the others were beaten just by the soldiers. Then they closed the shops, locked them. Many people were there. It was not the first time these sorts of things had happened. (Human Rights Watch 2003: 67–8)

Another example recounted by Human Rights Watch came from a wedding in Lachikhel, a village in Paghman district, when soldiers arrived at midnight to break up a wedding party:

> They beat up the musicians, who had come from Kabul. They made them lie down, and put their noses on the ground, and swear that they would not come back to Paghman to play music. Then they destroyed their instruments. (ibid., p. 68)

Not surprisingly, musicians from Kabul became very wary about where they would go to play and for whom; they had to feel adequately protected. Such precise information as that provided by Human Rights Watch for southeast Afghanistan was not available for other parts of the country, but it is clear that the situation varied greatly from place to place. Ironically, at that time the one city where women were able to perform on local radio and television was Kandahar, formerly a Taliban stronghold, the reason being that the Governor of Kandahar, Gul Agha Sherzai, was himself a great music lover.

By 2004 things were changing. On 12 January 2004, a few days after the ratification of the new constitution for Afghanistan by a *Loya Jirga* (National Assembly), RTA broadcast old video footage of female singers Parasto and Salma (Reuters, 13 January 2004). Explaining the reasons for this dramatic break with the recent past, the Minister for Information and Culture Sayed Makdoom Raheen told Reuters, 'We are endeavouring to perform our artistic works regardless of the issue of sex.' However, the action provoked an immediate backlash from the Supreme Court. On the same day Deputy Chief Justice Fazl Ahmad Manawi told Reuters that the Supreme Court was 'opposed to women singing and dancing as a whole' and added 'This is totally against the decisions of the Supreme Court and it has to be stopped' (*Saudi Gazette*, 16 January 2004). On 23 January, the press agency AFP reported that Ismail Khan, the Governor of Herat, supported the Supreme Court's judgement and had banned the sale of audio and videotapes featuring women singers in Herat. Despite these statements, however, the radio and television persisted with the new policy (Graham 2004: 34).

In the post-Taliban era a number of independent radio and television stations were established, usually financed by outside agencies, such as Voice of America. The most significant of these was *Tolo TV* (Sunrise TV), a commercial television station operated by the MOBY group, an Afghan-Australian owned company operating from Dubai, launched in 2004. By 2007 it had extended its coverage from Kabul to many cities in Afghanistan via satellite. From the outset it had a strong emphasis on programmes for young people and quickly established itself as a controversial institution, challenging the values of *mujahideen* ideology in Afghanistan. The most extreme example of *Tolo* confronting traditional Afghan values concerns the female presenter Shaima Rezayee, a young woman who presented the daily television show *Hop*, targeted at a young Afghan audience. Shaima Rezayee was known for appearing on *Tolo TV* in western dress, wearing make-up, and sometimes with no scarf covering her head. Her show was condemned by the clerics. For example, Fazl Hadi Shinwari, a chief justice of the Afghan Supreme Court declared:

> It [*Hop*] will corrupt our society, culture and most importantly, it will take our people away from Islam and destroy our country … . This will make our people accept another culture, and make our country a laughing stock around the world.[15]

Under this kind of pressure, Shaima was laid off by *Tolo* in 2005. Two months later (18 May 2005) she was shot dead at home. Her two brothers were arrested as suspects. The usual explanation is that this was an honour killing: through her work as a presenter on *Tolo* Shaima had brought dishonour and shame to her family. *Tolo TV* seemed to thrive on these controversies. Another case concerned Shaima's colleague Shakeb Issar, who had to flee for his life after presenting footage of western female singers. He was granted political asylum in Sweden, and became *Tolo TV*'s Europe entertainment correspondent.

Probably *Tolo TV*'s most successful show was *Setâra-ye Afghân* (*Afghan Star*), a singing competition based on the *Pop Idol* format. The first time the competition took place was in 2005, with auditions, then a series of eliminatory rounds with

---

[15] See http://en.wikipedia.org/wiki/Shaima_Rezayee.

live accompaniment, with the audience voting by text messages from their mobile telephones. The third season (2007) was the subject of the award winning documentary film *Afghan Star* and proved to be particularly controversial. In one of the earlier rounds the woman singer Setara from Herat performed rather too freely for Afghan public opinion. At the start of her final song she very obviously danced on stage. Backstage, *Tolo* employees watching the programme on a monitor were horrified, 'Oh my God. Why are you dancing?' one of them exclaims. Furthermore, while her head was covered with a large headscarf at the beginning of this song, it slowly fell back as she sang, coming to rest on her shoulders, leaving her face and hair completely exposed to view.

Men interviewed in the bazaars of Herat described Setara as a 'loose woman' who had brought shame on the Herati people and deserved to be killed. Setara was evicted by her landlord from her apartment in Kabul and returned to Herat, to the consternation of her family, who feared for her life. The eventual winner of the third series of *Afghan Star* was Rafi Naabzada, from Mazar. Two other finalists were the Hazara Hamid, and Lema Sahar, a woman from Kandahar. She also received death threats for taking part. It is claimed that 11 million Afghans, a third of the population, watched the final round of *Afghan Star*.

The Aga Khan Music School 2003–06

On my return from Kabul in 2002 I edited the film *A Kabul Music Diary* (Baily 2003) from video I had shot during my visit. I also wrote a report on my findings for The British Academy's Committee for Central and Inner Asia, the organization that had funded my visit. This unpublished report made a number of recommendations to help restore a normal life of music in Afghanistan and to recreate a culture in which people had the freedom to make music. As we have seen, this was something they had enjoyed to a considerable degree in the past, when live music was a common occurrence at wedding festivities, concerts and private parties, a time when music flourished on radio and television, and shops and street vendors were free to sell cassettes and music videos. My recommendations dealt with, amongst other things: the consolidation of audio music archives at the radio station, the collection of oral history from musicians living in the Kucheh Kharabat, the re-establishment of music education, and bringing back musicians from abroad for concerts and to teach. It was apparent to me that in the post-Taliban period the rapid reappearance of popular music, particularly using modern electronic instruments such as keyboards, showed that that kind of music hardly required outside support beyond the provision of musical instruments. On the other hand, the art music of Kabul, especially the style of performing classical *ghazal*s in Persian and Pashto that had developed in the court of the Amirs of Kabul from the late nineteenth century, was certainly in a fragile state and required some positive intervention.

I sent a copy of my report to the Aga Khan Trust for Culture (AKTC), with whom I had already had some contact, having attended a meeting in Geneva with other ethnomusicologists to discuss a possible Central Asian CD series. AKTC liked my report and I was summoned to Geneva to meet with Fairouz Nishanova and Luis Monreal. They also liked *A Kabul Music Diary* and I was invited to serve as a part-time consultant to the Aga Khan Music Initiative in Central Asia (AKMICA). This was a new role for me and one that allowed little scope for original research. I made a preliminary visit to Kabul for AKMICA in July 2003, with three main objectives: (1) to set up a Tradition Bearers Programme similar to one established by Jean During in Tajikistan; (2) to explore the possibilities of digitizing the RTA music sound archive; (3) to arrange for the reprinting of Madadi's book *Sar-guzasht Musiqi Mu'âsir Afghânistân* (*The Story of Contemporary Music in Afghanistan*) (1996) that had been published in Tehran and was out of print. It was only possible to implement the first of these projects, as discussed below.

The strategy of the AKMICA Tradition Bearers Programme was to identify a small number of master musicians as teachers of Kabuli art music, that is, the art of *ghazal* singing, accompanied by *rubâb* and *tabla*, set up a teaching space, and find students, who would be paid a small stipend intended to cover the costs of attending the classes, travel and perhaps loss of income.

In 2003 I travelled to Kabul at the end of July for 10 days. Ezat Mir met me at the airport; I had arranged to hire him again as my driver, and settled back in AFSC. Kabul seemed much the same as it had the year before. I made several visits to the musicians in Shor Bazaar. Ghulam Hussain was busy with rebuilding the house he and his family occupied in the Shor Bazaar, close to the Kharabat, and he had rented a small shop next door that he used for teaching purposes, holding a regular early-morning *rubâb* class. Regarding the reprinting of Madadi's book I contacted Mohammad Rais, the bookseller of Kabul, later made infamous by Norwegian journalist Åsne Seierstad, and the Saba Printing Press. From the latter I got an estimate for the cost of the reprint. However, there were issues about the copyright for Madadi's book that discouraged AKTC from going ahead with the reprint. I visited the music archive at RTA twice to find out more about the tape catalogue but realized that the people there were becoming anxious about my lack of a valid permit. I tried without success to get permission to work in the archive from the Ministry of Information and Culture. In any case, I discovered that there was a French proposal to digitize the music sound archive, and the Head of AKDN in Kabul did not want to undermine this initiative.[16]

On a more positive note, I was impressed by the newly established Foundation for Culture and Civil Society (FCCS), located in two attractive old houses with their gardens, conveniently close to the centre of Kabul. FCCS had been established in March 2003 by a group of Afghans concerned with the fate of Afghan culture and the need to strengthen Afghan civil society. The Foundation worked in areas of culture, research, civil society and human rights. Timur Shah

---

[16] The archive was digitized some years later with the help of Lorraine Sakata, who organized a programme at Indiana University in the USA to train RTA staff to digitize the recordings themselves (Sakata 2013: 123–5).

Hakimyar, Head of the Artists' Union and a filmmaker was (and remains) Director of FCCS's Cultural Centre. By the time I got there it had organized a play, concerts, poetry readings, a photo exhibition and a film screening, and was showing a keen interest in promoting music. On 2 August 2003 FCCS put on a concert in their garden of Kabul art music performed by a large group of musicians from the Kharabat: Bashir Olfat, vocal and *'armonia*, Salim Sheydai, vocal and *'armonia*, Alem-e Shauqi, vocal and *tanbur*, Ghulam Hussain, *rubâb*, Wali Nabizada, *tabla*, Amruddin, *delrubâ*, Sharif, *doholak*, and Qand Agha, *'armonia*. I was asked to give an introductory talk, in English, for the mainly non-Afghan audience and to introduce the members of the band. This was my first opportunity to see who was available in Kabul, and I felt encouraged about the prospects for the AKMICA Tradition Bearers Programme. I decided to investigate hiring a room in this oasis of cultural activity to start the Programme, and this proposal was accepted, with some reluctance, by Geneva, who would have preferred to have their own building rather than share with another organization.

The first step was to recruit the teachers. I appointed Ustad Ghulam Hussain as the *rubâb* teacher, and Ustad Wali Nabizada as the *tabla* teacher. Wali was from a famous family of musicians in the Kharabat and I had close links with him, for his father, Ustad Nabi Gol, had been the teacher of Amir Jan Khushnawaz in Herat in the 1930s, and many of the compositions I learned from Amir Jan (Baily 1997b) derived from Nabi Gol. I had last seen Wali three years earlier in Khalil House, Peshawar. For vocal teaching I had in mind Qassem Bakhsh, who had been amongst that wave of Kabuli musicians seeking refuge in Peshawar in 1991 (see Chapter 3). He was a student of Ustad Rahim Bakhsh, was a very good *ghazal* singer, and had an agreeable warm personality. However, when I approached him he told me that he was soon going back to Peshawar for the winter months, where his family was still based. Like many Afghans at that time who had returned to Kabul to see what life there would be like, he had maintained his base outside the country. So I approached somebody I hardly knew, Ustad Salim Bakhsh, a son of Ustad Rahim Bakhsh, and he agreed to join the team. The three *ustâd*s insisted that the *delrubâ* player Ustad Amruddin should also be appointed, arguing that the *delrubâ* was an essential part of the Kharabat sound.

In October I returned to Kabul to continue my work for AKMICA and get the Tradition Bearer's Programme started. Time was short because I also had to arrange for Ghulam Hussain and the singer and *tanbur* player Alem-e Shauqi to go to Paris for two AKMICA concerts in the Odéon Théâtre, and to convey the musicians there. The concerts also featured groups from Tajikistan, Uzbekistan, the Kyrgyrz Republic and Iran and were attended by His Highness Prince Shah Karim Al Hussaini, The Aga Khan, whom I had the honour of meeting (for the first time). Before leaving for Paris I arranged to hire a room at FCCS. It had the disadvantage that it was close to a large and noisy generator used when the main electricity supply failed. I was assured this was only needed occasionally and that FCCS was soon to have the luxury of 24-hour electricity. I bought a large factory-made carpet, cushions, two sets of *tabla*, two *'armonia*s and two *rubâb*s for teaching. No *delrubâ*s for Ustad Amruddin could be found, but he had two instruments of his own. A young Iranian woman married to an Austrian, Roja Affolter, was hired to run the programme and to supervise payments of the *ustâd*s and their *shâgerd*s from AKMICA funds.

I did not instruct the *ustâd*s to follow a particular music curriculum; I left it to them to teach in their own way, using Indian *sargam* and *tabla bol* notations. In doing this I followed the Ustad Mohammad Omar model that I described earlier. I had also observed teaching sessions in Khalil House and knew these musicians were used to teaching and to running their own music courses. The following guidance was issued to them, translated into Dari by Mrs Affolter:

> 1. The purpose of this Training Programme is to support and encourage the art of music in Kabul as practised by the musician families of the Kucheh Kharabat. Central to this is the art of *ghazal* singing in the Kabuli style, an art associated with many of the singers of the Kharabat, such as Ustad Qassem, Ustad Ghulam Hussain, Ustad Natu, Ustad Nabi Gol, Ustad Rahim Bakhsh, Ustad Sheyda, Ustad Sarahang, and others. The performance of *ghazal* also requires advanced skills in playing *rubâb*, *tabla* and *delrubâ*. Your students should be doing their best to become excellent performers of this traditional music.

> 2. The music theory underlying the art of *ghazal* singing in the Kabuli style is very close to the music theory of Indian music. It is not your primary job to teach your students to perform Indian music, but Afghan music, which may be close to Indian music but has many important differences.

> 3. In addition to playing *ghazal* your students should also learn to play instrumental pieces of the *naghma-ye chahârtuk* genre. Your *tabla* students should be able to play solo performances, and your *rubâb* students should be able to play classical music (*naghma-ye klâsik*) in some common modes (*râg*s). Your vocal students should have some skill in singing Indian classical music. But the main objective is to learn to sing and accompany *ghazal* in the style of the great masters of Kucheh Kharabat.

> 4. Each of you is budgeted to have ten students. These should be amongst your advanced students rather than beginners. And the intention is that most of the students should be from musician families of the Kucheh Kharabat.

My contention that the Kabuli *ghazal* should be considered as a distinct form of Afghan art was originally made in Baily (1988a: 79–80), and reiterated in greater detail in Baily (2011a Chapter 5), and is clearly expressed in these instructions.

In 2004 I visited Kabul again, this time with Veronica, carrying two *delrubâ*s purchased in London for Ustad Amruddin's students. I observed and documented on video the teaching of the *ustâd*s, and I was impressed with how well things were going, even though the generator seemed to be on rather a lot, its sound disrupting the classes to some extent. But the *ustâd*s were not satisfied. They wanted more instruments, more space, more teaching hours and more students. In 2005 I resigned from my position as Consultant to AKMICA, feeling that I had done as much as I could at a distance. Jolyon Leslie, Head of the Aga Khan Trust for Culture in Kabul, took over running the programme temporarily, while he looked for a suitable Coordinator. After a long search, Mirwaiss Sidiqi was appointed to this position and has done a marvellous job in developing the programme.

In 2006 I was back in Kabul. I was impressed with how much progress had been made at the Aga Khan Music School with Mirwaiss in charge. The programme had been moved from FCCS and had now become a fully-fledged school, housed in a modern building next to the AKTC offices, with more students, and many more instruments. The original four *ustâd*s were teaching, and had been joined temporarily by Ustad Asif, who was now spending much of his time in Kabul. Mirwaiss Sidiqi had also established a regional music instrumental group (*Goldasteh Kharâbât*) under the direction of Ustad Ghulam Hussain, which brought together instrumentalists from various parts of the country. The mode of teaching had also changed markedly from my original concept. Instead of one-to-one interaction between *ustâd* and *shâgerd*, with other *shâgerd*s observing and learning from one another's mistakes, they had adopted group teaching, with up to a dozen students practising exercises and compositions in unison together. A curriculum had been established, with a sequence of *râg*s or *tâl*s to be learned, and examinations that had to be passed before the *shâgerd* proceeded to the next level. In 2009 a second AKMICA school was established, in Herat, with local Herati musicians as teachers. In 2012 Mirwaiss told me there were 70 students enrolled in Kabul, and 87 in Herat. When I next visited the School, in February 2014, I found that teaching had now been extended to some of the regional musics of Afghanistan, with teachers of *tanbur*, *ghaichak*, *dutâr*, *tulak* and *dambura*.

When I retired from my part-time consultancy with AKMICA, which had paid a quarter of my salary for two years, I returned to full-time teaching at Goldsmiths. In 2003 I had been awarded a Personal Chair and became the first Professor of Ethnomusicology in the UK. I felt that AMU had accomplished its main objectives, to conduct research on the re-emergence of music in public life in Afghanistan, and to provide educational support in the re-building of Afghan music culture. I had witnessed the surprisingly quick return to a more normal life of music at least in Kabul, though there were undoubtedly changes, especially in the capital, where the new modern music that was favoured in the diaspora seemed to be taking over from more traditional forms. I had played a modest role in supporting the practice of traditional art music through my work with AKMICA. It was time to consolidate what I had learned since my visit to Peshawar in 1985, and to examine what it all meant in an academic rather than a practical sense. But my naval-gazing was interrupted by the emergence of new academic initiatives on the research scene.

Chapter 6
The Global Circulation of Afghanistan's Music

Music and Migration

At this point in my ethnographic narrative I have to declare a change of direction and emphasis. By 2005 I felt that the AMU's main objectives had been accomplished. AMU had documented the return of music after the Taliban, and had helped to secure the future of Kabul's art music by setting up the AKMICA Tradition Bearers' Programme. At this point in my narrative I do not feel it necessary to discuss political events after my visit in 2004, except to mention Karzai's re-election for a second (and final) term as President, the resurgence of the Taliban and the fighting with NATO forces in Helmand and other regions of southern Afghanistan. But these events have had little direct impact on the lives of musicians.

Hitherto, since 1985, I had followed in a rather haphazard manner the lives of musicians in the Afghan diaspora as they were affected by political developments in Afghanistan itself. There had been no master plan; it had been a matter of keeping abreast of current political events and documenting the effects on Afghan musicians in Pakistan (1991, 1992, 2000); Afghanistan (1994); Iran (1998, 2004) and California (2000). A gradual realization of the significance of what I was doing began to emerge: this was all about music and forced migration. Several of my graduate students at Goldsmiths were involved with the music of refugee communities: Matthaios Tsahourides and the music of the Pontic Greeks exiled from their Black Sea homeland in the 1920s; Sarah Mannasseh and the music of the Jewish communities who left Iraq after 1948; and Maria da Silva and the music of East Timorese exiled in Portugal after the Indonesian invasion of 1975. In addition, in the 1990s I had been working 'at home' in Bradford, Leicester and Nuneaton, with members of the Gujarati Khalifa community. The members of this small encapsulated community were technically 'twice migrants', having emigrated from India to East Africa in the 1940s–50s, and who came to the UK as refugees after the Africanization policies in Uganda and Kenya in the 1960s. In 2006 Dr Michael Collyer and I edited a special issue of the *Journal of Ethnic and Migration Studies* on 'Music and Migration', which included my paper on Gujarati Muslim musicians in the UK (Baily 2006).[1]

---

[1]   Adelaida Reyes' work on Vietnamese exiles is the outstanding example of the study of music in refugee life, see Reyes (1999).

'Afghanistan' was no longer the population of a specific geographical location, but an amorphous virtual globalised disbursement that after many years of conflict was beginning to gain a sense of itself as a transnational community, made possible in part by the advent of new communications technology. In making sense of what I had done so far, I realized that I needed more data about the wider diaspora and an understanding of how music flowed within the Afghan transnational community.

Good luck came to my aid. In 2005 the Arts and Humanities Research Council (AHRC) launched a multi-million pound research programme on Diasporas, Migration and Identities. This was indicative of an increasing academic interest in the crucially important issue of migration and its social, cultural and economic consequences. I applied and the following year was awarded £10,000 for a research project on 'Afghan music in London and its ongoing communications with Kabul and the Afghan Transnational Community'. The stated aims of the project were to focus on musical innovation, the feedback of new music from the periphery (the diasporic community) to the centre (Kabul), and the connection between the creation of new music and transformations in the construction of cultural identity. The proposed research included visits to Kabul, Hamburg and Dublin; the research outputs included a film, a concert at Goldsmiths, and written publications. The grant included provision for me to employ a young Afghan poet and engineer, Yama Yari, as my part-time research assistant.

Having completed this project I was in 2008 awarded a Leverhulme Emeritus Fellowship. These highly competitive and much sought-after Fellowships were awarded to recently retired academics who had significant research projects to complete. In my case, the project was to review all my research on Afghan music from 1985 onwards and write a monograph that somehow brought the data together. The grant allowed me to employ Yama Yari again as my part-time research assistant. It also included a budget for me to conduct fieldwork on Afghan music in Australia for two months, which combined neatly with invitations to Veronica and myself to be Visiting Scholars at Monash University in Victoria. I knew there to be Afghan communities in Melbourne and Sydney to be researched into. Together, the AHRC and Leverhulme grants allowed me to examine Afghan musical life at extreme antipodean sites, London and Melbourne–Sydney.

London 2006

> This house is beautiful but it's not my house
> This land is so beautiful but it's not my homeland

Profile: Haroon Yousofi (BBC World Service Presenter and Singer)

Given the crucial role of the BBC in reporting on the war in Afghanistan, and as I had had many opportunities to work with the BBC Dari and Pashto Services, it was natural that I should start my work in London's Bush House, then home to

Figure 6.1   Haroon Yousofi in the BBC studio, London 2006

the BBC World Service (BBC WS). This Service supported a number of music programme directed to an Afghan audience. My most productive contact at the BBC was Haroon Yousofi, one of the best-informed Afghans about the music of the Afghanistan transnational community, a man with a pocketbook filled with the phone numbers and email addresses of Afghan musicians around the world. Besides working for the BBC he frequently served as master of ceremonies at concerts of Afghan music in London, was well known as a writer of satires and comic sketches, and occasionally performed as a stand-up comedian. I discovered he was also a very good amateur singer.

Haroon Yousofi (Figure 6.1) was born in Kabul in 1950, studied literature at Kabul University and was sent to Moscow State University to complete his BA and MA degrees. On his return to Kabul he taught the history of western literature at Kabul University. In later years he was Head of the Arts and Literature section of RTA until leaving Afghanistan in 1990 and making his way to London, where he was able to find a job with the BBC WS. He became famous for his radio show *Studio Shomara Haft*, 'Studio Number Seven', hereinafter referred to as *Studio 7*.

Studio 7 was a pioneering weekly live interactive radio show, technically a 'music and phone-in programme'. Each week a special guest was connected to the studio in London via ISDN satellite telephone. The guest's name was announced beforehand on the programme's website,[2] and Afghans from across the world phoned in to indicate they would like to speak to that week's special guest. When the programme was broadcast, a succession of these people were phoned back from London, and they talked to the guest and to Haroon, who was as much an attraction to listeners of *Studio 7* as his guests, because of his witty presentation and jokes. Others phoned in during the course of the programme. A *Studio 7* show usually included a few recordings of the artist in question, and sometimes a singer would sing over the phone, even accompanying himself on the *'armonia*. The programmes were broadcast on Friday afternoons, from 2.15pm to 3.00pm GMT, which due to the time difference of about four hours was heard in the early evening in Afghanistan, prime listening time on the day of rest. For my research I attended six of these shows, sitting in the studio just across the table facing Haroon. On another occasion Veronica and I were the guests and had to play live in the studio.[3]

Up to 2006 the programme's guests were almost all singers, old and young, international super-stars like Farhad Darya, and the locally famous, male and female. The only instrumentalist was Ustad Asif Mahmoud, the *tabla* player. On one occasion the guest was the Quranic reciter Qeri Barakatullah in Kabul. On another occasion it was the Australia-based musicologist Dr Ahmad Sarmast. After 2006 it appears that a wider variety of artists, writers and filmmakers were guests. Very few of the guests were resident in Afghanistan. *Studio 7* was a way for the Afghan transnational community to talk to itself about music, and about musicians.

It so happened that the Afghan singer Ali Shah Sadozai, generally known by his stage name Khushhal (Happy Disposition), was engaged to perform at the annual Festival of World Cultures in Dun Laoghaire (Dun Leary), Ireland, on 27 August 2006. I was not familiar with the name of Khushhal, who I later discovered had lived in Hamburg for more than 30 years. He was a popular local singer in Hamburg's large Afghan community and also worked as a teacher for Afghan children in a music school in the city. His invitation to Dunleary came through Nasruddin Saljuqi, now resettled with his family in Ireland. Nasruddin had soon emerged as a leader in the small Afghan community in Dublin. He organized exhibitions and concerts, and had written a book on music and theatre in Herat that was published in Tehran (Saljuqi 2004). Nasruddin had recommended that the Festival should invite Khushhal to give a concert. The scenario looked promising in terms of my undertaking to the AHRC to research into Afghan music in Dublin. I informed Haroon about Khushhal's impending visit and told him I would be there. Haroon was sent by the BBC to report on the Festival.

I arrived two days before the concert and visited the Festival with Nasruddin. There was an international fashion show, which included, as well as a number of

---

[2]   See http://www.bbbpersian.com/Afghanistan.

[3]   Haroon's wife, Amina Yousofi, had a somewhat similar show called *Zamzama* (*Whisper, Murmur*) aimed principally at women in the Afghan transnational community. This programme did not have a weekly guest. Women phoned in to talk to Amina, who encouraged them to sing to the listeners over the phone.

glamorous young ladies modelling national dress from various parts of the world, Zadran, a bulky Pashtun, the proprietor of an Internet café in Dublin. He was modelling the *piran o tâmbân* (long shirt and baggy trousers) typical of his home in Paktia. The night Khushhal and his accompanists (electronic keyboard and *tabla*) arrived from Hamburg, Nasruddin held a small *mehmâni* at his house for the visitors, including Haroon and me. It was a typical *shauqi* evening, with lots of jokes and music making. After an excellent meal, Haroon sang a set of songs, including the following:

This house is beautiful but it's not my house
This land is not our homeland
This land is so beautiful but it's not my homeland
This is not my house

Listen!
Paris is beautiful but it's not like Kabul, Ghazni or Zabol
London is not as pleasant as ancient Herat
This land is not our homeland
This land is so beautiful but it's not my homeland
This is not my house

Listen!
In Maimana, Kunduz, Farah and Badakhshan, in the hills of Paghman
There's an elegance that's not in Delhi, Berlin or Yeman
This land is not our homeland
This house is beautiful but it's not my house
This land is not our homeland

Listen!
For whom shall I sing? For whom shall I sing?
The *ghazals* of Sadi, Jami, or Nizami
In a foreign city where there's no understanding of such poetic discourse
This land is not our homeland
This land is so beautiful but it's not my homeland
This is not my house

Listen!
Let's hope our country soon comes out of this misery and grief
What can I do here, it's not my country, and it's not my house
This land is not our homeland
This house is beautiful but it's not my house
This land is not our homeland
This land is so beautiful but it's not our homeland

This is not my house
It's Mr Saljuqi's house
(Poetry by Haroon Yousofi)

At the end of the song Haroon apologized to Nasruddin, explaining that Khushhal had whispered the idea of the last line to him.[4]

The concert took place the next day in a large upstairs auditorium in an old municipal building in Dun Leary. It did not attract a large audience, and those who came were mostly Afghans. The Festival organizers had specifically requested there should be no dancing, but their concerns were disregarded. For much of the time a group of Afghan youths squatted in a circle, clapping strongly to the music, while a succession of them took turns to dance solo in their midst. Next day Nasruddin told me this type of dance was from the Panjshir. I reminded him that dancing was not allowed but had occurred. He laughed, and said, 'They did it because they are Afghan', as though that explained everything.

When I got back to London Haroon called me to say that Khushhal was going to be the next guest for *Studio 7*. This was an opportunity not to be missed; I needed video footage of Haroon in the studio for the film I had undertaken to make as a research output for the AHRC. Haroon gave me his consent and I videoed the whole programme. It was particularly useful that Khushhal talked about his concert in Dublin and even mentioned his pleasure at meeting me there. I used some of the footage to frame my film *Scenes of Afghan Music: London, Kabul, Hamburg, Dublin*. In 2009 the BBC axed *Studio 7* and its sister programme *Zamzama*, explaining that while *Studio 7* and *Zamzama* 'were pioneering programmes in their time, there were now a number of television and FM radio stations in Afghanistan offering similar programmes, including chat shows with Afghan singers and musicians abroad. It was important that BBC WS remain distinctive, contemporary and relevant, and periodic changes of programming were inevitable' (Baily 2011b: 191).

The Transnational Community's Conversation about Music in Studio 7

Most *Studio 7* callers wanted to know about the biographies of the guest artists. 'Where were you born, where are you living now, how many children do you have, how did you learn your musical art? When did you leave Afghanistan? Have you been back? What did you do there? How was it? When are you coming to give a concert in Hamburg, Rotterdam, Toronto, Sydney, London … ?' There were questions about particular songs broadcast by RTA in the past, or to be found on recent CD/DVD releases.

---

[4]   My visit to Dublin, including Haroon's song, is documented in the film *Scenes of Afghan Music: London, Kabul, Hamburg, Dublin* (Baily 2007b), not included on the DVD that comes with this book. But Haroon's song can be found on http://www.youtube.com/watch?v=OPTblMDy8–4.

But *Studio 7* was also a forum for serious discussion about the current state of Afghan music, both in the country itself and in the Afghan diaspora. There was concern about standards of musicianship, the lack of training opportunities and the need for institutional support, the poetic quality of current song lyrics, and the use of modern instruments like the electronic keyboard. It is significant that these discussions were mainly about Afghan popular music and expressed a concern to get back to the music of Radio Afghanistan as it was up until about 1992, when the last communist government fell to the *mujahideen* parties. There was little discussion of Afghan art music, or of the various regional 'traditional' musics associated with different ethnic/language groups. Only a few guests had much to say about these matters and I have been highly selective in what I present here, choosing programmes with the following guests:

- Abdul Wahab Madadi, former Director of Music for RTA. Living in Germany. We met him in Chapter 3.
- Dr Ahmad Naser Sarmast, Founder and Director of the Afghanistan National Institute for Music, in Kabul. Living in Australia.
- Wahid Qassemi, singer and composer, a grandson of Ustad Qassem, a former star of RTA. Living in Canada.
- Amir Jan Sabori, singer, poet and songwriter, also a former star of RTA. Living in Canada.

Madadi and Sarmast had a good deal to say about the present state of Afghan music:

Madadi: Amongst millions of Afghans, we can say we have about 10 great musicians in the new generation. I am not saying that we do not have good musicians, we do have good musicians, like Farhad Darya … Wahid Qassemi … Najim … Shadkam … Haidar Salim … Salma … Rahim Jahani … Ehsan Aman … And there is Amir Jan Sabori, who released a CD last year that in my opinion is a masterpiece. The good thing about him is that he writes his own songs and he sings so well. He is a very good poet himself. He has written the lyrics, he has composed the songs and he has sung them accompanied by the Tashkent orchestra, a modern orchestra. But these kinds of singers who have these advantages and facilities available to them are rare. The thing is even if there are 10 of them it is not sufficient for a nation. For a country torn apart and its singers scattered around the world, 10 singers are not enough.

Sarmast: Despite all the positive opinions expressed by some musicians on *Studio 7*, by taking a deep and broad view of the current state of Afghan music one can draw the precise conclusion that in the same way in which the past 30 years of war has affected different aspects of people's lives, culture, art and country, in the same way it has affected our music, too. The war, the collective exile of musicians, and the death of several musicians who could have played a fundamental and important role in the training of today's musical generation, these have all had their negative effects on our music ... [Our music] is in a disorganized and chaotic state. Like any other part of Afghanistan's culture, music needs serious attention and care on the part of both governmental and non-governmental organizations.

Madadi: [Of course] Afghan music is important for those Afghans who live in the West ... But they have lost the real Afghan music. If good Afghan music, with the same songwriters and orchestras as there were in Kabul, was sung by singers, then people would cry for it. People love that music. But they don't have it. ... There are many singers from Afghanistan, hundreds of them. There are many in Hamburg. But they have some problems. Some of them don't have a good voice, some who have a nice voice don't know good poetry, some don't have new songs. They have the passion for singing, but they have no guidance, no compositions and no familiarity with music. They come with a keyboard and they make some noises to which people dance and content themselves ... If a keyboard player knows how to play it well and plays according to the rules [of music], then I like keyboard. What I don't like is for a singer to always sing with a keyboard with a loud rhythm that deafens the ears.

Sarmast: The creation of one-man-bands, which is common practice among Afghan musicians in the West, is now also being practised inside Afghanistan, and forces out our very talented, skilled and good musicians who play other instruments.

Afghan music is predominantly vocal rather than instrumental, and a good deal of concern was expressed about the quality of new songs as judged from the point of view of the lyrics:

Madadi: Very poor and low-grade lyrics are used [today]. The singers themselves usually put words together to suit their music, but it is not poetry. Poetry has meaning, it is a big thing; it is no less important than music. In the new music, poetry has been ruined and lost. You hear a bit of musical interest in the new music, but you don't hear good poetry, with the exception of a limited number of musicians ... Some of the artists who live in some countries have even forgotten the Farsi language. They have no knowledge, because they cannot write Farsi poetry with Farsi alphabet; they write Farsi lyrics in Roman alphabet. So if they are removed from their language then they do not know the poetry.

Sabori: When we had only one radio and television station, there was a skilled board that checked the songs in terms of quality. They decided which song should go on the radio and which on television. We also had a literary team who checked the poetry and lyrics. If the poem was not up to scratch, then they would reject it and one would have to take the poem to someone for correction. But what is damaging our music these days more than anything is the language that goes with the music, which is poetry. Few of our musicians pay attention to this, now they concentrate more on the rhythm.

Qassemi: As a composer myself, I am available to work with musicians, whether they are beginners or professionals ... The lyrics that I normally choose to sing belong to Dari [Farsi] poets like Rumi, Bedil, Hafiz, Ashghari, Sarwar-e-Dehqan, Nader Naderpur, Faraidun Mosheri. I don't limit myself to singing lyrics from one poet only. I use some contemporary poets too, such as Raziq Sani, Naim Mihrzad, S.A. Muzafari, Humaira Nekhat and many others.

As already discussed, in the past the radio station in Kabul was a crucially important centre for musical creativity and innovation that was undermined by the anti-music stance of the Coalition and Taliban governments (1992–2001). Those who remembered the creative role played by RTA in the past looked to the recreation of such an institution in Kabul:

Madadi: Provided that we create a proper music school in Kabul, we do have Afghan music teachers who live abroad [to staff it] ... but who is going to invite them to Kabul? Who is going to organize something for them? The government needs to take responsibility ... The music of Afghanistan is not going to be saved by a handful of teachers teaching *rubâb* and *tabla* in Kabul. We need more; we need the keyboards, saxophones, violins, flutes, clarinets and so on. Our music cannot be saved just by *rubâb* and *tabla*. This is not enough. We had people [in the past] who played the *delrubâ*, *sârang*, *sarinda*, *sarod* and *sitâr*. Now we have nothing. All these instruments are lost.

These voices articulated a very clear critique of the situation of Afghan music in 2006. It is worth noting that the weakening of Afghan music culture was attributed to the effects of 30 years of warfare on the institutions that promoted music in the past, rather than blamed on the anti-music policies of Islamic fundamentalists, and there was an acknowledgement that there had been a loss not only of music but also of musical sensibility.

Afghan Music in London

The BBC WS may have been an important disseminator of Afghan music in 2006, but London itself was not a great centre for live Afghan music, even though it had a number of musicians from the Kucheh Kharabat as residents. They included *tabla* players Ustad Asif Mahmoud, his brother Ustad Arif and Asif's son, Yusuf, who was also a good singer and married to a daughter of Ustad Sarahang. In addition, there was the singer Timor Sheydai, a grandson of Ustad Sheyda, who had been one of the most eminent of the Kharabat vocalists, and percussionist Shafi Nabizada, a grandson of Ustad Nabi Gol. Only Toronto could rival London as a new home for Kharabat musicians, with Olfat Ahang (vocal), his brother Fazal Ahmad (*tabla*), and Ustad Sarahang's son Eltaf Hussain (also a vocalist). Although the Kharabat musicians in London were respected in the Afghan community they were not much in demand to play the art music of Kabul; though the *tabla* players amongst them were sometimes called upon by non-Afghan patrons to accompany visiting Indian musicians and/or dancers. Until 2006 my knowledge of Afghan music in London was largely based on my interactions with Ustad Asif and Yusuf, both of whom had been employed as *tabla* teachers to our students at Goldsmiths, and with whom I had given many concerts.

Afghan audiences in London preferred the new popular music, played with modern instruments like electronic keyboards and drum pads. In 2006 there were several well-known semi-professional singers in London who regularly performed such music, such as Belqis, Hashmat, Mahmud Kamen and Obaid but there were no 'international superstars' amongst them. They performed mainly at wedding parties and on festive occasions such as concerts held during the two *'Eids, Now Ruz* (Afghan New Year, 21 March), and the western New Year (1 January). At the wedding parties they fulfilled a ritual function, since music was an essential part of such festivities. Such local singers were not of great appeal for concerts; in part they were too well known by the local audiences. For concerts, singers were usually brought from abroad, from elsewhere in the diaspora.

An Afghan concert was a big event. It was usually held in a banqueting suite with an elaborately decorated stage, very loud amplification and one or more professional video cameras on dollies recording the event for later release in DVD format. If brought from outside the UK (as was usual), singers would sometimes bring one or more accompanists; otherwise they used local Afghan musicians. In the space of three months in 2006 I attended concerts in London by Faiz-e Karezi (Germany), Seema Tarana (Canada), Habib Qaderi (USA), Ehsan Aman (USA), Shahna (Netherlands) and Asad Badie (Austria). They performed very much in the style of the new Afghan music, dominated by keyboards, drum machines, and drum pads; though the singers themselves tended to play the *'armonia* on these occasions. Tickets cost between £15 and £20. It is clear that considerable amounts of money were involved in organizing these business ventures, with the hire of the hall, lighting and PA systems, security, travel and accommodation of visiting artists, and, of course, their payment.

Much of the music played at such concerts was dance music; which brings us to an important distinction between two types of event, which I designate the 'family concert' and the 'open concert'. To attend a family concert one had to be a member or guest of a family group. The groups sat around large circular tables for 10, and it was a fairly restrained event. There would be dancing, but usually only for small numbers of dancers at a time. It was very much a middle-class family occasion, the guests smartly dressed and well behaved.

The open concert, in contrast, was open to anybody who could afford a ticket. Here the audience would be seated in long rows, and the area in front of the stage was dominated by large numbers of young men dancing together – perhaps 100 or even 200 at a time. Their dress was casual, jeans and a leather jacket being typical. Many of these young men were asylum seekers and illegal immigrants, cut off from their families, living in hostels or cheap flats provided by local councils. Given that they represented the various ethnic groups that made up the

London Afghan community, and in view of the rivalries that existed between such groups, it is not surprising that arguments sometimes flared up: fights were not unknown, hence the need for several security men to maintain order.[5] The point of the family concert was to cut out the 'riff-raff'. The audience at either type of concert, open and family, consisted almost entirely of Afghans: the concerts were not intended for people outside the Afghan community, who simply did not know that such events were taking place, for they were not part of the 'world music' concert scene in London.

One of the research outcomes for my AHRC award was to organize a concert of Afghan music at Goldsmiths. This took place on 23 November 2006, with our own Goldsmiths' based group, with the addition of singer Timor Shaydai, billed for this occasion as Yusuf Mahmoud's Afghan Music. We played the first half of the evening, and the woman singer Bilqis, accompanied by her husband on keyboard and brother on drum pads played the second half. Haroon Yousofi came along to compere the show, which he did, speaking and joking in Dari. For once there was a mixed Afghan and non-Afghan audience. Bilqis's set attracted a good deal of dancing from a group of young Afghan men of the type normally excluded from family concerts, and the evening concluded with a performance of the *attan*.[6]

Australia 2009

> I am the axis of needs, I am the wheel of all souls
> I am the saint of Kharabat, I am the happy lover

Early in 2009 Veronica and I travelled to Australia to take up our Visiting Scholar positions in Monash University, located about 30 miles from Melbourne. One of the attractions of Monash was the presence of Dr Ahmad Sarmast in the Monash Asia Institute, the Afghan musicologist whose work I have cited extensively in Chapter 1. We also had a wonderful contact in Sydney: Safar Sarmed, who had worked as my research assistant in Herat in 1974. A graduate in engineering from the Technical Institute in Kabul, which taught in the medium of English, he had made his way to Australia and gained a master's degree in engineering in 1977 from the University of New South Wales. After the *Saur* Revolution of 1978

---

[5]   For example, at one open concert I attended somebody let off a mace or teargas canister by the box office. The concert was brought to a halt for half-an-hour. The windows were opened, an ambulance was called for somebody who had fainted, and then the music resumed. It is noteworthy that the first song to be performed after the gas attack was Awal Mir's patriotic *This is our Beautiful Homeland, This is our Lovely Homeland,* perhaps to remind the audience of who they were.

[6]   Some months later the complete Yusuf Mahmoud's Afghan Music half of the concert was shown by *Noor TV*, an Afghan satellite channel broadcasting from California.

he had remained in Australia. Many years later I had managed to make contact with him and he had subsequently visited us in Brighton and given me a detailed account of the Afghan music scene in Australia, insisting that we make a visit. Through him we had a direct entrée into the Afghan communities near Melbourne and Sydney, particularly to those from Herat.

The first Afghan migrants to Australia were cameleers in the 1860s. The camel had an important role in opening up the interior of much of the country, initially for purposes of exploration, and later for the movement of agricultural and construction materials and merchandise. Camels were shipped from Karachi and with them came the cameleers. Some were Pashtuns from Afghanistan or the North-West Frontier Province of British India, others were Baluchis and Punjabis. This diversity notwithstanding, they were generally known collectively as 'Afghans', a term often abbreviated to 'Ghan', commemorated in The Ghan, a train running between Adelaide and Alice Springs, along a rail track that was originally constructed following one of the cameleers' transit routes.

Between 1860 and 1920 more than 2,000 cameleers went to Australia, with around 20,000 imported camels. Many of the Afghans went on three-year contracts and returned home after fulfilling their terms. Others stayed on and in due course set up their own camel transport businesses and imported animals for themselves. There was some inter-marriage with Aboriginal women. This migrant community has been fully documented in two publications, Stevens (1989) and Jones and Kenny (2007). The descendants of these pioneers remain today, as do a few of the 'tin mosques' and 'ghantowns' their predecessors built. As far as we know, the interaction with Aboriginal culture did not have any musical repercussions (see Stevens 1989: 259–60 on family life in the ghantowns). The Afghan cameleers are part of Australian history and folk memory. 'The Ghan cameleer theme is stamped all over the Central Australia brand with bronze statues, logos etc.' (Gavin Gatenby, personal communication 16 November 2009). This folk memory perhaps gave Afghans some advantage over other recent migrant communities in Australia.

After the *Saur* Revolution of 1978 a number of Afghans studying in Australia stayed put, like our friend Safar. At that time it was relatively easy to be granted political asylum in Australia, as was also the case for a number of other western countries. Those already in Australia were able to sponsor family members and others for resettlement in their new home. Over the years Safar had helped more than a hundred people in this way. This became more difficult after 1992 and even more so after 2001. Recently, there had been a wave of illegal immigrants traveling via the southern islands of Indonesia, then on to Australia by boat, a process of migration described in detail by Najaf Ali Mazari in *The Rugmaker of Mazar-e-Sharif* (Mazari and Hillman, 2008).

The number of Afghans living in the whole of Australia in 2009 was small, probably no more than 25,000.[7] The small size of the Afghan-Australian community

---

[7]   Australia is one of the few countries to have precise statistics about migrants from Afghanistan. In 2009 the South Eastern Region Migrant Resource Centre published the

turned out to have some significance for the life of Afghan music in its new home, as discussed later. All four of the main ethnic groups in Afghanistan – Pashtuns, Tajiks, Uzbeks and Hazaras – were represented, as were the two main branches of Islam, Sunni and Shia. While Afghan-Australians were obviously aware of differences between these groups, this had not become a major source of conflict, from which one might conclude that the tolerance supposedly characteristic of multicultural Australian society extended to these groups. Afghan culture in Australia was generally liberal, and women did not seem to be too restricted, especially in matters of dress. The major conflicts that arose within the Afghan community were the usual inter-generational differences in the diaspora, with tensions between the traditionalism of the older generation and the modernism of the younger. Another common problem concerned marriage breakdown and divorce, where traditional Afghan ideas about gender roles in marriage were contrasted with those of mainstream Australian society.

The two major areas of Afghan settlement in Australia were in the conurbations near Sydney and Melbourne. Since Monash University was near Melbourne I had the opportunity to make a number of visits to Thomas Street, the Afghan precinct in Greater Dandenong (named 'The City of Opportunity'), about 25 miles from Melbourne's city centre. In this street I counted 27 Afghan businesses: groceries, kebab shops, restaurants, carpet shops and hardware stores. This formerly dilapidated business area was now in the process of urban regeneration and designated The Afghan Bazaar Precinct. The municipality had designed an attractive logo, using the inevitable image of a camel. In April 2009 this logo suddenly appeared all over Thomas Street, in the form of business cards, posters in shop windows, and large billboards. It transpired that a documentary film was being made about the city.

To promote Afghan business and culture, Dandenong had established regular Afghan Bazaar Cultural Tours. The flyer for these read as follows:

> Experience the enchanting Afghan culture, fashion, food and music through the gracious hospitality of a wide variety of traders in Dandenong's Afghan Bazaar Precinct.
>
> Your tour guide will lead you on a journey to a far flung corner of the world throwing light on the captivating Afghan culture where exotic music, unique fashions and tantalizing food will be experienced.

---

following figures, derived from the Australian Bureau of Statistics Census of 2006. The total Afghan population was 17,865, of whom 5,848 were in Victoria, 6,699 in New South Wales, 2,339 in South Australia, 1,782 in Western Australia, and small numbers in Queensland, Northern Territory, Tasmania and Canberra Australia Capital Territory (Migrant Resource Centre 2009: 23–4). As the survey itself admits, these figures could not be entirely accurate, and they were now several years out of date. The same census for 2006 reported there to be about 330,000 Muslims in Australia.

> Tours occur once a month and include visits to specialty shops, an
> introduction to Afghanistan's long history with Australia, intriguing rugs and
> carpets, authentic Afghan music, including a variety of delicious food samples
> that will excite all your senses. Then share the fun of the tour over a meal in a
> local Afghan restaurant. Tours free, meals optional.

The tour guide was Bashir Keshtiar, an Afghan community leader, manager of
a local branch of the National Australia Bank, and also one of several presenters
of Afghan programmes on Special Broadcasting Service (SBS), Australia's
multicultural and multilingual community radio. Dandenong seemed to be an
admirable example of Australian multiculturalism in action.[8] In this milieu, with
its emphasis on multiculturalism, Afghan immigrants had been able to make the
most of Australia as 'a land of opportunity', a phrase frequently articulated (in
English) by Afghan-Australians. This was a major theme of Najaf Ali Mazari's
autobiography (Mazari and Hillman 2008), which brought him from a small
village in northern Afghanistan to become the proprietor of a successful carpet
business in Melbourne. The Afghans I met were relatively affluent, often living in
luxurious houses in well-heeled suburbs.

Profile: Zahir Yusuf (Taxi Driver and Singer)

My friend Zahir Yusuf, the last of my 10 *hamkârân*, was a good exemplar of
the semi-professional Afghan singer in contemporary Australia. He came from
a relatively well-off artisan family in Kabul: his father and cousins were in the
jewellery business. His was a musical family; his father and his uncle both played
the *tanbur*. Zahir had some contact with Radio Afghanistan when young and
recorded at least one song as a boy. He left Afghanistan for Pakistan in 1990 with
several male relatives of his age. At first they stayed in Peshawar, but finding the
jihâdi ambiance of that city strongly against music, they moved on to Islamabad.
Returning to Kabul in about 1992 he found the fighting between the *mujahideen*
factions too dangerous and persuaded his parents and other family members
to move to Pakistan. In 1995 he arrived in Australia, sponsored by an Afghan-
Australian family. Once established in his new home he married a close relative
living in Pakistan, and after several years of separation had been able to get her
to Australia. He lived in a suburb of Dandenong with his wife and two young
children, and like so many Afghans in exile, worked as a taxi driver.[9]

---

[8]   It is instructive to compare the attitude of the Dandenong authorities with Fremont's
refusal to rebrand Centreville as Little Kabul.

[9]   Taxi driving is a way of being your own boss, and is congruent with Afghan
ideas about non-subservience, autonomy and independence. My Anonymous Scribe who
transcribed, transliterated and translated a set of Sufi poems set to music in the Kabuli style,
was also a taxi driver, in Washington Airport (Baily 2011a: 54).

Zahir Yusuf proved to be a competent semi-professional musician who knew a certain amount about music theory, such as the scales of many of the *râg*s used for Afghan music, note names, metric cycles, etc. He was also something of a composer, having made up the melodies of many of the songs that he sang, and had written some lyrics too. He preferred to sing *ghazal*s but his work as a musician required him to perform mainly Afghan popular music, in both 'slow music' and 'fast music' styles, when people wanted to dance, rather than to listen to serious poetry. For gigs in Sydney he often played with the brothers Yama and Ali Sarshar on *tabla* and keyboard respectively. In Melbourne he played with Hosham, a *tabla* player, but for distant engagements, such as going to Perth, in Western Australia, then he went out alone, as a one-man-band, with his electronic keyboard.

I met Zahir about halfway through my two months at Monash University. We were both attending Khalil Gudaz's charity concert, which is described below. A few days later I phoned him and we arranged to meet in the Ariana Restaurant in Thomas Street, Dandenong. Having got there by a slow bus I waited a long time. Eventually my mobile rang, it was Zahir, asking where was I? He was waiting for me at the Aryan Restaurant across the road! He gave me a tour of the Afghan Bazaar Precinct and introduced me to many of the shopkeepers. Some of these shops I had visited before, but after he told them that I was a famous *prufesar* from London they were much more cooperative. Towards the end of my stay he organized a music party at his house in my honour, with a big barbecue in his garden. In preparation for this I had to learn several of songs from his own recordings.

By that time he had made three CDs (Figure 6.2), which gave me a good insight into his work. He had recorded two of these with Kharabat musicians during a visit to Kabul in 2004. The CDs were self-financed and privately produced and not to be found in the shops: he gave them to his friends and could send them to prospective patrons. The third CD he had recorded in Sydney's Sash Studios, whose recording methods are described below. He sang songs popularized by others, traditional folk songs, and his own compositions. The Afghan-Australian poet Wakil Nala wrote many of the lyrics he sang, including 'I am the saint of the Kharabat, I am the happy lover'. This, his favourite of the songs in his repertoire, was to be found on two of his CDs, and clearly referred to the memory of the Kharabat in Kabul. He told me that he preferred to sing *ghazals* but his audiences wanted pop music for their parties.

> The sheikh, the drunkenness and the brokenness have all become intertwined
> The mosque and the wine and the *khânaqâh*, the wine has gone sour
>
> I am the excitement of knowledge, I am the excitement of imagination
> I am the restlessness of knowledge, I am the excitement of imagination
> I am the happy lover, the saint of the Kharabat
>
> The way to save one from oneself is to go missing
> Being lost within oneself is to take one's life

I am the dance of the branches, I am absorbed in the divine state
I am the blood of Kharabat, I am the fulfilled lover

The workings of the world are in tune with me
Whichever way the heart goes, it is yet within me

I am the axis of needs, I am the wheel of all souls
I am the saint of Kharabat, I am the happy lover

The whisper of the instrument of truth beats in my veins
It tears the curtain of the heart, it drags life out of my body

I am the excitement of knowledge, I am the cunning hand of miracles
I am the saint of Kharabat, I am the happy lover
                            (poetry by Nala, composition by Zahir Yusuf)

Afghan Music in the Sydney and Melbourne Conurbations

According to Safar Sarmed, in the early days of Afghan immigration in the late 1960s and early 1970s, there were very few people with performance skills. When music was required for an *'Eid* or *Now Ruz* celebration – Afghan weddings were rare events – cassette recordings were played. But gradually Afghans arrived who had musical skills and abilities, such as Ghulam Sakhi Hasib Delnawaz, from Herat, who arrived in Sydney in the late 1970s. As an amateur singer he had had a number of songs broadcast on Radio Afghanistan under the name of Delnawaz (Player of the Heart), including his much admired *Qâlin Bâf*, which was about making carpets in the town of Aqcha in northern Afghanistan. For many years he was well known as a semi-professional singer in Sydney, performing at wedding parties and other festive occasions. By the time I met him he had become more committed to religious singing in Shia ceremonies, and at a festivity would only take the stage, by popular request, to sing a song or two.

In those early days Delnawaz was often accompanied on *tabla* by Nesruddin Sarshar, who had come to study in Australia in the late 1970s and stayed on after the *Saur* Revolution. In Kabul Nesruddin's family had been keen amateur musicians, and he had received some training in *tabla* playing from the Kharabat. In addition, he played *sitâr* (which he studied with a disciple of Ravi Shankar), *doholak, rubâb, tanbur, 'armonia, tulak* and he also sang. He sometimes worked for the Australian government as an interpreter, especially in the processing of new illegal arrivals who came from Indonesia by boat. Nesruddin had two highly talented musician sons, Yama and Ali, and together they ran the recording business Sash Studios, where Zahir Yusuf had recorded his third CD.

I found that in the Sydney and Melbourne conurbations public performances followed the pattern established in other parts of the wider diaspora, with occasional visits by the big stars of Afghan music, such as Farhad Darya, Mahwash and

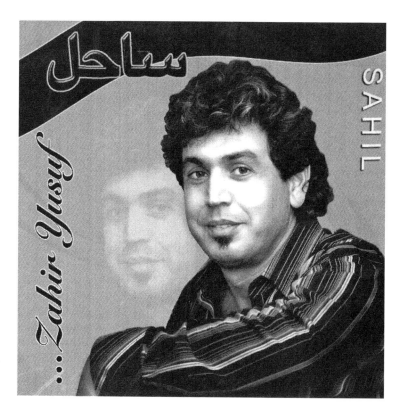

Figure 6.2   Zahir Yusuf, the cover of his Sash Music Studio CD *Sahil*.
© Sash Music Studio

Wahid Qassemi. These concerts were arranged by Afghan-Australian businessmen, who, of course, hoped to make good profits from such enterprises. Their concerts were attended by hundreds of young Afghans, who liked to dance en masse in front of the stage. Until recently young men and women were free to dance together, but by 2009 there seemed to be new pressure against this. Another kind of visit would be sponsored by a wealthy music-loving patron in Australia, who issued the invitation, arranged the visa, accommodated the artist, and organized small private house concerts. The visiting artist went 'home' (wherever that might be) with money donated by guests at those gatherings. The host-patron was likely to have put a lot of time, effort and finance into organizing such a visit, to be offset against the prestige gained within their local Afghan community. This kind of patronage was also to be found in other parts of the diaspora. For example, in 2003 Rahim Khushnawaz was invited by a group of Herati families in Darmstadt, Germany, to spend a month with them, to teach music to their children, and to entertain the adults. Australia-based Afghan musicians were engaged for weddings and other family celebrations, benefits and charity concerts. There were numerous private music sessions when groups of friends gathered for dinner and then played and sang deep into the night the old songs from home and the new songs of the diaspora, accompanied by *'armonia* and *tabla.*

Arguably, the only Afghan musician in Australia with an international profile was the *sitâr* player Ustad Khalil Gudaz. Born in Kabul in 1963 into a Kharabat musician family, he had learned to play *rubâb* and *tanbur* from Ustad Mohammad Omar and was employed as a musician at Radio Afghanistan in the 1980s. He started learning *sitâr* from Ustad Irfan Khan, who was teaching in the Indian Cultural Centre in Kabul in the 1980s (see Chapter 2). In 1988 he was awarded a scholarship to study *sitâr* in India, where he received a thorough training in the theory and practice of Hindustani music. He emigrated to Australia in 1998, sponsored by his brother, and settled in Melbourne. He performed both Hindustani and Afghan music. One of his specialties was the performance of Afghan folk and popular song melodies on the *sitâr*, which he did tastefully and sensitively, with a strong input of Hindustani music, especially with ornaments and short improvised passages. In this he was following the example of several key Afghan vocalists such as Ustad Qassem (the famous 1920s court singer) and Ustad Sarahang, both of whom performed Afghan folk songs with a strong imprint of classical music. In recent years Gudaz had presented himself as a singer, using mainly the poetry of Maulana Jalaluddin Rumi, sung to his own *râg*-based compositions, accompanying his singing with the *sitâr*. In this respect he was the unique performer of a new approach to Afghan classical music. He was a full-time professional musician, making his living from performances, and he also ran a small private music school, where he taught *sitâr*, *rubâb*, *tabla*, *'armonia* and vocal, and had a number of non-Afghan students.

I attended a remarkable charity concert given by Khalil Gudaz in Dandenong for victims of the bush fires that devastated large areas of Victoria in 2009. Many in the audience were not from Afghanistan. The concert was held in the local premises of the Retired Serviceman's League, a very important organization for war veterans in a country where the military occupies a position of great respect. The building itself was full of war trophies and photos of veterans, and a large Australian flag was draped across the back of the stage. The evening began with a speech by Bashir Kashtiar, the community leader mentioned above with respect to Afghan precinct tours, first in Dari, then in English. Then the sound system played the Australian national anthem; Bashir requested us all to stand up. This was followed by the new Afghan national anthem, composed by Babrak Wassa, and a speech by the Mayor of Dandanong, Councillor Pinar Yesil, a young woman of Turkish descent. There were various other speeches in the course of the evening, with expressions of sympathy for the victims of the bush fires, as though to say, 'We Afghans know what it is to suffer devastating experiences'. Then, as the main part of the programme, Khalil Gudaz played his *sitâr* and sang some of his Rumi compositions. At the end it was announced that the concert had raised AUS$1,715, and that the Dandenong mosque had donated another AUS$4,000 to the fund. This was an Afghan concert directed at both local Afghans and the wider community, with strong affirmations of solidarity. In the speeches there was lots of rhetoric from the Afghans about 'we are Australian'.

In Sydney there were a few Afghan musicians with some knowledge of Hindustani music. I have mentioned multi-instrumentalist Nesruddin Sarshar already. His son Yama was a talented *tabla* player who had been awarded scholarships by the Australian government for advanced training in India, where he had become a student of Zakir Hussain. Another son, Ali, was a keyboardist, composer, arranger and qualified sound engineer with a diploma from the Roland Company. They were successful as purveyors of both Indian and Afghan music and were able to address a range of audiences, Afghan, Indian, and 'white-Australians' that patronized the world music scene. They performed both within the Afghan community – at weddings and other festive occasions – and to the greater Australian community, for example, at world and international music festivals, such as the Mid-West Music Festival, the Aurora Music Festival, Womadelaide, and the Sydney Jazz Festival. Looking at Sydney and Melbourne as part of the wider Afghan diaspora I note that Afghan musical life in Australia, in comparison with the USA or Germany, was conditioned by the relatively small size of the community. It was unable to support a vigorous Afghan music profession. There were no big stars and very few full-time professional musicians. Such as there were supplemented their income by teaching in their own small privately run music schools. There were only two, very small, media companies, Aryan Music and Sash Studios. There was some state sponsorship for making commercial recordings and going abroad for musical training. And there were state-sponsored multicultural radio and television channels that had some Afghan music programming. The result was an active amateur music scene catering for a community of music lovers. Khalil Gudaz's Dandenong concert and the appearances of the Sarshars in world music and jazz events were significant because they revealed more engagement with mainstream society than usual; the Australian-Afghans seemed to be less encapsulated than some diasporic Afghan communities in other parts of the world. There is a comparison to be drawn with Dublin and Khushhal's concert in the Festival of World Cultures in 2006. These small communities need to make their presence known by engaging with the host community.

Audiocassettes and Compact Discs

During most of the period covered in this ethnographer's tale, the audiocassette and the compact disc had been the main media for the dissemination of commercial recordings of Afghan music. That era is coming to an end, with the increasing importance of the Internet.

As already noted in Chapter 1, a number of musicians from Afghanistan made 78 rpm records for the Gramophone Company's HMV label in the 1920s. In the 1960s, when quarter-inch tape recording machines were introduced to Radio Kabul, a number of recordings of Afghan music were made at the radio station, pressed as 78 rpm records in the USSR and shipped back to Kabul. They could be purchased from the radio station archive. From the 1960s some recordings of Afghan music were released on long-playing 33 rpm records in the West. These publications had scholarly and educational intentions, and were the outcome of anthropological or ethnomusicological research, and normally received institutional support. They were usually compilations, drawing together a number of different genres to give an overall view of the particular musical culture as a whole, and with very little attention paid to individual artists. Sometimes their names were not even mentioned in the liner notes. As far as I know, these recordings hardly reached an audience in Afghanistan.

By the late 1960s–early 1970s Japanese-made cassette machines were becoming quite common in Afghanistan. The standard models were what Manuel (1993: 60) describes as 'two-in-ones', often brought back by Afghan migrant workers from the Gulf or Iran, but also available for purchase in Kabul. These combined a radio and cassette recorder/playback machine, which allowed direct recording from the radio, and had a cheap external microphone, which the owner could attach to the extended aerial, serving as a makeshift microphone stand when recording live music. During my fieldwork in Herat in the 1970s I saw how these machines were brought by music enthusiasts to public concerts held during *Ramazân* and to the tented teahouses in the *Now Ruz* country fairs. Purchase of a ticket for admission to a concert, or ordering a pot of tea at a country fair, gave one the right to make one's own recording. And many recordings were made at weddings and at private parties. Such domestic cassette recordings made years ago of artists such as Ustad Sarahang and Ahmad Zahir were later released on commercial CDs in the wider diaspora. Not surprisingly, they varied greatly in technical quality.

The production of commercial audiocassettes of Afghan music in Afghanistan began in Kabul in the early 1970s. The Hamidi family owned a department store in Shahr-e Now, and the wide range of luxury goods on sale included some hi-fi audio equipment, turntables for playing LPs and cassette players. In addition, the store stocked a range of western LPs and audiocassettes, mainly to sell to foreigners connected with embassies and development programmes such as USAID. A younger member of the family, Ahmad Hamidi, who I met in Fremont in 2000, realized that there was a possibility for marketing audiocassettes of Afghan music. He imported some high-quality reel-to-reel recording equipment from London and established the first privately owned recording studio in Afghanistan, in about 1972. He called his recording business Music Center. His first release was of Ustad Sarahang; other early recordings were mainly of currently popular singers such as Ahmad Zahir and Salma, both of whom had reached prominence through radio broadcasting. The singers and musicians were paid a flat fee for their work. Music Center's business activities included cassette copying, and from the outset cassettes were released with an inlay in colour with a portrait of the artist. Following the example of Music Center, several other cassette companies were established in Kabul, such as Afghan Music, Aryan Music and Farhad Music.

Provincial cities had their own local music cassette businesses. In Herat in the 1970s there were a number of shops selling cassettes. Some cassettes were the products of companies like Music Center in Kabul, but these shops also made their own recordings of local artists, in what is best described as a cottage recording industry. These cassettes were replicated in small numbers, perhaps even copied individually to order. They had no special inlays but might be graced with a picture of an Indian or Pakistani female film star folded into the box. The name of the artist would be hand-written on the paper label stuck on the cassette itself. One night I attended a recording session for the visiting amateur Kabuli singer Khotam, a student of Ustad Sarahang. The recording session was organized by Azim, the proprietor of a cassette shop in the centre of the city and took place in Azim's home in a village near the city. Khotam, singing and playing *'armonia*, was accompanied by *dutâr*, *delrubâ* and *tabla*. Azim recorded on a stereo Sanyo cassette deck, with separate microphones for voice and *tabla*. He usually stopped the tape after a song had been recorded, and checked that the result was satisfactory. Material was carefully selected: Azim did not want any Indian classical music, and turned his machine off when Khotam sang a *râg* at my request. Azim's work showed the low level of technology involved in the production of cassettes outside the sophisticated studios of Kabul in the 1970s.

Madadi informed me that when the communists came to power in Kabul in 1978, the privately owned cassette businesses were closed down and their recording equipment, tape masters, and stocks of cassettes confiscated, on the grounds that their kind of music was not suited to the new revolutionary times. A new organization was set up, called Afghan Music, which was in effect a collective of singers, instrumentalists and composers, under the directorship of Mashor Jamal, a well-known singer and composer. Afghan Music established its own cassette production unit, releasing cassettes under the name of Afghan Music (not to be confused with the pre-revolutionary label with the same name). In this way the Government exercised tight control over what appeared on cassette.

With the steady increase in the size of diasporic Afghan communities in the West, there arose the need to supply them with Afghan music. An early entrepreneur in this field was the Afghan singer Ahmad Tahir, who made his way to Germany in about 1980. He started importing cassettes from Kabul, brought to him by the flight crews working for Ariana Afghan Airlines. He would have these copied in Germany and then travel round Germany and Austria to sell them to local Afghan businesses. In 1982 he went to the USA and settled in Alexandria, Virginia. By the late 1990s he started producing Afghan music DVDs and set up Tarana Film and Music Production. This company, and others that followed, established Alexandria as the main centre for the production of CDs of Afghan music in the USA, on labels such as Marco Polo and Afghan Music Production.

The other centre for Afghan CD production was Hamburg, which has a wealthy Afghan business sector. In 2006 I visited Hamburg for the first time, to meet with Madadi. He gave me a conducted tour of the Steindamm area, near the central railway station, where there are many Afghan and Turkish businesses in a part of the city well known for prostitution and sex shops. We visited a large shop devoted to music CDs and DVDs. This was the recently opened Kayhan Music, owned by Aref Kayhan. The shop itself did not seem to have been economically viable. A year later I found it shared its space with an Afghan travel agency, and in 2008 it had closed altogether, perhaps an indication of the general demise of the CD and the DVD. But the record shop was only part of the Kayhan enterprise. Aref and his family promoted concerts of Afghan music and also ran a recording business, with a large studio in the basement of the family home in a suburb of the city. Aref Kayhan had had some role as a singer on RTA in the 1980s, and he ran the studio with his two sons Farhad and Khaled, both of whom also worked as semi-professional musicians.

When I visited the Kayhan studio in 2006 we discussed amongst other matters the problems of getting the CD master that the studio produces pressed into CDs for sale. While it would be possible for them to get their CDs reproduced more cheaply in, for example, Pakistan, or China, the Kayhans were very aware of the need to maintain a high quality of product. Various faults could develop in the replication process, tracks might disappear and distortions appear. Things could go wrong with printing the label. Dealing with a far-away company made it hard to keep a check on these matters, so Kayhan Music preferred to deal with a local German company. Maintaining a reputation as the provider of a reliable product was very important (perhaps reflecting German standards of manufacture). In this respect their products contrasted markedly with the cheap CDs produced in flimsy cardboard covers in Pakistan, which are very often pirated copies of recordings made in the West and frequently turn out to be faulty. Kayhan Music was a good example of a small media company, recording and disseminating music CDs and also involved in the promotion of concerts by Afghan artists in Germany.

During my visit to Australia in 2009 I made a point of collecting locally produced Afghan-Australian CDs. Some of them were recorded in the Sash Studio in Sydney, a business I had the opportunity to look at in some detail. In this I was helped by Zahir Yusuf, who came over from Dandenong to work on his new CD. He wanted me to add some *rubâb* to two of the tracks. The tiny studio was located in the garage of the luxurious large new house occupied by the Sarshar family in the Glenwood suburb of the Sydney conurbation. Unlike Afghan CD production companies in Germany and the USA, Sash Studio did not offer their artists an advance. It catered for those who wanted to produce their own CDs. Normally a singer such as Zahir Yusuf approached the studio to discuss making a recording. The singer recorded the songs he wanted on his CD to a click track, accompanied by his own *'armonia*. Then over the next few weeks Ali Sarshar created what he called 'the music', that is, the accompaniment, using as many tracks as he needed, getting his brother Yama to lay down some percussion tracks playing *tabla* and/or *dohol*. Once the accompaniment had been finalized the singer would return to the studio and re-record his vocals without *'armonia*, singing over 'the music'. In 2009 the cost was $300 per track; typically the singer wanted 10 tracks. In theory, according to the deal, the singer could go back to the studio as often as he liked to make any changes he wanted in the accompaniment or his own performance, but no doubt there were limits to which this was possible. When the work was finished, the artist then paid $3,000 for the audio master plus artwork for the CD's cover, also designed by the multi-talented Ali Sarshar. The artist paid a CD replication company $2,000 to get 1,000 copies made, and it was then up to the artist to arrange about distribution. CDs sold for $7–$8 in the shops, and by the time the shopkeeper had taken his cut there was little if any profit to be made by the artist. Thus the CD in itself was not a commercial proposition; it was used to promote the artist and get bookings for gigs.

Retail Outlets

During my visits to Kabul after 2002, I found numerous retail outlets for audiocassettes and CDs, especially in Nader Shah Pashtun Street, near the city centre. Here there were shops and street vendors selling music in various formats, and a row of nearly identical open-fronted music shops nearby. In 2006 I had a productive conversation with Salim, the young proprietor of one of those shops. He told me he sold lots of cassettes of singers like Sarban and Nashenas, and of Hindi film music. Ahmad Zahir continued to be very popular, even with modern youth. During the Taliban era he had sold cassettes of Quranic recitation, and Taliban *tarânas*, and also sold 'real music' under the counter, for which he had twice been caught and imprisoned. He still had a stock of Taliban tapes at home, ready to put on his shelves should the Taliban return to power. Most of the CDs on sale in his shop were pirated copies of recordings made by Afghan studios in the West

In Fremont in 2000 I was introduced to the type of store known in the USA as an 'Afghan market'. This was typically a large supermarket stocked with all the necessary ingredients for Afghan cuisine, the herbs and spices, the dried fruits and nuts, pulses, dried milk products, *halal* meat, and freshly baked Afghan bread, often from a bakery at the back of the store. They sold Afghan national costumes for young girls to wear on festive occasions, books in Dari, Pashto and Arabic, ornaments and items such as wall-clocks in the shape of Afghanistan. Such stores usually also stocked a large selection of music CDs, VHS cassettes and DVDs, including many of Indian films. In the downtown area of Fremont there were half a dozen such Afghan markets.[10] I observed there to be a number of similar stores in the Steindamm area of Hamburg, and in Australia in the Auburn suburb near Sydney and in Dandenong, where they were called Afghan groceries. It is surely significant that music should be sold in food shops, and there is an interesting connection here between diet and identity; 'you are what you eat'.[11]

---

[10]   Ustad Asif can be seen visiting an Afghan market in *Tablas and Drum Machines*, 32′ 20″ (Baily 2005).

[11]   The phrase originated as a slogan for healthy eating but seems very apposite in the context of diet, culinary practices, ethnic identity and migration.

Likewise, music and dance CDs and DVDs also confer and express identity. In any case, music is often described as *qazâ-ye ruh* in Afghanistan, meaning 'spiritual food' or 'nourishment', an idea derived from Sufism. The connection between groceries and music can be found in some other immigrant communities, too.

Perusal of the recordings on sale in such outlets in the USA, Canada, Australia and Germany showed a variety of products. Some of the CDs were releases or re-releases of old recordings, either copied from audiocassettes originally published by Kabuli companies such as Music Center or Afghan Music, or from the original quarter-inch masters. There were many CDs of Ustad Sarahang, Afghanistan's greatest singer of *ghazals* and Indian classical music in the later twentieth century. Many of these were domestic recordings made at private parties where Sarahang was invited to sing. Likewise, there were numerous CDs of Ahmad Zahir, some of which were also of domestic origin. In addition, there were CDs of many singers from the past singing traditional genres – either 'albums' devoted to a particular artist, or compilations. However, there were many more CDs of the *new* Afghan music – vocal (male or female) accompanied by keyboards, drum machines and drum pads – and it is these which crowded the racks in the shops where the CDs were sold.

Audio and video piracy of cassettes, CDs, VHSs and DVDs was rife in the Afghan transnational community and was frequently a matter of complaint by musician and record producers. No sooner did a popular singer release a new album that cheap copies of it appeared in the retail outlets. Although this was obviously a matter of commercial exploitation, the pirates could offer their own justifications. I noticed that an Afghan grocery in Auburn had a set of DVDs, *Best of Afghani Hits*, Vols 1 to 10, which the shopkeepers had compiled themselves, from a variety of video sources from Afghanistan, Tajikistan and Uzbekistan. The provenance of these was obvious from the logos displayed on the footage. When I asked what *Tolo TV* (in Kabul) might say about the appropriation of *Tolo* materials I was told, 'It's okay, this is our culture and it's dying out and in this way we are supporting it.'

There are two largely separate worlds of audio recordings of Afghan music made for the Afghan market and Afghan music recordings that have found their way into the 'world music' market. Recordings aimed at the two domains have remained largely independent, and various suggestions can be offered as to how and why this should be. The new Afghan popular music on CD, privileging the use of electronic keyboards with their programmable percussion libraries, is of little interest to the world music audience, which seeks the exotic timbres and 'authencity' of non-western instruments. Packaging, lack of content information and the marketing of Afghan produced recordings are also part of the explanation. Conversely, recordings of traditional music represent an Afghan culture that Afghans have moved away from in their quest for modernity. The matter is discussed at greater detail by Baily 2010).

Creativity and the Flow of Music as Information

Music in Afghanistan in the past was by no means static. While there may have been genres that had remained relatively stable over long periods of time, such as rural *chahârbeiti* or unaccompanied religious singing (*na't khâni*), the history of music in Afghanistan since the 1860s describes a process of musical change, not just a succession of celebrated musicians and singers. As we have seen in earlier chapters, in the 1860s musicians, singers and dancers from British India brought with them knowledge of Hindustani music theory and practice, replacing the former Khorasani music of the court. It was probably at this time that the *'armonia* and *tabla* were introduced. They were to become two essential instruments of Afghan music. In the early twentieth century Ustad Qassem and others created the distinctive Kabuli *ghazal* style that in due course became the core of a pan-Afghan urban art music. The establishment of Radio Kabul in the 1940s saw the consolidation of the Afghan *tarz* style of popular song, often accompanied by a studio orchestra of western, Indian and Afghan instruments. The radio station emerged as the centre of musical creativity in Afghanistan, as discussed in Chapter 1. Amongst other innovations made at the radio station was the 14-stringed Herati *dutâr*, attributed to Mohammad Karim Herawi (Baily 1976). In the late 1960s – early 1970s Ahmad Zahir developed a more modern style of popular music, often playing electric organ or accordion, accompanied by small groups with western instruments such as trumpet, saxophone, flute and trap set. I have tried to show the flow of music as information at that time in Figure 1.3.

The communist takeover in 1978 and the start of the *jihâd* marked a turning point in the creative process. Despite the accelerating civil war, perhaps even because of it, Kabul remained the centre of musical creativity in Afghanistan, with activity focused on the newly established RTA organization, controlled by the Ministry of Information and Culture. The new hi-tech television studios and broadcasting network promoted the further development of popular music, modelled to some extent on trends in Uzbekistan and Tajikistan, and a number of young Afghan singers became prominent. Meanwhile, amongst the exiles, musicians were struggling to continue with their profession. In the near diaspora they were held back by the anti-music attitudes of the Afghan *mujahideen* parties in Pakistan and the new revolutionary government in Iran.

In due course the migratory movements that began after the communist take-over in 1978 placed Afghan musicians in contact with other kinds of music – in Pakistan, in Iran and in the West. The interactions led to various instances of interculturalism. In Pakistan, Afghan music became more strongly connected with its Hindustani roots and Afghan musicians began to adopt the Pakistani style *qawwâli* performance of Sufi music. In Mashhad there were interactions between Herati and Iranian musicians, exploring their common heritage, and this probably reinforced the former Iranian connections that were evident in the 1920s, as discussed in Chapter 1. The most significant interactions took place in the wider diaspora, where young Afghans were confronted by western popular music.

The difficulties of obtaining traditional Afghan instruments such as *rubâbs*, *dutârs* and *tanburs* encouraged the adoption of electronic keyboards manufactured by companies such as Yamaha, Technics and Korg, to which *'armonia* keyboard skills could be easily transferred. California became an important site for the development of a new keyboard-based Afghan music, as exemplified in the work of Qader Eshpari, who claimed to have innovated the 'one-man-band', a phenomenon criticized by Ahmad Sarmast in his *Studio 7* programme.

In the wider diaspora Afghans also encountered western dance culture, which led to the development of a new dance music, often called *fast muzik* or *musiqi-ye mast* (intoxicating music), or even *musiqi pop*. The development of the new dance music was closely connected with a new interest in dance. In western societies dancing is generally regarded as a normal part of social life, though one can certainly find many examples of puritanical condemnation of dance. Men and women dancing together is an accepted part of many kinds of social occasion, and we are familiar with the institutions of *the dance* and *the ball*, where social dancing itself is the main activity. Dance is respected and respectable and part of the curriculum in many schools in the West. It seems that Afghans in the wider diaspora adopted some of these relaxed views about dance, discovered the pleasures of social dancing and found a new freedom in expressing themselves through highly skilled aesthetically pleasing dance movements. This freedom of expression applies to men and women dancing together at wedding or birthday parties, and to the massed dancing by young men at concerts.

Another aspect of innovation in the wider diaspora was the concert presentation of visiting stars. This included the hire of the space, usually a banqueting hall in an area near where many Afghans live, the elaborate stage show, the lighting and PA system, security, travel and accommodation of visiting artists, and their payment, posters, and leaflets, adverts in local radio and television. These were new ways of presenting music, building a new kind of image, one much influenced by western popular music culture. That new image was also clearly evident in the design of many CD covers.

As we have seen from ideas voiced in the *Studio 7* programmes, the new music was not without its critics: with poor poetry, played by self-taught amateurs who knew nothing about the theory of music. Other commentators were less critical. When in 2006 I asked an Afghan BBC journalist in Kabul where the centre of creativity of Afghan music today is located he said:

> Inside Afghanistan there isn't any creativity, all the creativity comes from Afghan singers living in western countries. Farhad Darya, Wahid Qassemi, Qader Eshpari, Nasrat Parsa ... . They have creativity. These are the new people who are creating new things, the food for the new generation, the source for these young people, they feed from them.

To which one might reply, in the words of Salim the cassette seller of Kabul:

The singers who are abroad are also very good, Habib Qaderi is good, Qader Eshpari is also good, but they are not Ahmad Zahir's equals; they're not as popular as Ahmad Zahir. They copy his songs; they have some songs of their own but still they copy him. They have not been innovative; they have not made anything new. But they're okay.

In terms of innovation in recent times one could mention the following: Eshpari's invention of the one-man-band; Amir Jan Saburi's album *This is Life*, with his own compositions, recorded with the State Orchestra in Tashkent; Khalil Gudaz's Rumi songs with his own *sitâr* accompaniment; Geneva-based Khaled Arman's re-modelled *rubâb*, with four melody strings and frets all the way up the neck; Homayun Sakhi's development of new techniques for the *rubâb* and his involvement with the Kronos Quartet. All these innovations were made by musicians in the diaspora. The one innovation that may have taken place within Afghanistan itself is the expansion of a genre of instrumental composition in northern Afghanistan associated with the *dambura* and used to accompany solo dance. This kind of piece, which I knew in Herat in the 1970s as *Uzbeki*, has now proliferated into a group of pieces with names such as *Dard-e dandân dâram* (*I've got toothache*), *Parda Awal* (*First Fret*) and *Parda Dovum* (*Second Fret*).

In Chapter 1 I discussed the flow of popular music within Afghanistan in the 1970s. Figure 1.3 represented the flow of music from the centre to the periphery, and around the periphery. After my AHRC research in 2006 I had to update my ideas in the light of changed circumstances. The size of the network had expanded enormously: the centre of the Afghan transnational community was still Kabul, but now the periphery included geographically and culturally distant cities like London, Hamburg, Fremont, Toronto and Melbourne, as well as cities in Pakistan and Iran. Where now were the centres of musical creativity that were in any way equivalent to Radio Kabul/Radio Afghanistan in the middle of the twentieth century? It is clear that the centre of creativity was now a multi-sited series of hubs located in the periphery, in the wider diaspora, particularly in North America and Germany. The flow of music after the Taliban was now mainly *from* the periphery *into* Afghanistan. The community in exile in the West had become a dynamic centre for cultural innovation and change. The new music, westernized and modernized, was much in demand in post-Taliban Kabul, for concerts and wedding parties, with a strong emphasis on dancing.[12]

The fieldwork in Australia in 2009 allowed me to refine the model further. There was certainly circulation between the various sites (communities) in the periphery – especially between those located in the wider diaspora. But different places in the periphery had different saliencies, depending upon local conditions

---

[12]   The flow of music followed a more general pattern of economic flow – from the diaspora into Afghanistan. Here I do not refer simply to economic aid from the wealthier countries that were trying to support Afghanistan, but also to the remittances that Afghans abroad sent to support their families back home (Oeppen 2010).

and the size of the Afghan community. Afghan-Australian musical life was conditioned by the relatively small size of the community and Australia was not a significant hub of creativity of Afghan music. Ireland, with not more than a few hundred exiles from Afghanistan, was an extreme case in point. There was only one significant singer, Hakim Sanehi from Herat.[13] He had recorded a CD in Iran in 2007. London had a mixture of a few hereditary professional musicians from Kabul, and a number of semi-professionals who provided music for weddings and other celebrations. Only a few of these musicians had made CDs. In contrast, Fremont and Hamburg had large and relatively wealthy Afghan communities that could support an Afghan music industry. The circulation between the various sites in the periphery was asymmetrical. Germany and the USA were the major sources of musicians and new products, which flowed into less productive sites in the periphery. Music products manufactured in countries such as Australia had little chance of being distributed in Germany or the USA, though they might find their way to Afghanistan.

This updated view of the flow of music is represented in Figure 6.3. When in the future Afghanistan has the infrastructure to support professional music making, the flow chart will need to be redrawn, with Kabul again as the centre for musical creativity.

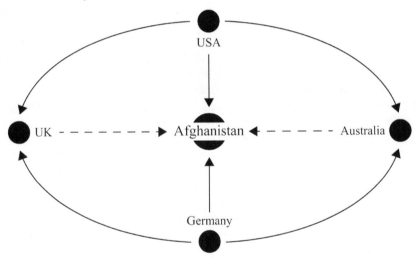

Figure 6.3   The global circulation of Afghan music around 2009

---

[13]   Hakim Sanehi was one of the first singers to appear on Afghan television. Clips of his performances can be found on YouTube.

Chapter 7
The Summing Up[1]

And so I reach the end of my journey through forty years of Afghan music history. By the time this book is published it will be 2015, the year in which USA and ISAF combat troops are to be finally withdrawn and the Afghans left (largely) to their own devices. What lessons have we learned about the music of Afghanistan in relation to its wider social and cultural contexts and what outcomes can we predict for its future?

Music and Politics

Whether by accident or design, music and politics are closely linked. The relationship is convincingly demonstrated by the experience of Afghanistan, where music is clearly a sensitive indicator of broader socio-political processes. Music making fluctuated widely in frequency and intensity according to the dominant ideology of the time. From the 1950s to the 1970s, during the heyday of Radio Afghanistan, music was relatively unconstrained and flourished. Women were free to sing over the radio and in the theatres. *Ramazân* may have been a month of fasting austerity, but it was also was a time for nightly concerts. Many amateur musicians became professional. The cassette industry was booming. Things changed dramatically with the communist takeover in 1978. In Kabul and other urban sites, music was promoted as a positive aspect of the new socialist polity, though song lyrics were carefully controlled as to political content. In contrast, amongst the refugees in Pakistan and Iran, music was under pressure. The opposition of the *mujahideen* parties to music, and its proscription in the refugee camps under their control, was exacerbated when the *mujahideen* coalition came to power in Kabul. In a less extreme form this phenomenon also occurred in cities like Herat, where private music making was permitted. With the coming of the Taliban the ban on music was officially complete, although a good deal of clandestine musical activities, performing and listening to recordings, continued. Following the defeat of the Taliban in 2001, music quickly reappeared, though problems of censorship continued, especially concerning the place of women singers.

In all this we see a close link between music and modernization. From the time of Sher Ali Khan in the 1860s, the Amirs of Kabul were modernizers who advocated material progress and who were also great patrons of music. During Amir Habibullah's era the modernist project was promoted by the influence of

---

[1]   With thanks to the shade of Somerset Maugham.

the cosmopolitan Afghan intellectual Mahmud Tarzi, who introduced Afghans to the modern world through his writings (Wide, 2013). Besides founding the influential newspaper *Siraj al-Akhbar*, which published many articles advocating the necessity of modernization in Afghanistan, he translated four of Jules Verne's novels. Mahmud Tarzi's influence continued during the reign of Amanullah, when further attempts at modernization were made. Nadir Khan continued the project, and after his assassination his brothers further implemented it. Zahir Shah's programme of modernization included the introduction of a democratic parliamentary system, and this was also the heyday of music making.

However, there is a complicated relationship between liberalism, secularism and modernism. Modernization itself has several aspects: first, material – in the form of electricity, a postal system, industrialization, new roads, modern transport; second, social – justice and human rights, the education of girls and the unveiling of women; and, third, political – the introduction of new political systems, such as socialism or democracy. Music in the Afghan context was not *necessarily* associated with modernization; it had more to do with the liberalization and secularization that went along with modernization in Afghanistan than with the concept of modernism in itself. The communist rulers of Kabul may have promoted music as an aspect of the modern society they strove to establish, but society was to be tightly regulated. It was to be secularized but not liberalized. Patronage of music in itself is not necessarily a sign of modernization. The great development of vocal art music in India in the late nineteenth century was not driven by modernism but by competition between rival courts deprived of military might. The introduction of *nautch* girls to the Kabul court by Sher Ali Khan was not an obvious sign of modernization, either. Nevertheless, the Amirs of Kabul adopted a pro-music policy as part of their modernist aspirations. The fact that music flourished during this period is indicative of the generally liberal and modernist policies emanating from Kabul. While Islamist factions may have opposed music, much as they opposed many aspects of modernization, the vernacular Sufism that prevailed in Afghanistan sanctioned music from a religious point of view.

Afghan Identities

I approach the contentious and complicated subject of identity with some trepidation, for this takes us into areas of anthropology, sociology, psychology and cultural studies that are far beyond the domain of my narrative. The term *identity* is used with various qualifiers in many contexts: we speak of personal identity, individual identity, social identity, cultural identity, ethnic identity, national identity, transnational identity and even global identity. Thinking about the issue in the Afghan context embraces most of these possible meanings of 'identity'.

Afghanistan is notable for its ethnic diversity, which may have something to do with the mountainous terrain and past difficulties of communication between areas that are quite close geographically, allowing isolated communities to remain culturally intact over long periods of time. According to Glatzer (1998: 167) the most exhaustive list of the ethnic groups in Afghanistan was compiled by the German anthropologist Erwin Orywal, who identified 55 ethnic groups in Afghanistan. However, as Glatzer points out, many of these groups and identities were local, variable and relative. For present purposes the largest ethnic groups are Pashtun, Tajik, Hazara and Uzbek, followed by Turkmen, Pashai, Baluch, Kazakh, Kirghiz, Aimaq and Nuristani. This very diversity is itself problematic and challenging in modern times. As I wrote in an earlier paper on music and Afghan identity:

> Issues of cultural identity seem likely to constitute some of the major problems confronting humanity in the twenty-first century. In various places around the world we see heterogeneous political entities of various sizes – from large empires to relatively small countries – disintegrating into their constituent parts, a process often accompanied by a frightening degree of conflict. We become increasingly aware of the extraordinary tenacity of this phenomenon we call 'culture', and of the way its meaning and importance persist for the culture bearers.
>
> Afghanistan may be taken as a paradigm of this process. Confronted with the cultural and political fragmentation that has occurred since the Marxist *putsch* of 1978 one wonders what kind of unity ever prevailed in the past. What was it that held this country of 15 million people together? Was it a unity that was imposed and maintained by force, or was there a real degree of social consensus? And if one can identify the processes that gave political cohesion in the past, how can they be revived, assuming that would be the best outcome for the people of Afghanistan and their neighbours? (Baily 1994b: 45)

Part of the answer to the question of what held Afghanistan together in the past is the fact that although the country may have a multi-ethnic population it does not exhibit a great range of cultural diversity. Despite speaking a variety of languages the different ethnic groups shared basically the same worldview, the same religion (allowing for Sunni/Shia distinctions), the same material culture, the same agricultural methods and the same commercial organization of urban life. Nevertheless, the challenge of ethnic diversity was recognized. As discussed in Chapter 1, in the 1930s a new nationalist movement developed in Afghanistan in the wake of Mahmud Tarzi's earlier efforts in that direction. Nationalist writers of the time recognized that one of Afghanistan's problems was its ethnic diversity and they were preoccupied with establishing a common history, religious background and ethnic origin for all the peoples of Afghanistan, claiming that they were descended from the same Aryan stock (Gregorian 1969: 347). As the twentieth-century Pashtun poet Malang Jan put it:

Chay ay mor'i pa de khawra zagawalay
Ka pa har zhaban goyaa day, khow Afghan day
[That person who was given birth by his mother on this soil
Whatever language he speaks, he is still an Afghan][2]

---

[2]   I thank Nabi Misdaq for pointing out this couplet.

Music had a role to play in this attempt to create a national identity. Radio broadcasting opened up new possibilities for communication between Kabul and the rest of the country, and it allowed the government to inform the population of its policies and development programmes. It seems probable that music on air was promoted as a way of attracting an audience that could then be informed about local news and government edicts and policies; it was part of a modernizing package. Music was surely deliberately used to promote nationalism, modernity and secularism. Slobin discussed the role of music on radio in the following terms:

> Radio Afghanistan is one of the few unifying factors in a country unusually marked by ethnic and linguistic fragmentation ... For the Afghan villager or nomad ... the radio has drastically reduced the restrictions on the scope of his imagination ... he shares in the music of the Kabul studio, one of the few manifestations of an emerging pattern of national values and expression that may eventually comprise a pan-ethnic, distinctively Afghan society. (Slobin 1974: 247–8)

Slobin writes about 'an emerging pattern' that may eventually lead to a pan-ethnic society: I believe the pattern had in fact *emerged* already. It was the war that began in 1978 that jeopardized the success of the project.

One of the outcomes of the war was the exacerbation of inter-ethnic conflict, both inside Afghanistan and in the diaspora. For present purposes of simplification we can consider the two most significant ethnic groups inhabiting Afghanistan to be Pashtuns (the 'true Afghans'), speakers of the Pashto language, and the 'so-called' Tajiks, who are Persian speaking agriculturalists and townspeople to be found all over Afghanistan. The country has been dominated politically since it came into being in 1747 by Pashtuns, who in the 1970s made up about half of the total population of 15 million people, while Tajiks amounted to three or four million. Both groups were dispersed over much of the territory of Afghanistan, with the Pashtun heartland in the south and south-east.

The history of Afghanistan since its inception in 1747 is in part the story of relations between these two ethnic groups. The rulers of Afghanistan were Pashtuns, the military forces were mainly Pashtun, but Dari was the language of the court and the administration, inherited from the Durranis' sojourn as mercenaries in Iran. The Afghan royal family were 'Persianized Pashtuns', who by the twentieth century hardly spoke Pashto.[3] It is clear that at least for the elite there had been an accommodation between the cultures of the Pashtuns and Tajiks. Pashtun hegemony remained relatively unchallenged until the new constitution

---

[3]   'Although ... these leaders and rulers were originally Durrani Pashtun most spoke Dari as their first language and felt more like urban Kabulis than elite Pashtuns. For example [President] Daoud's brother Mohammad Naim, who was his foreign minister in the 1950s on a visit to Pakistan found himself highly embarrassed when the then President of Pakistan, Yaqob Khan, spoke with him in Pashto and he could not reply. Yaqob Khan then told him, "how come you want Pashtunistan but, do not speak their language!"' (Misdaq 2006: 82).

of 1964, which allowed greater freedom of expression, particularly in the print media. Ethnic differences were exacerbated after 1978, with rivalries between the two wings of the PDPA, and amongst the many *mujahideen* parties that were allied with one ethnic group or another. Of the Peshawar Seven, six were strongly Pashtun in terms of recruitment; the seventh was the Tajik party of Rabbani, supported by his most able commander, Ahmad Shah Massoud. And in the wider diaspora, freedom of speech and freedom of expression in print media, radio, television, and in due course Internet, has enabled people from Afghanistan to air old inter-ethnic grievances and stir up new ones.

Some non-Pashtuns in the diaspora resist being labelled as 'Afghan'. They are eager to point out that the territory was not called Afghanistan until comparatively recently: maps from the nineteenth century by European cartographers show that initially 'Afghanistan', if used at all, referred to the Pashtun heartland. Elphinstone's classic book of 1815 is entitled *An Account of the Kingdom of Caubul and its dependencies in Persia, Tartary, and India*. Persia, Tartary and India refer to the extended territories west, north and south in the Afghan 'Empire' established by Ahmad Shah Durrani after 1747. The territory to the west and north was historic Khorasan, with its four great cities of Herat, Balkh, Merv and Nishapur. Some in the Afghan diaspora want to call themselves Khorasani rather than Afghan; others advocate the new appellation 'Afghanistani' (Bezhan 2008: 21).

Music in the Afghan Diaspora: Mashhad, Peshawar and Fremont

Here I propose a simple model that tries to link together several kinds of identity. To start with, I assume that the individual human being needs self-identity, a sense of personhood that is necessary for a healthy psychological state of being. I would suppose this need is innate, part of the human condition. A person's individual identity is established in part through a process of enculturation, of growing up embedded in a particular culture, plus the individual's unique set of life experiences and chosen beliefs. Through combining received culture and personal experience the individual constructs a fluid sense of self-identity. In the context of a nation state, a socially constructed place assembled through the combination of its constituent cultural identities, one arrives at a national identity that is rooted in a geographical space, a homeland. And when, for whatever reason, through processes of migration we have diasporic communities, its people may or may not construct a transnational identity.

What does music have to do with all this? If, as Blacking posits, 'music is essential for the very survival of man's humanity' (see the Introduction to this volume), then we may suppose that music is an important component of identity, from individual to transnational. Moreover, music is a powerful tool in the transmission and construction of identity because of its special capacity to generate emotion. Music is a potentially strong symbol of identity; like language (and attributes of language such as accent and dialect), it is one of those aspects of culture that can, when the need to assert 'ethnic identity' arises, most readily serve this purpose. Its effectiveness may be twofold: not only does it act as a ready means for the identification of different ethnic or social groups, but it has potent emotional connotations and can be used to assert and negotiate identity in a particularly powerful manner (Baily 1994b: 48). There is nothing unique to Afghanistan and its diaspora on this point; the same applies in many other transnational communities. But what is special about countries such as Afghanistan, Pakistan, Somalia, Mali and others, is the repression of music by Islamists. Censorship endows music with fresh power and significance. The mere fact of music, the mere act of music making, become political statements.

It is worth looking in more detail at the issue of music and identity in Mashhad, Peshawar and Fremont, all visited by me during the period of Taliban supremacy (see Chapter 4). We begin with a comparison between the two sites of near diaspora, Mashhad and Peshawar. Both cities are geographically and culturally close to Afghanistan. Both afforded a temporary safe haven for a refugee population that would in all likelihood return to Afghanistan. In general terms, in both cases music seems to have been about normalization, reassurance, ticking over, keeping things going through difficult times in anticipation of going home. Traditional music reminded people of their cultural heritage and gave them a feeling of being connected to a relatively secure past. Herati musicians in Mashhad and Kabuli musicians in Peshawar were self-consciously keeping their cultural identity alive in the place of exile. Their performances were largely inward directed, both for themselves and for their Afghan patrons in exile. Music in this situation had a quasi-therapeutic influence and one might describe this as a classic role for 'culture in exile'.

When we look in more detail at the musicians themselves, their social organization and their relations to the host community, then some interesting differences emerge. The number of musicians from Kabul was much larger than from Herat. There were several large extended families of hereditary musicians, like the Nabizada family, the sons and grandsons of Ustad Ghulam Nabi, or the Hamahang family, Haji Hamahang himself, and his sons and grandsons. Although the hereditary musicians of the Kucheh Kharabat had originally come from a number of places, some were the descendants of indigenous Afghan musician families, many were from the Indian Subcontinent, others from Kashmir, and through inter-marriage they had come to constitute a large coherent musician community. They stuck together in Khalil House for a number of reasons. They had lived cheek by jowl in Kabul; now at least they worked cheek by jowl in Peshawar, crammed into the business centre of Khalil House. It gave them a feeling of solidarity and a sense of protection. It also enabled the musicians from Kabul to maintain and even develop key skills. Having little else to do in this small space, they spent a lot of time playing to and with each other and had ample opportunity to listen to and learn from and compete with one another. It was a time for retrospection and consolidation of the music they especially valued, the art music of Kabul. They were not just recreating the past, but using their enforced exile as a spur to excel and develop in certain directions. That was shown most clearly in the virtuosity and creativity of Homayun Sakhi.

In comparison, the number of Herati musicians in Mashhad was small. They were less cohesive and consisted basically of three families, the Khushnawaz family, its Hassanpur offshoot, and the Delahang (Golpasand) family. There had been rivalry between them in the past, with the Khushnawaz group tending to dominate, but by the year 2000 the scales were tipping in the other direction and Jalil Delahang was emerging as a very good singer. The Herati musicians from the three families had less opportunity for day-to-day contact and interaction than their colleagues in Pakistan. If Khalil House brought the Kharabat musicians together, in Mashhad it was Nasruddin Saljuqi and the Association of Actors and Musicians that encouraged collaboration between the musicians.

Another difference was that the Heratis were more 'at home' in Mashhad than the Kabulis were in Peshawar. This was in part a difference in mother tongue. The Dari spoken in Herat is close to the dialect of Persian spoken in Iranian Khorasan, while the Dari speakers of Kabul were embedded in a largely Pashto speaking Peshawari population. There seems to have been more interaction between Herati and local Mashhadi musicians than between Kabuli and local Peshawari musicians. And quite possibly the Heratis enjoyed more patronage from Iranian institutions than did the Kabulis from the Pakistani equivalents. In both Mashhad and Peshawar the hereditary musicians retained control of the music business; music making was their traditional occupation, and they held on to it.

Fremont represents the wider diaspora at that time. For various reasons, these Afghans realized that they were not going back to live in Afghanistan, and they had got to make the most of the new opportunities they had in America. For older Afghans in Fremont, those who had actually made the long journey from Kabul to California, music culture had the same quasi-therapeutic benefits discussed for Mashhad and Peshawar, providing a link with the past. But for the younger generation, who had grown up in Fremont, music also provided a means through which to create a new identity as permanent citizens. Musical performances in Fremont addressed the future, using newly available technical resources in an innovative manner to construct a new 'Afghan-American' popular music that helped to consolidate a new Afghan-American identity. Afghans in Fremont lived in a cultural milieu which placed a high value on music, and they had become free from the hereditary professional musicians who had controlled the music business in the past and who were custodians of musical traditions they maintained could only be learned *sina be sina* (chest to chest), through direct one-to-one teaching. Reyes (1986: 91) argued that the difficulties of refugee life, 'impede the usual channels through which traditions pass from one generation to the next'. One could argue that in Fremont young Afghan musicians were liberated from the strictures of the past. The economic advantages they enjoyed allowed them to invest in expensive electronic equipment and they took advantage of the creative opportunities this provided. In the process they were able to free themselves from the protocols of the Kharabat epitomized in the formal institution of the *ustâd-shâgerd* relationship established through the *gormâni* ritual.

The Ten *Hamkârân*

I have once again to acknowledge my debt to the *hamkârân*, my panel of experts, my advisory board. Let me name them again, in order of their appearance in my tale: Amir Jan Herati, Nashenas, Sattar Khan, Rahim Khushnawaz, Madadi, Homayun Sakhi, Ustad Asif, Ghulam Hussain, Haroon Yousofi and Zahir Yusuf. They, amongst others, were my links to the scenes of Afghan music I encountered; some of them were my teachers or people from whom I learned specific pieces or techniques. From their lives we gain insight into the recent history of Afghanistan's music; their experiences and life stories amount to a history of music in Afghanistan since the 1970s.

Between them my musician friends embraced the whole range of musician recruitment and roles in Afghan society, from amateur (*shauqi*) to professional (*kesbi*), and from non-literate to the highly educated. They were all male, since (quite properly) I had so little contact with Afghan women in general, let alone women singers or musicians. Six of them were from hereditary musician backgrounds. Amir Jan and Sattar Khan, his father-in-law, were from barber-musician families, low ranking in terms of social status. Rahim was from a non-barber musician background.[4] The other three, Ustad Asif, Ghulam Hussain and Homayun Sakhi, were denizens of Kabul's Kucheh Kharabat. Ustad Asif traces his ancestry back to Gamuddin Khan from Kasur in the Punjab, while the backgrounds of Ghulam Hussain and Homayun Sakhi are unclear. As Kharabatians they had an advanced knowledge of classical music and sat comfortably on the cusp between Afghan and Indian traditions.

Nashenas and Madadi were from educated backgrounds and relatively cosmopolitan in experience: Nashenas, with his study of Pashto linguistics in Moscow, and Madadi, with his technical training as a radio journalist in Germany. Nashenas and Madadi both experienced strong pressure from their families and others not to engage in music making when they were young. Neither can be said to have crossed the *shauqi/kesbi* divide, since they did not come to depend upon money earned from performing music for their livelihoods. Madadi was a staff member at Radio Afghanistan for most of his working life, was often on air as a singer and had a large number of songs in the archive. Certainly when in exile he was happy to perform professionally (that is, for payment) at concerts in Germany, France and the UK. Nashenas was in a similar position. From a wealthy family he also held various positions at Radio Afghanistan and other government posts. In exile he has given concerts in the USA and Germany but performs only for small private parties at home in the UK. Zakir Yusuf is a true semi-professional, earning a living as a taxi-driver and as a singer. Haroon Yousofi is perhaps the

---

[4]   It is not quite clear but his grandfather appears to have been an amateur turned professional from the early twentieth century, at a time when Iranian *dastgâh* music was in vogue in Herat.

only genuinely amateur singer amongst the *hamkârân*. He is otherwise famous as a radio presenter, radio personality and stand-up comedian.

Most of the *hamkârân* nurtured me as a musician, sustained me, stuffed me full of *qazâ-ye ruh*, 'food for the soul', or 'spiritual nourishment'. I learned all sorts of things from them about music and musicians. While I count Ustad Mohammad Omar as my first *rubâb* teacher, more than 20 years later I became the 'official' *shâgerd* of Rahim Khushnawaz through an informal *gormâni* ceremony conducted by Ustad Asif Mahmud in London. Through Rahim I trace my musical lineage to Ustad Nabi Gol of the Kucheh Kharabat, the teacher of Rahim's father, Ustad Amir Jan Khushnawaz, the source of many of the old compositions I collected.

The *hamkârân*, too, have been responsible for putting very good *rubâb*s in my hands. Acquiring good Afghan instruments is no simple matter; they are not usually available in shops that sell musical instruments. You have to commission an instrument maker to make you an instrument, or purchase one from a musician. In 1995 Rahim exchanged the excellent *rubâb* he had brought to Paris and London in 1995 for an instrument I had bought from his father in 1975. Rahim's was the better instrument but he wanted, for sentimental reasons, to have the one his father had owned and played. Amir Jan Herati, generous as ever, gave me another very nice *rubâb* that he had brought to Switzerland for his concerts in 1999. It is the twin of the *rubâb* that Amir himself plays so touchingly in the final scene of the film *Amir* (Baily 1985a). Being relatively small, it is the instrument I usually take with me for concerts, especially when air travel is involved.

So, amongst other things I became a kind of semi-professional Afghan *rubâb* player, similar in status to Nashenas or Madadi. I have played in many concerts in many countries: in the USA, Canada, Australia, Germany, Italy, Ireland, Denmark, Finland, Switzerland, Greece, Iran and Afghanistan, usually with Veronica. For some years we had a Goldsmiths-based group, Ensemble Bakhtar, with my Greek PhD student Matthaios Tsahourides, a virtuoso of the Pontic *lyra*, and Yusuf Mahmoud, *tabla*. I realize that I am living in a world where many musicians are deeply involved with other people's music, and I am one of them. My work as a practising musician has also had a direct impact on Afghan culture, in nurturing the spirit of Afghan music during the last 35 years. For Afghans it was important that there should be recognition and respect for their rich traditions, including music. Refugees, exiles, need to be reminded that they have an admirable and valuable culture with deep historical roots. Because 35 years of war destroyed, changed and transformed so much, the gaps in the record mean that the researcher becomes a resource, the archive of field recordings holds invaluable remnants of a cultural heritage, the fieldwork of the ethnographer becomes part of the informants' own music history. The skills and knowledge acquired in the process of learning to perform can then be handed back to those from whom they were borrowed in the first place. And as with any intangible cultural heritage, it is important that it should not be preserved unchanged as a museum piece, but retain its dynamic potential for development (Howard 2012: Chapter 1).

Future Prospects for the Music of Afghanistan

Finally, we come to the question of the future of Afghanistan's music, a matter that is intimately tied to the destiny of Afghanistan itself. I have no intention here of getting involved in the debate about the rights and wrongs of western intervention in Afghanistan after 9/11. Early on, Johnson and Leslie (2004) could detect how things were *not* working out as envisaged by the West. Both authors had spent years working in Afghanistan, including the era of Taliban rule, and were well placed to see what was going wrong. Cowper-Coles, British Ambassador in Kabul and then the Foreign Secretary's Special Representative to Afghanistan (serving from 2007 to 2010) gives a masterly account of the conduct of the war against the Taliban, and points out the many mistakes that were made, especially in US policy (Cowper-Coles 2011).

From my visits to Kabul between 2002 and 2006 I was aware of the increasing sense of disappointment following the initial euphoria. My friend Aziz Yaqubi, the administrator of AFSC, was there every time I visited Kabul. We had long discussions every morning over breakfast, and he kept me up to date with the latest scandals involving corruption at the highest levels, and all the other complaints voiced by the Afghan people about what was happening and what was not happening. On the other hand, I am aware of many improvements in that period in terms of human rights, education and the availability of medical facilities. Kabul may have grown without planning, but some of that growth is impressive in terms of rebuilding a ruined city. The way the denizens of the Kharabat have found the means to rebuild their houses is a case in point.

The upgrading of the media and media growth are regarded as one of the success stories of the new Afghan state. After 2001 there was a plethora of new independent radio and TV stations operating in Afghanistan, a trend well documented by Page and Siddiqi (2012). Western countries saw free media as a pillar of the new democracy they sought to bring to Afghanistan. The government granted broadcasting licences more or less on demand. The USA encouraged a strong commercial media sector, while the Europeans saw media as a way to strengthen the influence of civil society. According to statistics provided by Page and Siddiqi (2012: 6), by 2010 there were 75 terrestrial TV stations, 30 in Kabul, eight in Herat. There were 175 FM stations in the country, 34 of them owned by the Ministry of Information and Culture. There was also an extraordinary growth in the use of mobile telephones.[5] A country that had been dogged by poor communications for so long suddenly had the resources to enter the cutting edge of the modern world. A range of financial backers and audiences supported these radio and TV broadcasters. External donors funded some local radio and TV stations; advertising financed others. There were the so-called 'warlord channels',

---

[5]　By 2011 there were four mobile telephone networks: 66 per cent of the population had access to a mobile, 88 per cent in the cities, 60 per cent in rural areas. On the other hand, only 4 per cent of the population had access to the Internet (ibid., p. 6).

connected with former militia and major *mujahideen* leaders such as Dostam, Hekmatyar and Rabbani. Some channels had specific religious affiliations, and some were sectarian and vehement in their ethnic affiliations, accused of stirring up sectarian conflicts. There was, and remains, the problem of a lack of regulatory framework. Only occasionally was a channel closed down because of its promotion of sectarian propaganda, and then only for a short while.

In the midst of this media frenzy the Taliban did not have its own TV channel, but it did have a strong website presence. Page and Siddiqi (2012: 10) note the popularity of Taliban *tarāna*s with users of their website. The growth of media is particularly relevant because modernization in Afghanistan in the twentieth century was closely linked to improvements in communication, from roads to radio. In contrast to the development of private sector media, state-owned RTA showed a steady decline in popularity, due to poor funding and disputes about content, especially in the early days regarding women singers, as we have seen in Chapter 5. Many of RTA's younger staff left to join more dynamic independent radio and TV channels, leaving RTA saddled with an aging workforce, many of whom worked from 1992 to 2002 with little if any emolument. The institution that was so central to the musical life of Afghanistan in the past has become largely moribund.

Kabul Once Again, 2011

In 2011 I paid another visit to Kabul, after an absence of five years. I had not felt the need to go back; I was trying to digest what I had already garnered over the years rather than gathering new data. This time my mission was to visit the Afghanistan National Institute of Music (ANIM), a co-educational vocational music school that teaches Afghan, Indian and western music, founded by musicologist Dr Ahmad Sarmast. The UK-based Society for Education, Music and Psychology Research (SEMPRE) had taken a keen interest in ANIM and invited me to visit Kabul in October 2011 as their 'Special Ambassador to Afghanistan'. This was not an official inspection but an informal visit over a period of 12 days, in part to explore ways in which SEMPRE could further support ANIM in the area of staff development. During this time I had the free run of the Institute, and visited many classes, small group rehearsals, orchestral rehearsals and non-music classes.

ANIM is located in a large compound very close to Kabul University, and is housed in a modern two-storey building erected in the 1970s, now totally refurbished, with a library, IT room, classrooms, performance spaces and studios for faculty members. The school's founder is the son of the celebrated musician, composer, conductor and teacher, Ustad Salim Sarmast (see Chapter 1). Ahmad Sarmast received a training in western music in this former Vocational School of Music opened by the Ministry of Education in 1974.[6] He went on to study music

---

[6] This school provided tuition in western music theory, solfege, piano, guitar, saxophone, drums, flute, trombone and accordion. It was under the tutelage of Faqir

in Moscow, this during the time of the communist governments of Afghanistan when many young Afghans were sent to the USSR for higher education. In 1992 he emigrated to Australia, studied at Monash University, and was awarded his PhD degree for an important historical survey of music in Afghanistan, referred to frequently in Chapter 1 (Sarmast 2004). Working subsequently as a post-doctoral fellow in the Monash Asia Institute, Dr Ahmad Sarmast established the Revival of Afghan Music (ROAM) project, aimed at rebuilding vocational music education in the Islamic Republic of Afghanistan. According to ROAM's statement of 2008:

> After almost three decades of war, the musical culture of Afghanistan and its music institutions have been shattered. Music education and the promotion of music are tasks requiring urgent attention. To establish a vocational school of music it is important to identify and assist Afghan children with special musical gifts, regardless of their gender, personal and social circumstances. Such children, especially orphans, can benefit greatly from receiving specialist music training as part of their general education. Such training will enable them to proceed towards careers in music, and in this manner also promote job creation in Afghanistan. (http://www.monash.edu.au/mai/roam/)

With generous funding from the World Bank and many other sources, especially in Germany and the USA, Dr Sarmast has been able to implement the ROAM project. The former Vocational School of Music had been reopened as the Vocational Secondary School of Fine Arts in about 2004. Though supported financially by a Polish NGO the school was seriously under-funded and little music teaching was taking place. Sarmast took over the two-storey building and raised money to completely refurbish it. He then hired a number of international staff, mostly American music educators, to teach western music, and he also acquired a large stock of brand new musical instruments, Afghan, Indian and western. In 2010 ANIM was officially inaugurated. The whole process of planning, fund-raising and implementation is recorded in the remarkable documentary directed by Australian film maker Polly Watkins, *Dr Sarmast's Music School* (Watkins 2012), from which I quote in the following paragraphs.[7]

Mohamad Nangyalai, Salim Sarmast, Mohammad Ismail Azami, Abulrazaq Zafaryar, and a number of others. In 1987 training in instruments of Afghan music such as *'armonia, rubâb, tanbur, dilrubâ* and *zirbaghali* was introduced. A number of Afghan musicians working in the western musical idiom were trained in the Vocational School of Music, such as the composer Babrak Wassa, now in Germany, Khaled Arman, who later studied classical guitar in the Prague Conservatory, and is based in Geneva, Wahid Samandari, trumpet player and conductor in the Czech Republic, and Dr Sarmast himself. This school was closed down in 1992 when the Coalition government came to power.

[7]   I also edited a film from video I shot during my visit, *Return of the Nightingales* (Baily 2013). One of the main differences between Polly Watkins's epic and my own much more modest effort lies in Colin Young's distinction between telling a story and showing the viewer something (see Chapter 2).

At the time of my visit there were 140 ANIM pupils, from a variety of backgrounds. Some were recruited from AFCECO (Afghanistan Children Education and Care Organization), a progressive orphanage that has its own music programme. Ahmad Sarmast evinces a special vocation to help orphans gain a training in music, saying, 'My father Ustad Mohammad Salim Sarmast was a well known and respected Afghan musician. And I'm proud to say that my father was an orphan whose life was changed thanks to music.'[8] Some of the school's pupils came from a so-called 'street working children' background, who helped support their families by selling newspapers, magazines, chewing gum or plastic bags on the streets of Kabul. Sarmast made a special effort to enrol such children, but they proved to be so behind in other aspects of education they had great difficulties with schoolwork and tended to drop out, ashamed of their educational backwardness. ANIM also inherited a number of pupils from the former Vocational Secondary School of Fine Arts it came to replace.

New pupils were selected through an audition process that assessed a sense of rhythm, a sense of pitch, a curiosity about musical instruments, and an initial impulse of what instrument the child might like to learn. Recruitment also required engagement with parents, to get them to realize the opportunities study at ANIM would provide and to overcome prejudice against music. As Sarmast says to a group of prospective applicants, 'We will explain to them that times have changed and the art of music can have a very important role in your education and guarantee your future.'[9]

As well as music, ANIM pupils study the normal Afghan school curriculum: Religious Studies, Dari, Pashto, Maths, Physics, History, Geography, and a little Chemistry and Biology. There is a strong emphasis on learning English. At the time of my visit ANIM employed 35 teachers, 10 for general education and 25 for music, including seven international faculty, six of them Americans teaching violin, viola, cello, piano, oboe, trumpet, flute and percussion, and one Indian, Ustad Mohammad Irfan, teaching *sitâr* and *sarod*. Ahmad Farid Shefta, an Afghan trained in Ukraine, teaches clarinet and serves as choirmaster.

One of the justifications for the emphasis on western music is the fact that it had been part of Afghan music culture since the early twentieth century. But there are other reasons. As Sarmast explains in Polly Watkins's film: 'Some people told me why does Afghanistan need Bach or Beethoven or Mozart? You should concentrate on Afghan traditional music. But Bach, Beethoven, Mozart, they don't belong to Europe, they don't belong to America, they belong to all the world and I want Afghan kids to have access to the musical heritage of the world.'[10]

Ahmad Sarmast has clear ideas about the linkage between music and democracy: 'An important element of democracy is to give people a chance to

---

[8]   *Dr Sarmast's Music School* – 16' 42" (Watkins 2012).
[9]   *Dr Sarmast's Music School* – 15' 54" (ibid.).
[10] *Dr Sarmast's Music School* – 24' 09" (ibid.).

express themselves via arts and music.'[11] Under the Taliban people were deprived of 'a very basic human right of expressing themselves freely with music'.[12] He attaches great importance to the fact that ANIM has its own elected student advisory board, appointed by secret ballot. The counting of the votes is conducted in front of the board members in the interests of transparency. In this way ANIM students learn about the meaning of democracy in a very direct practical manner:

> There's a lot of challenges but there's a lot of positive changes. The positive changes we created here, returning the musical rights of Afghan children back to them and allowing them to learn the type of music that they love to play, really, it's a positive change. Every small step like that is going to make a great change to the country.[13] ... It is now for the government and the clergy of this country to make a clear statement about the status of music. It should be clearly reflected in all laws and regulations of this country. If it's not going to happen it might come again under fire and still music will be considered as a loose practice and loose activity.[14]

During my visit the students were practising a major work, *Prayer for Peace*, with choir and orchestra. Ahmad Farid Shefta coached the choir, mainly girls, and William Harvey, the violin and viola teacher, conducted the orchestra. This piece was videoed for the International Conference on Afghanistan held in Bonn in December 2011. As Shefta says about this work:

> We made this peace song to have the same voice as the voice of Afghanistan's people. Through this song we want to raise our voice together with Afghanistan's people and make the people of the world hear our voice of peace so that one day Afghanistan will become peaceful. The more we stay with music the further we will get away from war.[15]

In 2013 ANIM pupils gave a series of high-profile concerts in the USA, including one in Carnegie Hall. In the same year Sarmast's contribution to music and child development was recognized by his being awarded an Honorary Membership of the Royal Philharmonic Society in London. It is clear that ANIM is the answer to Madadi's plea in the *Studio 7* programme for the creation of 'a proper music school in Kabul' (Chapter 6). It is significant that ANIM, while nominally under the aegis of the Ministry of Education, is not an Afghan government initiative but the work of a single gifted individual from Afghanistan (Figure 7.1).

---

[11]   *Dr Sarmast's Music School* – 61′ 09″ (ibid.).
[12]   *Dr Sarmast's Music School* – 71′ 49″ (ibid.).
[13]   *Dr Sarmast's Music School* – 93′ 36″ (ibid.).
[14]   *Dr Sarmast's Music School* – 86′ 59″ (ibid.).
[15]   *Dr Sarmast's Music School* – 79′ 59″ (ibid.).

Figure 7.1   Ahmad Samin Zefar (*rubâb*) and Nadim Nabizada (cello) at ANIM, 2011

These reflections on Dr Sarmast's Music School lead me to end my tale on a positive note. At the time of my visit in 2011 I was also able to participate in the first National Folkloric Music Seminar and Festival held in the historic and recently renovated Queen's Palace in the famous Bagh-e Babur, Kabul, on 23–24 October 2011. The organization of this important event brought together a number of institutions, notably the Ministry of Information and Culture, the Aga Khan Music Initiative, the Afghanistan National Institute of Music, the Foundation for Culture and Civil Society, and the Music Department of Kabul University. On the mornings of both days, Afghan scholars, intellectuals and academics presented short papers on various regional musics, in Pashto, Dari, and in my case, English.[16] In the early afternoons there were discussion sessions and a number of resolutions were passed concerning matters such as copyright and censorship. In the late afternoons and early evenings it was time for the Festival, when 20 groups from many parts of Afghanistan performed their local regional musics.

---

[16]   The subject of my talk was 'Recent changes in the *dutâr* of Herat', the subject of my original fieldwork in 1973–74.

The Seminar and Festival were significant events, for several reasons. They showed that local traditions were not, as many might have supposed, moribund after so many years of armed conflict but had simply gone 'underground', to be replaced by the new keyboard-based popular music. Now, despite the political uncertainties of the current situation, practitioners of these traditions had come out of hiding, and we saw the reappearance of the wonderful regional music traditions of Afghanistan. This suggests that the regional musicians in different parts of the country are feeling confident to come out from under the shadow of ultra-orthodox disapproval and repression, to make their contribution to the gradually strengthening life of music in Afghanistan. Moreover, not only have traditional regional musics reappeared, we see the emergence of an indigenous Afghan musicology, with local experts studying and writing about their local traditions. One could connect all this with a renewed sense of national identity. While distinct in themselves, the regional musics have many elements in common, comparable to different dialects of a single language. Collectively, they are an important part of that intangible notion of what it is to be a person from Afghanistan, despite differences of language and ethnicity. The Seminar and Festival are markers of deep processes of national cohesion. Afghan music today is a bellwether of better things to come in terms of reconciliation and political stabilization. Let the Kabuli singer Qassem Bakhsh have the last word, in his own prayer for peace.

> O God, bring peace to this country
> Whose people are tired of war

Glossary of Musical Instruments

'Armonia   Small portable Indian harmonium, a free-reed aerophone, with bellows pumped by one hand, the digitals fingered with the other.

Chahârtâr   Herati term for the Iranian *târ*.

Chimta   Idiophone consisting of metal tongs with circular metal jingles attached. Used for religious music in Paksitan, India and Afghanistan.

Dâira   Frame drum, with jingles (iron rings and pellet bells) attached inside the frame. Played mainly by women.

Dambura   Fretless two stringed long-necked lute strongly associated with northern Afghanistan.

Delrubâ   An Indian bowed lute having the finger-board of the *sitâr*, with wide curved frets arched over sympathetic strings.

Dohol   Double-headed frame drum beaten with a heavy stick on the upper head and a thin flexible stick on the lower one.

Doholak   Twin-headed barrel or cylinder drum played with the hands. Often referred to as a *dohol*.

Dutâr   Long-necked plucked lute, often in modern times equipped with sympathetic strings.

Ghaichak   Term for three types of bowed lute: (1) *sarinda*, (2) *kemâncheh*, (3) spike-fiddle with large tin can as resonator found in northern Afghanistan.

Kemâncheh   Iranian spike-fiddle of the *rabâb* family.

Naqqârakhâna Archaic ensemble of drums, trumpets and shawms playing royal, ceremonial, civic or military music, usually from a tower or gateway.

Nay	Rim blown oblique flute.
Qairaq	Polished stone clappers.
Qânun	Plucked board zither, common today in Arab and Turkish music.
Rabâb	Family of spike-fiddles having a membranous belly.
Rubâb	Short-necked, double-chambered plucked lute. The Afghan *rubâb* is strongly associated with Pashtun music, and is considered to be the 'national instrument' of Afghanistan.
Santur	Dulcimer (hammered zither). An important Iranian instrument, also found in Kashmir, and formerly in Afghanistan.
Sârang	Term for (1) *sârangi*, (2) *sarinda*.
Sârangi	Bowed lute with a skin belly and many sympathetic strings, fretless, usually used to accompany vocal music in Pakistan and India.
Sarinda	Double-chambered bowed lute, member of the *rubâb* family, the small lower chamber has a skin belly, the upper chamber is open. Strongly associated with Pashtun music in Afghanistan.
Sarod	Plucked lute, an instrument of North Indian classical music, a modern development of the Afghan *rubâb*, with metal strings and a fretless metal finger-board.
Sitâr	Large, long-necked plucked lute of North Indian classical music.
Sormandel	A board zither used as a drone instrument in Afghanistan, Pakistan and India.
Sornâ	Double reed aerophone of the shawm family.
Tabla	Pair of small kettle drums, played with the hands. Very common in Pakistan and North India.
Tanbur	Large long-necked lute with sympathetic strings. Characteristically Afghan and especially common in Mazar-e Sharif and Shomali regions.

Tânpurâ	Large long-necked lute used as a drone instrument in Pakistan and India.
Târ	Long-necked double-chambered plucked lute of Iran and the Caucasus.
'Ud	The Arabian lute.
Zirbaghali	Single-headed goblet drum, usually of pottery.

Bibliography

Allen, Charles (ed.), *Plain Tales from the Raj. Images of British India in the Twentieth Century* (London: Futura, 1976).

——, *Soldier Sahibs. The men who made the North-West Frontier* (London: Abacus, 2000).

Anwar, Raja, *The Tragedy of Afghanistan. A First-hand Account* (London: Verso, 1988).

Baily, John, *Krishna Govinda's Rudiments of Tabla Playing*, with accompanying audiocassette published by Sussex Tapes (Brighton: Unicorn Books, 1974).

——, 'Recent changes in the *dutâr* of Herat', *Asian Music*, VIII/1 (1976): 29–64.

——, 'Professional and amateur musicians in Afghanistan', *World of Music*, 21/2 (1979): 46–64.

——, 'Cross-cultural perspectives in popular music: the case of Afghanistan', in Richard Middleton and David Horn (eds), *Popular Music 1* (Cambridge: Cambridge University Press, 1981): 105–22.

——, *The Annual Cycle of Music in Herat*, DVD (London: Royal Anthropological Institute, 1982).

——, *The City of Herat*, DVD (London: Royal Anthropological Institute, 1983a).

——, *The Shrines of Herat*, DVD (London: Royal Anthropological Institute, 1983b).

——, *Amir: An Afghan refugee musician's life in Peshawar, Pakistan*, DVD (London: Royal Anthropological Institute, 1985a).

——, 'Music structure and human movement', in Peter Howell, Ian Cross and Robert West (eds), *Musical Structure and Cognition* (London: Academic Press, 1985b): 237–58.

——, 'Principes d'improvisation rythmique dans le jeu du *rubâb* d'Afghanistan', in Bernard Lortat-Jacob (ed.), *L'Improvisation dans les musiques de tradition orale* (Paris: SELAF, 1987): 175–88.

——, *Music of Afghanistan: Professional musicians in the city of Herat*, with accompanying audiocassette (Cambridge: Cambridge University Press, 1988a).

——, 'Amin-e Diwaneh: the musician as madman', *Popular Music*, 7/2 (1988b): 133–46.

——, 'Film making as musical ethnography', *World of Music*, XXXI/3 (1989a): 3–20.

——, 'The role of a motor grammar in the performance of music', in Frank Wilson and Franz Roehmann (eds), *Music and Child Development: Proceedings of the 1987 Denver Conference* (St. Louis: MMB Music, 1989b): 202–13.

——, *The making of 'Amir: An Afghan Refugee Musician's Life in Peshawar, Pakistan'. A Study Guide to the Film* (Boston: Documentary Educational Resources, 1990).

—, *AFGHANISTAN. Le rubâb de Hérat / The rubâb of Herat*. VDE CD-699 (1993).

—, *John Blacking: Dialogue with the Ancestors* (London: Goldsmiths, 1994a).

—, 'The role of music in the creation of an Afghan national identity, 1923–73', in Martin Stokes (ed.), *Music, Ethnicity and Identity. The Musical Construction of Place* (Oxford: Berg Publishers, 1994b): 45–60.

—, 'Using Tests of Sound Perception in Fieldwork', *Yearbook for Traditional Music*, 28 (1996): 147–73.

—, 'Afghan perceptions of birdsong', *World of Music*, 39/2 (1997a): 51–9.

—, 'The *naghma-ye kashâl* of Afghanistan', *British Journal of Ethnomusicology*, 6 (1997b): 117–63.

—, 'Music and refugee lives: Afghans in eastern Iran and California', *Forced Migration Review*, 6 (1999): 10–13.

—, 'Bring Back the Rubab', *Afghanistan Reflections*, 1 (2000a): 12–15.

—, *John Baily & Ustad Asif Mahmoud: From Cabool to California*, CD (Brighton: BOLBOL CD1, 2000b).

—, *'Can you stop the birds singing?' The censorship of music in Afghanistan*, with accompanying CD (Copenhagen: Freemuse, 2001a).

—, 'Learning to perform as a research technique in ethnomusicology', *British Journal of Ethnomusicology*, 10/2 (2001b): 85–98.

—, *A Kabul Music Diary*, DVD (London: Goldsmiths, 2003).

—, *Tablas and Drum Machines: Afghan Music in California*, DVD (London, Goldsmiths, 2005).

—, '"Music is in Our Blood": Gujarati Muslim Musicians in the UK', *Journal of Ethnic and Migration Studies*, 32/2 (2006): 257–70.

—, 'The circulation of "New Music" between Afghanistan and its transnational community', paper read at Conference on Music in the world of Islam, Assilah, Morocco, August 2007a. http://www.mcm.asso.fr/site02/music-w-islam/articles/Baily-2007.pdf

—, *Scenes of Afghan Music. London, Kabul, Hamburg, Dublin*, DVD (London: Goldsmiths, 2007b).

—, *Across the Border: Afghan musicians exiled in Peshawar*, DVD (London: Goldsmiths, 2007c).

—, '*Târ-e Irâni va Robâb-e Afghâni: Tahavvolât-e Moshabeh dar Qarn-e 19?*' ('Iranian *târ* and Afghan *rubâb*: Parallel developments in the 19th century?'), *Mahoor*, 10/40, (1387, 2008a): 18–22.

—, *Ustad Rahim: Herat's Rubab Maestro*, DVD (London: Royal Anthropological Institute, 2008b).

—, 'Two different worlds: Afghan music for '*Afghanistanis*' and '*Kharejis*'', *Ethnomusicology Forum*, 19/1 (2010): 69–88.

—, *Songs from Kabul: The Spiritual Music of Ustad Amir Mohammad*, with accompanying CD (Farnham: Ashgate, 2011a).

—, 'Music, migration and war: the BBC's interactive music broadcasting to Afghanistan and the Afghan diaspora', in Jason Toynbee and Byron Dueck (eds), *Migrating Music* (Abingdon: Routledge, 2011b): 180–94.

—, *Return of the nightingales*, DVD (London: SEMPRE & Institute of Education, 2013).

Bezhan, Faridullah, 'A contemporary writer from Afghanistan: Akram Osman and his short stories', *British Journal of Middle Eastern Studies*, 35/1 (2008): 21–36.

Blacking, John, *How Musical is Man?* (Seattle: University of Washington Press, 1973).

Blanc, Jean-Charles, *Afghan Trucks* (London: Mathews Miller Dunbar, 1976).

Bony, Jérome, and Christophe de Pontfilly (filmmakers), *Afghanistan: A Valley Against an Empire* (London: BBC2, 3 May 1983).

Braithwaite, Rodric, *Afghansty. The Russians in Afghanistan 1979–89* (London: Profile Books, 2011).

Broughton, Simon, *Breaking the Silence. Music in Afghanistan*, Director, Simon Broughton, Music consultant, John Baily (London: A Songlines Films MWTV production for BBC, 2002).

—, 'Farhad Darya returns to Kabul', *Songlines*, 50 (2008): 47.

Burnes, Sir Alexander, *Travels into Bokhara. Being an account of a Journey from India to Cabool, Tartary and Persia. Also, narrative of a Voyage on the Indus from the Sea to Lahore* (3 vols, London: John Murray, 1834).

—, *Cabool. Being a Personal Narrative of a Journey to, and residence in, that City in the Years 1836, 7 and 8* (London: John Murray, 1842).

Byron, Robert, *The Road to Oxiana* (London: Macmillan, 1937).

Centlivres, Pierre and Micheline Centlivres-Demont, 'The Afghan Refugees in Pakistan: A Nation in Exile', *Current Sociology*, 36/2 (1988): 71–92.

Conolly, Arthur, *Journey to the North of India, Overland From England, Through Russia, Persia, and Affghaunistaun* (2 vols, London: Richard Bentley, 1834).

Cowper-Coles, Sir Sherard, *Cables from Kabul. The Inside Story of the West's Afghanistan Campaign* (London: Harper Press, 2011).

Dalrymple, William, *Return of a King: The Battle for Afghanistan 1839–42* (London: Bloomsbury, 2013).

Darr, Robert Abdul Hayy, *The Spy of the Heart* (Louisville, KY: Fons Vitae, 2006).

Doubleday, Veronica, 'Women and music in Herat', *Afghanistan Journal*, 9/1 (1982): 3–12.

—, *Three Women of Herat* (London: Jonathan Cape, 1988).

—, 'Continuity and Change in the Frame Drum Traditions of Afghanistan', in Richard Graham (ed.), *Transculturation and Organology: Frame Drums in Time, Space and Context* (Farnham: Ashgate, forthcoming).

Doubleday, Veronica and John Baily, 'Patterns of musical development among children in Afghanistan', in Elizabeth Warnock Fernea (ed.), *Children in the Muslim Middle East* (Austin: University of Texas Press, 1995): 431–44.

Dupree, Louis, *Afghanistan* (Princeton, NJ: Princeton University Press, 1973).

Eastwick, Edward B., *The Gulistān, or, Rose-garden, of Shekh Muslihu'd-dīn Sâdī of Shīrāz, Translated for the First Time into Prose and Verse, with an Introductory Preface and a Life of the Author from the Ātish Kadah* (Hertford, 1852, reprinted London: Octagon Press, 1974).

Elphinstone, Mountstuart, *An Account of the Kingdom of Caubul and its dependencies in Persia, Tartary, and India* (1815), reprinted with bio-bibliographical notes by Alfred Janata (Graz: Akademische Druck – u. Verlagsanstalt, 1969).

Farhat, Hormoz, *The Dastgâh Concept in Persian Music* (Cambridge: Cambridge University Press, 1990).

Farmer, Henry George, *A History of Arabian Music* (1929, reprinted London: Luzak and Co., 1973).

Fraser-Tytler, W.K., *Afghanistan. A Study of Political Developments in Central and Southern Asia*, 3rd edition revised by M.C.Gillett (London: Oxford University Press, 1967).

Gall, Sandy, *Afghanistan: Agony of a Nation* (London: Bodley Head, 1988).

Gilmour, Benjamin, *Warrior Poets. Guns, movie-making and the Wild West of Pakistan* (Pier 9: Millers Point, Australia, 2008).

Glatzer, Bernt, 'Afghanistan: Ethnic and tribal disintegration?', in William Maley (ed.), *Fundamentalism Reborn? Afghanistan and the Taliban* (London: Hurst, 1998): 167–81.

Gommans, Jos J.L., *The Rise of the Indo-Afghan Empire: 1710–1780* (Leiden: Brill, 1995).

Graham, Stephen, 'Conservative Backlash as Afghan TV Airs First Female Singer in 10 Years', *The Independent* (14 July 2004: 34).

Gray, John A., *At the Court of the Amir: A Narrative* (London: Richard Bentley and Son, 1895).

Griffin, Michael, *Reaping the Whirlwind. The Taliban Movement in Afghanistan* (London: Pluto Press, 2001).

Gregorian, Vartan, *The Emergence of Modern Afghanistan. Politics of Reform and Modernization, 1880–1946* (Stanford: Stanford University Press, 1969).

Guinhut, Jean Pierre, 'Musicians Go to Afghanistan. Healing the Wounds of War', *Azerbaijan International*, 13/1 (2005): 38–9.

Halliday, Fred, 'Revolution in Afghanistan', *New Left Review*, 112 (1978): 3–44.

Hancock, David and Herbert DiGioia (filmmakers), *Naim and Jabar* (Ipswich: Concord Media, 1974).

Henley, Paul, 'The origins of observational cinema: conversations with Colin Young', in Beate Engelbrecht (ed.), *Memories of the Origins of Visual Anthropology* (Frankfurt: Peter Lang, 2014): 139–61.

Herawi, Mayel, *Siahmu, Litan, Mariam* (Kabul: Daulat Matb'a, 1347AH, 1968).

Hopkirk, Peter, *On Secret Service East of Constantinople. The Plot to Bring Down the British Empire* (Oxford: Oxford University Press, 1994).

—, *The Great Game. On Secret Service in High Asia* (London: John Murray, 2006).

Hood, Mantle, 'The challenge of bi-musicality', *Ethnomusicology*, 4/2 (1960): 55–9.

Howard, Keith (ed.), *Music as Intangible Cultural Heritage. Policy, Ideology, and Practice in the Preservation of East Asian Traditions* (Farnham, Ashgate, 2012).

Human Rights Watch, '"Killing You Is A Very Easy Thing For us": Human Rights Abuses in Southeast Afghanistan', *Human Rights Watch*, 15/5 (c) (2003): 1–102.

Hyman, Anthony, *Afghanistan under Soviet Domination, 1964–83* (London: Macmillan, 1984).

Janata, Alfred (1969), see Elphinstone (1815).

Johnson, Chris and Jolyon Leslie, *Afghanistan. The Mirage of Peace* (London: Zed Books, 2004).

Johnson, Thomas J. and Ahmad Waheed, 'Analysing Taliban taranas (chants): an effective Afghan propaganda artifact', *Small Wars & Insurgencies*, 22/01 (2011): 3–31.

Jones, Philip, and Anna Kenny, *Australia's Muslim Cameleers. Pioneers of the Inland 1880s–1930s* (Kent Town, South Australia: Wakefield Press, 2007).

Kaiser, Tania, 'Songs, Discos and Dancing in Kiryandongo, Uganda', *Journal of Ethnic and Migration Studies*, 32/2 (2006): 183–202.

Kaye, Sir John William, *History of the War in Afghanistan* (2 vols, London: Richard Bentley, 1851). Revised 3rd edition (3 vols, 1874).

Lecomte, Henri. Booklet accompanying CD *Mahwash. Radio Kaboul. Hommage aux compositeurs afghans* (ACCORDS CROIOSÉS, ACC100, 2003).

Lipson, Juliene G., and Patricia A. Omidian, *Afghan Community Health Assessment San Francisco Bay Area* (California: Department of Health Services, 1993).

Lo, Bobo, *Axis of Convenience: Moscow, Beijing, and the new geopolitics* (London: Chatham House and Brookings, 2008).

Loizos, Peter, *Innovation in ethnographic film. From innocence to self-consciousness, 1955–85* (Manchester: Manchester University Press, 1993).

Loyn, David, *Butcher & Bolt. Two Hundred Years of Foreign Engagement in Afghanistan* (London: Windmill Books, 2009).

Lubtchansky, J.C. and S., *Afghanistan et Iran*, vinyl LP (Paris: Musée de l'Homme, 1957).

McMahon, Sir A. Henry, *An account of the entry of HM Habibullah Khan Amir of Afghanistan into Freemasonry* (London: Silk Road Books and Photos, 2013).

Madadi, Abdul Wahab, 'Uruj wa nuzul-e musiqi dar Afghânistân' ('The rise and fall of music in Afghanistan'), *Pashtun Jakh* (Kabul: Ministry of Information and Culture, 1972).

—, *Sar-guzasht Musiqi Mu'âsir Afghanistan* (*The Story of Contemporary Music in Afghanistan*) (Tehran: Hauza Honari, 1375/1996).

Maley, William (ed.), *Fundamentalism Reborn? Afghanistan and the Taliban* (London: Hurst, 1998).

Manuel, Peter, *Cassette Culture. Popular Music and Technology in North India* (Chicago: University of Chicago Press, 1993).

Marsden, Peter, *The Taliban: War, religion and the new order in Afghanistan* (London: Zed Books, 1998).

Martin, Frank A., *Under the Absolute Amir of Afghanistan* (London: Harper: 1907, reprinted New Delhi: Bhavana Books & Prints, 2000).

Masson, Charles, *Narrative of Various Journeys in Balochistan, Afghanistan and the Panjab, including a Residence in those Countries from 1826 to 1838* (3 vols, London: Richard Bentley, 1842, reprinted Karachi: Oxford University Press, 1977).

Mazari, Najaf, and Robert Hillman, *The Rugmaker of Mazar-e-Sharif* (Elsternwick, Vic.: Insight Publications, 2008).

Merriam, Alan P., *The Anthropology of Music* (Chicago: Northwestern University Press, 1964).

Migrant Resource Centre, *Afghan people in south east Melbourne. Perspectives of a migrant and refugee community* (Dandenong, Victoria: South Eastern Region Migrant Resource Centre, 2009).

Misdaq, Nabi, *Afghanistan. Political frailty and external interference* (London: Routledge, 2006).

Moin, Baqer, 'An Afghan cultural renaissance?', *The Middle East* (January 1985): 29.

Morgan, Llewelyn, *The Buddhas of Bamiyan* (Cambridge, MA: Harvard University Press, 2012).

Mousavi, Sayed Askar, *The Hazaras of Afghanistan. An Historical, Cultural, Economic and Political Study* (London: Curzon, 1998).

Nettl, Bruno, *Theory and Method in Ethnomusicology* (New York: Free Press of Glencoe, 1964).

Neuman, Daniel, *The Life of Music in North India. The Organization of an Artistic Tradition* (Detroit: Wayne State University Press, 1980).

Nicod, M.R., *Afghanistan* (Innsbruck: Pinguin-Verlag, 1985).

Niedermayer, Oskar von, *Afghanistan* (Hiersemann: Leipzig, 1924).

Nooshin, Laudan (ed.), *Music and the Play of Power in the Middle East, North Africa and Central Asia* (Farnham: Ashgate, 2009).

Oeppen, Ceri, *A Stranger at Home. Integration, Transnationalism and the Afghan Elite* (D.Phil. thesis in Migration Studies, University of Sussex, 2009).

—, 'The Afghan Diaspora and its Involvement in the Reconstruction of Afghanistan, in Ceri Oppen and Angela Schlenkoff (eds), *Beyond the 'Wild Tribes': Understanding Modern Afghanistan and its Diaspora* (London: Hurst & Co. 2010): 141–56.

Page, David, and Shirazuddin Siddiqi, *The media of Afghanistan: The challenges of transition* (London: BBC Media Action, Policy Briefing #5, 2012).

Pennell, T. L., *Among the wild tribes of the Afghan frontier; a record of sixteen years' close intercourse with natives of the Indian marches* (London: Seeley, Service & Co. 1922).

Popular Mechanics Magazine, 'Around the World on a Motorcycle', *Popular Mechanics Magazine* (1937): 236–8, cont. 142A.

Pourjavady, Amir Hosein, 'Indian and Afghan Influences on Persian Music Culture during the 18th and 19th Centuries', paper presented at Conference on Music in the world of Islam, Assilah, Morocco (August 2007). www.mcm.asso.fr/site02/music-w-islam/articles/Pourjavady-2007.pdf

Powers, Harold S., 'Classical music, cultural roots, and colonial rule: an Indic musicologist looks at the Muslim world', *Asian Music*, XII/1 (1979): 5–39.

Rashid, Ahmed, *Taliban. Islam, Oil and the New Great Game in Central Asia* (London: I.B. Tauris, 2000).

Reshtia, Sayed Qassem, *Between Two Giants. Political History Of Afghanistan In The Nineteenth Century* (Peshawar: Afghan Jehad Works, 1990).

Reyes, Adelaida, 'Tradition in the guise of innovation: Music amongst a refugee population', *Yearbook of Traditional Music*, 18 (1986): 91–101.

—, Reyes, Adelaida, *Songs of the Caged, Songs of the Free: Music and the Vietnamese Refugee Experience* (Philadelphia: Temple University Press, 1999).

Robson, James, *Tracts on Listening to Music* (London: Royal Asiatic Society, 1938).

Said, Benham, 'Hymns (*Nasheeds*): A Contribution to the Study of the *Jihadist* Culture', *Studies in Conflict & Terrorism*, 35 (2012): 863–79.

Sakata, Hiromi Lorraine, 'The Concept of Musician in Three Persian-speaking Areas of Afghanistan', *Asian Music*, VIII/1 (1976): 1–28.

—, *Music in the Mind: the Concepts of Music and Musician in Afghanistan* (Kent: Kent State University Press, 1983). With two accompanying audio cassettes. Reprinted with a new foreword and preface and with CD (Washington and London: Smithsonion Institution Press, 2002).

—, *Afghanistan Encounters with Music and Friends* (Costa Mesa: Mazda Publishers, 2013).

Saljuqi, Nasruddin, *Musiqi wa te'âtr dar Herât: Sarâindegân wa âwâzkhânân harfehây wa shauqi honar te'âtr wa honar âfrinân herâti* (*Theatre and music in Herat: professional and popular musicians, singers and theatre art of Herat*) (Tehran: Toos, 2004).

Sarmast, Ahmad Naser, *A Survey of the History of Music in Afghanistan, from Ancient Times to 2000 A.D., with Special Reference to Art Music from c. 1000 A.D.* (PhD thesis in Musicology, Monash University, 2004).

—, 'The *Naghma-ye Chârtuk* of Afghanistan: A New Perspective on the Origin of a Solo Instrumental Genre', *Asian Music*, 38/2 (2007): 97–114.

Schofield, Victoria, *Afghan Frontier. At the crossroads of conflict* (London, New York: Tauris Parke Paperbacks, 2010).

Sikorski, Radek, *Dust of the Saints* (London: Chatto & Windus, 1989).

Singer, André (dir.), *Khyber* (UK: Granada International, 1979).

Skuse, Andrew, 'Radio, politics and trust in Afghanistan. A Social History of Broadcasting', *Gazette: The International Journal for Communication Studies*, 64/3 (2002): 267–79.

Slobin, Mark, 'Music in contemporary Afghan society', in Louis Dupree and Linette Albert (eds), *Afghanistan in the 1970s* (New York: Praeger, 1974): 239–48.

—, *Music in the Culture of Northern Afghanistan*, Viking Fund Publications in Anthropology No. 54 (Tucson: University of Arizona Press, 1976).

—, Review of *Amir: An Afghan refugee musician's life in Peshawar, Pakistan*, *Ethnomusicology*, 32/1 (1988): 161–2.

Steele, Jonathan, *Ghosts of Afghanistan. The Haunted Battleground* (London: Portobello Books, 2011).

Stevens, Christine, *Tin Mosques & Ghantowns. A History of Afghan Cameldrivers in Australia* (Melbourne: Oxford University Press, 1989).

Stewart, Jules, *On Afghanistan's Plains. The Story of Britain's Afghan Wars* (London: I.B. Tauris, 2011).

Swinson, Arthur, *North West Frontier* (London: Hutchinson & Co., 1967).

Thakston, Wheeler M., *The Baburnama. Memoirs of Babur, Prince and Emperor* (New York: Modern Library Paperback Editions, 2002).

Toynbee, Polly. 'Was it worth it?', *The Guardian*, 13 November 2002. http://www.guardian.co.uk/world/2002/nov/13/afghanistan.comment

Van Aken, Mauro, 'Dancing Belonging: Contesting *Dabkeh* in the Jordan Valley, Jordan', *Journal of Ethnic and Migration Studies*, 32/2 (2006): 203–22.

Van Hear, Nicholas, 'From durable solutions to transnational relations: home and exile among refugee diasporas', *New Issues in Refugee Research Working Papers*, 83 (Geneva: UNHCR, 2003).

Walker, Rowland, *Stories of British History*. London: A. & C. Black, 1928).

Watkins, Polly (dir.), *Dr Sarmast's Music School* (The Netherlands: Circe Films, 2012).

Wide, Thomas, 'Around the World in Twenty-nine Days: The Travels, Translations, and Temptations of an Afghan Dragoman', in Roberta Micaleff and Sunil Sharma (eds), *On the Wonders of Land and Sea: Persianate Travel Writing* (Cambridge: Ilex Foundation, 2013), 89–113.

Young, Colin, 'Observational Cinema', in Paul Hockings (ed.), *Principles of Visual Anthropology* (The Hague: Mouton, 1975): 65–80.

Zemp, Hugo, Review of *Amir: An Afghan refugee musician's life in Peshawar, Pakistan* and *Lessons from Gulam: Asian Music in Bradford, Yearbook for Traditional Music*, XX (1988): 257–60.

Index

References to illustrations are in **bold**.